WHY STUDY THE HOLOCAUST?

For years, the Holocaust was considered too difficult a subject to discuss in schools, too painful an event to relive through dramatic presentation. But it has also been recognized that the world could all too easily forget the sufferings of the Holocaust victims. This would be a great injustice to their memory—and a foolish invitation for history to repeat itself.

Now, in schools and other organizations across the country, teachers have chosen to discuss the political, psychological, and ethical implications of the Holocaust. Millions of Americans have chosen to educate themselves about it —many for the first time—by watching a televised fictional dramatization. Here, in cooperation with the Anti-Defamation League of B'nai B'rith, two teachers have compiled this collection of readings which give the facts, the theories, the parallels found in literature and life. Also included is new material which suggests the urgency of this topic in the world today.

THE
HOLOCAUST YEARS:
Society on Trial

Edited by Roselle Chartock
and Jack Spencer

*In cooperation with
the Anti-Defamation League
of B'nai B'rith*

BANTAM BOOKS
TORONTO · NEW YORK · LONDON · SYDNEY

RL 10, IL 9-up

THE HOLOCAUST YEARS: SOCIETY ON TRIAL
A Bantam Book / November 1978
2nd printing .... March 1979
3rd printing .... February 1981

ACKNOWLEDGMENTS

For permission to reprint all works in this volume by each of
the following authors, grateful acknowledgment is made to the
holders of copyright, publishers or representatives named below
and on the following pages (page v–vii), which constitutes an
extension of the copyright page. Every reasonable effort has
been made to obtain appropriate permission to reproduce those
copyrighted materials included in this volume. If notified of
omissions, the editor and publisher will make the necessary
corrections in future editions.

"The Death House," from The Rise and Fall of the Third
Reich *by William L. Shirer; copyright © 1959, 1960 by William*
L. Shirer. By permission of Simon & Schuster, a Division of
Gulf & Western Corporation, and Martin Secker & Warburg
Limited.

"The Final Solution of the Jewish Question" *and* "The
Jews in Hitler's Mental World," *from* The War Against the
Jews *by Lucy S. Dawidowicz; copyright © 1975 by Lucy S.*
Dawidowicz. By permission of Holt, Rinehart and Winston,
Publishers.

"The 'Final Solution' in Action, Testimony," *from* The
Harvest of Hate *by Leon Poliakov; copyright 1954 by Leon*
Poliakov. By permission of American Jewish Committee.

"Dehumanization and Starvation" *and* "The Decent and
the Indecent," *from* Man's Search For Meaning *by Viktor*
Frankl; copyright © 1963 by Viktor Frankl. By permission of
Hodder & Stoughton Limited and Beacon Press.

ISBN 0-553-20129-8

Published simultaneously in the United States and Canada

Bantam Books are published by Bantam Books, Inc. Its trademark, consisting of the words "Bantam Books" and the portrayal of a bantam, is Registered in U.S. Patent and Trademark Office and in other countries. Marca Registrada. Bantam Books, Inc., 666 Fifth Avenue, New York, New York 10103.

PRINTED IN THE UNITED STATES OF AMERICA

12 11 10 9 8 7 6 5 4

Contents

Acknowledgments

These readings comprise an eight-to-twelve week unit of required study for ninth graders and was developed by the Social Studies Department of Monument Mountain Regional High School, in Great Barrington, Massachusetts. With the assistance of a $2,135 grant from the National Conference of Christians and Jews and the efforts of one of its leaders, the late Dr. Bernhard Olsen, members of the Department, John Beacco, Bill Fields and Larry Webb, devoted many hours to research, reading, and the compilation of the related literature. Following this initial grant, we were assisted by Judith Muffs of the Anti-Defamation League of B'nai B'rith in revising and reorganizing some of the materials. Theodore Freedman, Program Director of ADL, and Stan Wexler, Publications Director, provided the groundwork for this publication. Special thanks must go to Benjamin Epstein, National Director of ADL, whose initial positive response to the project led the Anti-Defamation League to this point as well as to the inclusion in pilot projects of this material throughout the country. We are also most grateful to Ruth Routtenberg Seldin whose good judgment and editorial skills were of inestimable help.

The National Council for the Social Studies and Daniel Roselle, editor of its journal *Social Education,* also played a significant role in disseminating Holocaust materials by devoting the April, 1978, issue to the subject.

We know that all who contributed to this publication feel as we do about the importance of finally bringing the subject of the Holocaust out in the open for discussion and debate. For more than any other subject, the Holocaust can truly teach us about ourselves.

Special praise also goes to the administration and school committee of the Berkshire Hills Regional School District for having the sensitivity to encourage the teaching of a unit. The material has also been well taught for five years by Ray Shepardson and Jay Canning, members of the Social Studies Department.

ROSELLE CHARTOCK
JACK SPENCER

Fall, 1978

...
...
...

Introduction

If we are to learn from history how to improve the
quality of human life, then we must examine both the
positive and negative chapters in human history. The
readings in this anthology have been excerpted from
over 100 primary (first-hand) and secondary sources
so that the reader can begin to learn about the Nazi
Holocaust, an example of a negative chapter that remains unparalleled. Genocide and racial persecution
have always been a part of the past, but never before
the Holocaust has such persecution been practiced on
so large a scale or with such calculated cruelty. The
term "Holocaust" is formally defined as "the complete
destruction of people and animals by fire" and has
come to refer specifically to that destruction which was
perpetrated on the Jews of Europe during World
War II.

"How could the Holocaust have happened?" is the
question immediately asked by someone who has just
confronted the facts of this grotesque picture of man's
inhumanity to man. There are no easy answers to the
question of why six million Jews and six million non-
Jews were systematically slaughtered in Nazi Germany
and elsewhere under the leadership of Adolf Hitler. Nor
are there simple answers to the other complex questions
raised by this historical phenomena which defies comprehension, questions such as:

Who were the dead? Why were they killed? Had
they tried to escape?

Who were the murderers and their accomplices?
How could they?

What makes some people resist and others obey authority?

What would I have done under similar circumstances?

Could such a thing happen here—'or anywhere—again?

And there are the broader questions:

What can such a catastrophe tell us about human nature?

Are there comparable examples of man's inhumanity?

What is the role and responsibility of the individual in society?

Where does one draw the line between obeying the law or obeying one's conscience?

The readings in this anthology have been selected with these and other disturbing questions in mind. More and more students, and the general public as well, now want to know why country after country sat silently by as millions of innocents were murdered. They are asking why this chapter in history was left out of their history books with not even one line of reference.

As teachers introducing Holocaust material in classrooms, we have seen students—some for the first time—become seriously interested in reading, research, discussion, and problem-solving, when confronted with ideas that touch their very lives and the lives of everyone in their community. For example, haven't we all had to deal at some time or other with the issues of tolerance and intolerance, obedience and resistance to authority, conformity and individualism, freedom and the repression of freedom, and, of course, good and evil on several levels, both within our family roles and in our roles as citizens of a free country and citizens of the world? In addition, we are constantly facing questions of morality—of what is the right thing to do or the "good" thing to do in a given situation. Our moral dilemmas obviously don't deal with whether or not to disobey the law by hiding a Jew from the Nazis—a question many Germans faced. Instead, we may have to decide if we'll refuse to pay taxes which we know are going to finance a war we can't morally support, or if we'll speak out against our country's contributions to a totalitarian government, or if we'll do business with a known racist in our community. We may not have to decide whether to obey an authority figure as pervasive as Hitler, but don't all of us have to deal with authority figures? As students, we are often in conflict with parents and teachers. As employees, we must decide how to react to the orders of employers, local officials, even doctors and others whose services we depend on. Thus a study of the Holocaust goes beyond the specific events of the time period, 1933–1945, by relating these events to the universal and timeless issues of society. By tackling both the unique and universal aspects of the Holocaust, the reader can grapple with a very microcosm of history.

In seeking resolution to the difficult, often unanswerable, dilemmas raised here, it becomes necessary for the concerned student and citizen to bring to bear on these inquiries as much information as possible from such diverse fields of knowledge as philosophy, literature and poetry, religion, psychology, government, geography, and science. The readings herein are taken from every one of these fields, thus enabling one to see how differing issues actually interrelate; how, for example, an economic depression relates to the generating of fear, prejudice, and eventually violence. By linking these excerpts together there evolves a cohesive foundation for answering the question, "How could the Holocaust have happened?"

No doubt many people will ask while reading this material, "Why is it necessary to paint for the public such a bleak picture of humanity? Isn't it best to sweep this part of history under the rug and forget about it?" It is our emphatic belief that we cannot forget about the Holocaust for our own sake and the sake of generations to come. Philosopher George Santayana wrote, "Those who do not remember the past are condemned to relive it." We must tell the story to be on our guard so we might recognize the signals of when it might happen again. It is only through an exploration of both the positive and negative chapters in world history that we can ever expect to learn from the past. What lessons will be gleaned from these selections will depend both on what the reader brings to this anthology, and the desire of the reader to discover the truth about himself and his world. There is, however, one idea all will readily grasp from a study of this subject: that the courage and morality of a society are constantly on trial, and in crises society is often tested to its limits. One student, after being asked if events surrounding the Watergate burglary could ever lead to something of Holocaust proportion, answered:

"Could be. Maybe it wouldn't be the Jews again; maybe it would; but if what went on in Auschwitz could happen in a civilized country in 1944, why couldn't it happen in any civilized country at any time—even 1978 —if people are really blinded by their own problems and hate?"

I

WHAT HAPPENED?

"Six million were wiped off the face of the
earth. And there is the danger that they will
also be annihilated from our memories. Are
they doomed to a two-fold annihilation?"

—ABRAHAM JOSHUA HESCHEL

THE EXTERMINATION
OF THE JEWS

The first three readings in this collection plunge the reader immediately into the physical world of the concentration camp. Be forewarned—much of the material is shocking and ugly, and it is intended to be so, for that is exactly what life in the camps was. The concentration camps were the device invented by German scientific genius to carry out the mass murder of millions of "undesirables," with maximum efficiency and as little mess as possible.

To secure cooperative behavior, the Nazis employed outright lies. Those loaded on trains for shipment to the gas chambers were told that they were being "resettled" in labor camps in the east. Outside Germany, few people believed the reports that began trickling out about the existence of extermination camps. The very idea was preposterous.

The first and third readings are from Bernd Naumann's book *Auschwitz*. The second reading is from William Shirer's *The Rise and Fall of the Third Reich*. The first three paragraphs are quotations from the testimony of Rudolf Hoess, one-time commanding officer of Auschwitz.

1. Auschwitz: A Concentration Camp
Bernd Naumann

With every step one took one sank more deeply into the viscous mud. There was practically no water for washing. The prisoners slept on three tiers of wooden slabs, six to each tier, and for the most part without any straw pallets. Roll call twice a day meant that the prisoners had to stand for hours in the wet, cold mud. When it rained the prisoners had to lie on their wooden bunks in their wet garments. No wonder hundreds died daily. The guard towers around Auschwitz I and Birkenau formed the so-called "small guard chain." They were not used during the day; instead, the "big guard chain" encircled a huge perimeter encompassing most of the prisoners working in factories and in the fields, supervised by capos and foremen. Posters decorated with skulls and the warning "Auschwitz Concentration Camp Area—Do not cross this line—Fire will be opened without warning" dotted the big guard chain. But no such warnings were needed to keep civilians from approaching this eery tract, because of the ever-present threat of being suspected of trying to make contact with prisoners or of spying—charges that could land one in the camp. The work details outside the big guard chain were accompanied by as many guards as there were prisoners. At night after all the work details had returned, the guards left the towers of the big guard chain and the small guard went into operation. The returning prisoners were counted by the block leaders at the block leader offices in front of every compound. If a prisoner was missing, the guards of the big chain remained at their posts and a search party was sent out with dogs. Every now and then, however, a prisoner who had managed to steal away from his work detail succeeded in getting through the guards posted

4

100 feet apart and escaping. When that happened, the other prisoners were kept standing out in the open all night. And next morning, after spending the night in this fashion, they had to go right back to work.

Because of the barbaric sanitary conditions and the completely inadequate diet, combined with the hard labor and other tortures, most prisoners died a miserable death a few weeks or at most a few months after their arrival. Even the women, dressed in Russian blouses and rags, had to perform heavy labor, such as carrying rocks and digging ditches. Only those who managed to become trustees and get assigned to one of the few better details were able to stay alive for longer periods. Auschwitz was an extermination camp, the biggest in all of history. Between 2 and 3 million Jews were murdered there in the course of time, as well as thousands of Poles, Russians, Czechs, Yugoslavs, etc.

2. The Death House

William Shirer

We had two SS doctors on duty at Auschwitz to examine the incoming transports of prisoners. These would be marched by one of the doctors, who would make spot decisions as they walked by. Those who were fit to work were sent into the camp. Others were sent immediately to the extermination plants. Children of tender years were invariably exterminated since by reason of their youth they were unable to work.

Always Herr Hoess kept making improvements in the art of mass killing.

Still another improvement we made over Treblinka was that at Treblinka the victims almost always knew that they were to be exterminated, while at Auschwitz we endeavored to fool the victims into thinking that they were to go through a delousing process. Of course, frequently they realized our true intentions and we sometimes had riots and difficulties. Very frequently women would hide their children under the clothes but of course when we found them we would send the children in to be exterminated.

We were required to carry out these exterminations in secrecy, but of course the foul and nauseating stench from the continuous burning of bodies permeated the entire area and all of the people living in the surrounding communities knew that exterminations were going on at Auschwitz.

The gas chambers themselves and the adjoining crematoria, viewed from a short distance, were not sinister-looking places at all; it was impossible to make them out for what they were. Over them were well-kept lawns with flower borders; the signs at the entrances merely said BATHS. The unsuspecting Jews thought they were simply being taken to the baths for the delousing which was customary at all camps. And taken to the accompaniment of sweet music!

For there was light music. An orchestra of "young and pretty girls all dressed in white blouses and navy-blue skirts," as one survivor remembered, had been formed from among the inmates. While the selection was being made for the gas chambers this unique musical ensemble played gay tunes from *The Merry Widow* and *Tales of Hoffmann*. Nothing solemn and somber from Beethoven. The death marches at Auschwitz were sprightly and merry tunes, straight out of Viennese and Parisian operettas.

To such music, recalling as it did happier and more frivolous times, the men, women and children were led into the "bath houses," where they were told to undress preparatory to taking a "shower." Sometimes they were even given towels. Once they were inside the "shower-room"—and perhaps this was the first moment that they may have suspected something was amiss, for as many as two thousand of them were packed into the chamber like sardines, making it difficult to take a bath—the massive door was slid shut, locked and hermetically sealed.

Through heavy-glass portholes the executioners could watch what happened. The naked prisoners below would be looking up at the showers from which no water spouted or perhaps at the floor wondering why there were no drains. It took some moments for the gas to have much effect. But soon the inmates became aware that it was issuing from the perforations in the vents. It was then that they usually panicked, crowding away from the pipes and finally stampeding toward the huge metal door where, as Reitlinger puts it, "they piled up in one blue clammy blood-spattered pyramid, clawing and mauling each other even in death."

Twenty or thirty minutes later when the huge mass of naked flesh had ceased to writhe, pumps drew out the poisonous air, the large door was opened and the men of the *Sonderkommando* took over. These were Jewish male inmates who were promised their lives and adequate food in return for performing the most ghastly job of all. Protected with gas masks and rubber boots and wielding hoses they went to work. Reitlinger has described it.

> Their first task was to remove the blood and defecations before dragging the clawing dead apart with nooses and hooks, the prelude to the ghastly search for gold and the removal of teeth and hair which were regarded by the Germans as strategic materials. Then the journey by lift or rail-wagon to the furnaces, the mill that ground the clinker to fine ash, and the truck that scattered the ashes in the stream of the Sola.

3. The Horrors of Daily Life
Bernd Naumann

Billions of fleas tortured the prisoners in Auschwitz, and those who had shoes gave them away because the vermin prevented the use of this valuable possession. "Those who had only stockings or rags could at least scratch. The bugs didn't get much to eat, but still they were well-nourished.

"In Birkenau we didn't have fleas. Instead we had rats. They gnawed not only at corpses but also at the seriously sick. I have pictures showing women near death being bitten by rats. These animals were bold and impudent; they were not deterred by anything and at night even helped themselves to the bread the prisoners had saved in their pockets from the evening meal because at 'breakfast' there was nothing except a coffee-like brew. Then the prisoners would often accuse each other of having stolen bread from each other, but it was the rats. . . ."

The morning washing up: a row of wooden troughs under an iron pipe with holes through which some water trickled.

"Just enough so that one couldn't say it dripped. Then one hurried to get to the latrine. That was a concrete trough across which lay boards with round holes. There was room for 200 to 300 at one sitting. Latrine details watched to see that no one stayed too long and used sticks to chase the prisoners away. But some couldn't move so quickly, and others weren't through, and because of the strain a portion of the rectum would still protrude. When the latrine detail hit them they would run away and then once more get on line. There was no paper. Those who had jackets with linings would tear off a little piece at a time to clean themselves. Or they would steal a piece from somebody during the night to have some in reserve. The waste water of the washrooms was piped into the latrines to wash away the excrement. But again and again there were major stoppages, especially in places where the water pressure wasn't strong enough. When that happened a terrible stench spread throughout. Then pump details—'shit details'—would come to pump out the mess. . . .

"The people in the camp were so hungry that if a

bit of soup spilled over, the prisoners would come running from all sides and like a swarm of wasps converge on the spot, dig their spoons into the mud, and stuff the mess into their mouths. Hunger and extreme want made them into animals."

———————

It is impossible to imagine that a government would coldbloodedly plan to destroy an entire people, innocent and defenseless, and yet that was exactly the intention of Hitler's regime in Germany. All the complex and costly machinery of the concentration camps was used for that purpose. As Lucy Dawidowicz makes clear in this selection from her book, *The War Against the Jews*, the destruction of the Jews was no mere side-effect of the war; it was a carefully planned objective. Hitler's maniacal dream of world domination called for total annihilation of the Jews. In order for Germany to rule the world, he felt he had to first make the German people racially pure, and that required purging it of "internal enemies," chief among whom he listed the Jews.

4. "The Final Solution of the Jewish Question"
Lucy Dawidowicz

"The Final Solution of the Jewish Question" was the code name assigned by the German bureaucracy to the annihilation of the Jews. The very composition of the code name, when analyzed, reveals its fundamental character and meaning to the Germans who invented and used it. The term "Jewish question," as first used during the early Enlightenment/Emancipation period in Western Europe, referred to the "question" or "problem" that the anomalous persistence of the Jews as a people posed to the new nation-states and the rising political nationalisms. The "Jewish question" was, at bottom, a euphemism whose verbal neutrality concealed the user's impatience with the singularity of this people that did not appear to conform to the new political demands of the state.

Since a question demands an answer and a problem a solution, various answers and solutions were propounded to the "Jewish question," by foes and even friends, that entailed the disappearance of the Jews as such—abandonment of the Jewish religion or its essential elements, of the Jewish language, Yiddish, of Jewish culture, Jewish uniqueness and separatism. The histories of Jewish emancipation and of European anti-Semitism are replete with proffered "solutions to the Jewish question." The classic illustration is the "solution" offered by Constantine Pobyedonostsev, chief adviser to Czar Alexander III, in 1881: one-third of the Jews were to emigrate, one-third to convert, and one-third to die of hunger.

To this concept that the National Socialists adopted they added one new element, embodied in the word "final." "Final" means definitive, completed, perfected, ultimate. "Final" reverberates with apocalyptic promise, bespeaking the Last Judgment, the End of Days, the last destruction before salvation, Armageddon. "The Final Solution of the Jewish Question" in the National Socialist conception was not just another anti-Semitic undertaking, but a metahistorical program devised with an eschatological perspective. It was part of a salvational ideology that envisaged the attainment of Heaven by bringing Hell on earth. "The Devil is loose," Friedrich Reck-Malleczewen noted in his diary on October 30, 1942. The most important event of our time, André Malraux said, was *le retour de Satan,* citing the German system of terror.

To attain its heavenly Hell on earth the German dictatorship launched a war that engulfed the whole world. Over 35 million people were killed, more than half of them civilians. On the battlefields one out of

every 22 Russians was killed, one out of every 25
Germans, one out of every 150 Italians and English-
men, and one out of every 200 Frenchmen. The human cost of 2,191 days of war surpassed the losses
of any previous war in the world. That war brought
death to nearly 6 million Jews, to two out of every
three European Jews. Though one-third of them managed to survive, though the Jewish people and Judaism have outlived the Third Reich, the Germans nevertheless succeeded in irrecoverably destroying the life
and culture of East European Jewry.

The Final Solution transcended the bounds of
modern historical experience. Never before in modern
history had one people made the killing of another the
fulfillment of an ideology, in whose pursuit means
were identical with ends. History has, to be sure, recorded terrible massacres and destruction that one people perpetrated against another, but all—however cruel
and unjustifiable—were intended to achieve instrumen-
tal ends, being means to ends, not ends in themselves.

The German state, deciding that the Jews should
not live, arrogated to itself the judgment as to whether
a whole people had the right to existence, a judgment
that no man and no state have the right to make.
"Anyone who on the basis of such a judgment," said
Karl Jaspers, "plans the organized slaughter of a people
and participates in it, does something that is fundamentally different from all crimes that have existed in
the past."

To carry out this judgment, designated as the Final Solution, the German dictatorship involved and
engaged the entire bureaucratic and functional apparatus of the German state and the National Socialist
movement and employed the best available technological means. The Final Solution destroyed the East
European Jews. In doing so, it subverted fundamental
moral principles and every system of law that had governed, however imperfectly, human society for millennia.

What the Nazis did is fact, history. The evidence exists in eyewitness accounts that fill thousands of pages of testimony. The next two readings are descriptions of actual executions by Germans who were there, on the scene. What these accounts reveal about the behavior of all concerned—the victims, the murderers, and the passive observers themselves—is that a kind of mass hypnosis seems to have had nearly everyone in its grip.

The first account is from the testimony of a Nazi official assigned to work on the gas chambers at a camp in southern Poland. Before this man could be brought to trial, he committed suicide. The excerpt is from the book *The Harvest of Hate* by Leon Poliakov.

5. The "Final Solution" in Action
Testimony

This account is taken from the testimony of one of the Nazi executioners responsible for putting into effect Hitler's "final solution" to Germany's race problem. The site of the extermination camp he describes was Belzec, a village in southern Poland. Before this man could be brought to trial, he committed suicide.

Globocnik said: . . . "Your . . . duty will be to improve the workings of our gas chambers, which operate on the exhaust from a Diesel engine. We need a more toxic and faster working gas. . . . The Führer has ordered more speed. Dr. Herbert Lindner, who was here yesterday, asked me, 'Wouldn't it be more prudent to burn the bodies instead of burying them? Another generation might take a different view of these things.' I answered: 'Gentlemen, if there is ever a generation after us so cowardly, so soft, that it would not understand our work as good and necessary, then, gentlemen, National Socialism will have been for nothing. On the contrary, we should bury bronze tablets saying that it was we, we who had the courage to carry out this gigantic task!' ". . .

The next day we left for Belzec. . . .

The following morning, a little before seven there was an announcement: "The first train will arrive in ten minutes!" A few minutes later a train arrived from Lemberg: 45 cars with more than 6 thousand people. Two hundred Ukrainians assigned to this work flung open the doors and drove the Jews out of the cars with leather whips. A loud speaker gave instructions: "Strip, even artificial limbs and glasses. Hand all money and valuables in at the 'valuables window.' "

Then the march began. Barbed wire on both sides, in the rear two dozen Ukrainians with rifles. They drew near. Wirth and I found ourselves in front of the death chambers. Stark naked men, women, children, and cripples passed by. A tall SS man in the corner called to the unfortunates in a loud minister's voice: "Nothing is going to hurt you! Just breathe deep and it will strengthen your lungs. It's a way to prevent contagious diseases. It's a good disinfectant!" They asked him what was going to happen and he answered: "The men will have to work, build houses and streets. The women won't have to do that, they will be busy with the housework and the kitchen."

This was the last hope for some of these poor people, enough to make them march toward the death chambers without resistance. The majority knew everything; the smell betrayed it! They climbed a little wooden stairs and entered the death chambers, most of them silently, pushed by those behind them. . . . SS men pushed the men into the chambers. "Fill it up," Wirth ordered; 700–800 people in 93 square meters. The doors closed. . . . SS Unterscharführer Heckenholt tried to start the motor. It wouldn't start! . . . My

stopwatch clocked it all: 50 minutes, 70 minutes, and
the Diesel still would not start! . . . The men were
waiting in the gas chambers. You could hear them
weeping "as though in a synagogue." . . . The Diesel
started up after 2 hours and 49 minutes, by my stopwatch. Twenty-five minutes passed. You could see
through the window that many were already dead, for
an electric light illuminated the interior of the room.
All were dead after 32 minutes! Jewish workers on the
other side opened the wooden doors. They had been
promised their lives in return for doing this horrible
work, plus a small percentage of the money and valuables collected. The men were still standing, like col-
umns of stone, with no room to fall or lean. Even in
death you could tell the families, all holding hands. It
was difficult to separate them while emptying the rooms
for the next batch. The bodies were tossed out. . . . Two
dozen workers were busy checking mouths which they
opened with iron hooks. "Gold to the left, no gold to
the right" . . . Dentists knocked out gold teeth, bridges,
and crowns, with hammers. Captain Wirth stood in
the middle of them. He was in his element. . . .

From September 1941 until January 1944,
Herman Friedrich Graebe was manager and
engineer-in-charge of a branch office in Sdol-
bumow, the Ukraine, of a German building
firm. In this capacity it was his job to visit the
building sites of the firm. Under contract to an
Army Construction Office, the firm had orders
to erect grain storage buildings on the former
airport of Dubno, the Ukraine.

6. The Graebe Memorandum

Testimony

On 5 October 1942, when I visited the building
office at Dubno, my foreman Hubert Moennikes . . .

told me that in the vicinity of the site, Jews from Dubno had been shot in three large pits, each about 30 meters long and three meters deep. About 1,500 persons had been killed daily. All of the 5,000 Jews who had still been living in Dubno before the pogrom were to be liquidated. As the shootings had taken place in his presence he was still much upset.

Thereupon I drove to the site, accompanied by Moennikes and saw near it great mounds of earth, about 30 meters long and two meters high. Several trucks stood in front of the mounds. Armed Ukrainian militia drove the people off the trucks under the supervision of an SS man. The militiamen acted as guards on the trucks and drove them to and from the pit. All these people had the regulation yellow patches on the front and back of their clothes, and thus could be recognized as Jews.

Moennikes and I went directly to the pits. Nobody bothered us. Now I heard rifle shots in quick succession, from behind one of the earth mounds. The people who had got off the trucks—men, women and children of all ages—had to undress upon the order of an SS man who carried a riding or dog whip. They had to put down their clothes in fixed places, sorted according to shoes, top clothing, and underclothing. I saw a heap of shoes of about 800 to 1,000 pairs, great piles of underlinen and clothing. Without screaming or weeping these people undressed, stood around in family groups, kissed each other, said farewells and waited for a sign from another SS man, who stood near the pit, also with a whip in his hand.

During the 15 minutes that I stood near the pit, I heard no complaint or plea for mercy. I watched a family of about eight persons, a man and woman, both about 50, with their children of about one, eight and 10, and two grownup daughters of about 20 to 24. An old woman with snow-white hair was holding the one-year-old child in her arms and singing to it and tickling it. The child was cooing with delight. The couple were looking on with tears in their eyes. The father was holding the hand of a boy of about 10 years old and speaking to him softly; the boy was fighting his tears. The father pointed toward the sky, stroked his head, and seemed to explain something to him. At that moment the SS man at the pit shouted something to his comrade. The latter counted off about 20 persons and instructed them to go behind the earth mound. Among them was the family which I have mentioned.

I well remember a girl, slim and with black hair, who, as she passed close to me, pointed to herself and said, "Twenty-three!" I walked around the mound, and found myself confronted by a tremendous grave. People were closely wedged together and lying on top of each other so that only their heads were visible. Nearly all had blood running over their shoulders from their heads. Some of the people shot were still moving. Some were lifting their arms and turning their heads to show that they were still alive. The pit was already two-thirds full. I estimated that it already contained about a thousand people.

I looked for the man who did the shooting. He was an SS man, who sat at the edge of the narrow end of the pit, his feet dangling into the pit. He had a tommy gun on his knees and he was smoking a cigarette. The people, completely naked, went down some steps which were cut in the clay wall of the pit and clambered over the heads of the people lying there, to the place where the SS man directed them. They lay down in front of the dead or injured people; some caressed those who were still alive and spoke to them in a low voice. Then I heard a series of shots.

I looked into the pit and saw that the bodies were twitching or the heads lying already motionless on top of the bodies that lay before them. Blood was running from their necks. I was surprised that I was not ordered away, but I saw that there were two or three postmen in uniform nearby. The next batch was approaching already. They went down into the pit, lined themselves up against the previous victims and were shot.

When I walked back, around the mound, I noticed another truckload of people which had just arrived. This time it included sick and infirm people. An old, very thin woman with terribly thin legs was undressed by others who were already naked, while two people held her up. The woman appeared to be paralyzed. The naked people carried the woman around the mound. I left with Moennikes and drove in my car back to Dubno.

On the morning of the next day when I again visited the site, I saw about 30 naked people lying near the pit—about 30 to 50 meters away from it. Some of them were still alive; they looked straight in front of them with a fixed stare and seemed to notice neither the chilliness of the morning nor the workers of my firm who stood around. A girl of about 20 spoke to me and asked me to give her clothes and help her escape. At that moment we heard a fast car approach and I noticed that it was an SS detail. I moved away to my site. Ten minutes later we heard shots from the vicinity of the pit. The Jews still alive had been ordered to throw the corpses into the pit—then they themselves had to lie down in this to be shot in the neck.

The effects of prolonged brutal treatment and physical deprivation are vividly drawn in this excerpt from *Man's Search for Meaning* by Viktor E. Frankl. Dr. Frankl, a Viennese psychiatrist, was imprisoned in Auschwitz for three years. He survived, but his wife and most other members of his family perished in the camps.

7. Dehumanization and Starvation
Viktor E. Frankl

Suddenly there was a stir among my fellow travelers, who had been standing about with pale, fright-

ened faces, helplessly debating. Again we heard the
hoarsely shouted commands. We were driven with
blows into the immediate anteroom of the bath. There
we assembled around an SS man who waited until we
had all arrived. Then he said, "I will give you two
minutes, and I shall time you by my watch. In these
two minutes you will get fully undressed and drop
everything on the floor where you are standing. You
will take nothing with you except your shoes, your belt
or suspenders, and possibly a truss. I am starting to
count—now!"

With unthinkable haste, people tore off their
clothes. As the time grew shorter, they became increasingly nervous and pulled clumsily at their underwear,
belts and shoelaces. Then we heard the first sounds of
whipping; leather straps beating down on naked bodies.

Next we were herded into another room to be
shaved: not only our heads were shorn, but not a hair
was left on our entire bodies. Then on to the showers,
where we lined up again. We hardly recognized each
other; but with great relief some people noted that real
water dripped from the sprays.

While we were waiting for the shower, our naked-
ness was brought home to us: we really had nothing
now except our bare bodies—even minus hair; all we
possessed, literally, was our naked existence.

During the latter part of our imprisonment, the
daily ration consisted of very watery soup given out
once daily, and the usual small bread ration. In addition to that, there was the so-called "extra allowance,"
consisting of three-fourths of an ounce of margarine,
or of a slice of poor quality sausage, or of a little piece
of cheese, or a bit of synthetic honey, or a spoonful of
watery jam, varying daily. In calories, this diet was
absolutely inadequate, especially taking into consideration our heavy manual work and our constant exposure to the cold in inadequate clothing. The sick
who were "under special care"—that is, those who
were allowed to lie in the huts instead of leaving the
camp for work—were even worse off.

When the last layers of subcutaneous fat had vanished, and we looked like skeletons disguised with skin and rags, we could watch our bodies beginning to devour themselves. The organism digested its own protein, and the muscles disappeared. Then the body had no powers of resistance left. One after another the members of the little community in our hut died. Each of us could calculate with fair accuracy whose turn would be next, and when his own would come.

Prison camps of various kinds, well over a hundred by the end of the war, played a key role in the Nazi program to dispose of all people regarded as "undesirable." They were all located in Germany or Poland. In the middle 1930s, the camps were used mainly for internment or "protective custody" of Communists, other political dissidents, homosexuals, cripples, and the like. After 1939, many camps were used largely for forced labor: Jews and other prisoners, living at starvation levels, worked in German farms and war factories. Thousands of prisoners died of starvation, exposure, and illness. Countless others were shot to death. Following adoption of the Final Solution plan in 1941, six special camps (those marked with an "X" on the map) were equipped with gas chambers and crematoria. Auschwitz, the largest of these extermination camps, accounted for some 2 million deaths in a two-and-a-half-year period. A worker at Auschwitz said that "the stench given off by the pyres contaminated the surrounding countryside. At night the red sky over Auschwitz could be seen for miles." Yet people living in the vicinity of these camps claimed to know nothing of their existence.

Königsberg

Danzig
Stutthof

P O L A N D

Bialystok

Treblinka

Posen
Chelmno

Warsaw

Brest

Lodz

Sobibor

Lublin
Maidanek

Leignitz

Breslau

Gross
Rosen

Oppeln

Belzec

Gleiwitz
Kattowitz
Auschwitz

Plaszów

Krakau

Lwow

Teschen

O S L O V A K I A

Vienna

Bratislava

H U N G A R Y

MILES

0   20   60   120

Railroads

Main Concentration Camps

Extermination Camps

As soon as Hitler came to power in 1933, he began to put into effect various laws and regulations that deprived the Jews, bit by bit, of their rights and property. It was all done legally, because Hitler had absolute power. To stifle protest or criticism, from Jew or non-Jew, armed storm troopers were free to use violence and imprisonment. Particularly at the beginning, could anyone be certain where the chain of actions would lead?

This chronology was compiled from two sources: *Friedrich* by Hans Peter Richter, and *The Destruction of the European Jews* by Raul Hilberg.

9. Chronology of Laws and Actions Directed Against Jews in Nazi Germany 1933–45

Dates given for laws, decrees, and regulations are dates of public announcement.

(1933)

January 30, 1933	Adolf Hitler becomes Chancellor of the German Reich. He is the Supreme Leader of the NSDAP (National Socialist German Workers Party) and the SA (storm troopers).
March 5, 1933	Adolf Hitler receives a strong vote of confidence from the German people in the *Reichstagswahl* (parliamentary elections).
March 24, 1933	The Reichstag (German Parlia-

	ment) empowers Hitler to enact laws on its behalf.
April 1, 1933	Adolf Hitler proclaims a one-day boycott of all Jewish shops.
April 7, 1933	All non-Aryan civil servants, with the exception of soldiers, are forcibly retired.
April 21, 1933	Kosher butchering is forbidden by law.
April 25, 1933	Fewer non-Aryan children are admitted to German schools and universities.
June 16, 1933	There are 500,000 Jews living in the Third Reich.
July 14, 1933	German nationality can be revoked—for those considered "undesirable" by the government.

(1934)

| August 2, 1934 | Paul von Hindenburg, second president of the German Republic, dies. |
| August 3, 1934 | Adolf Hitler declares himself both President *and* Chancellor of the Third Reich. |

(1935)

March 16, 1935	Compulsory military service is reinstituted in Germany in open defiance of the Versailles Treaty.
September 6, 1935	Jewish newspapers can no longer be sold in the street.
September 15, 1935	Nuremberg Laws deprive Jews of German citizenship and reduce them to the status of "sub-

jects"; forbid marriage or any sexual relations between Jews and Aryans; forbid Jews to employ Aryan servants under the age of 35.

(1936)

March 7, 1936

Jews no longer have the right to participate in parliamentary elections.

The German army reoccupies the Rhineland.

August 1, 1936

The Olympic Games are opened in Berlin. Signs reading "Jews Not Welcome" are temporarily removed from most public places by order of the Führer— to present a favorable and misleading picture to foreign tourists.

(1937)

July 2, 1937

More Jewish students are removed from German schools and universities.

November 16, 1937

Jews can obtain passports for travel abroad only in special cases.

(1938)

March 11, 1938

German troops march into Austria.

July 6, 1938

Jews may no longer follow certain occupations such as broker, matchmaker, tourist guide, real estate agent.

July 23, 1938

As of January 1, 1939, all Jews must carry identification cards.

July 25, 1938	As of September 30, 1938, Jewish doctors can be regarded only as "medical attendants."
July 27, 1938	All "Jewish" street names are replaced.
August 17, 1938	As of January 1, 1939, all Jews must have only Jewish first names. If a Jew has a German first name, "Israel" or "Sarah" must be added to it.
October 5, 1938	Jewish passports are marked with a "J."
October 28, 1938	About 15,000 "stateless" Jews are "resettled" in Poland.
November 7, 1938	Herschel Grynszpan, a Jew, attempts to assassinate the German Attaché, vom Rath, in Paris.
November 9, 1938	Vom Rath dies. Goebbels, recognizing the propaganda value, issues instructions that "spontaneous demonstrations" against Jews are to be "organized and executed" throughout Germany —in retaliation! The pogrom begins.
November 10, 1938	Pogrom continues.
November 11, 1938	Jews may no longer own or bear arms. Destruction of synagogues in entire Reich.
November 12, 1938	Following the Nazi-organized pogrom, "reparations" of one billion Reichsmarks are imposed on the German Jews, and they must further repair all damages at their own cost. Jews may no longer head businesses. Jews may no longer attend

plays, movies, concerts, and exhibitions.

November 15, 1938   All Jewish children remaining in German schools are removed to Jewish schools.

November 23, 1938   All Jewish businesses are closed down.

November 28, 1938   Jews may no longer be in certain districts at certain times.

December 3, 1938   Local authorities allowed to bar Jews from the streets on Nazi holidays.

Jews must hand in their driver's licenses and car registrations.

Jews must sell their businesses, real estate, and hand over their securities and jewelry.

December 8, 1938   Jews may no longer attend universities.

(1939)

March 15, 1939   German troops march into Czechoslovakia.

April 30, 1939   Rent protection for Jews is reduced.

May 17, 1939   About 215,000 Jews still live in the Third Reich.

September 1, 1939   Germany declares war on Poland.

September 3, 1939   WORLD WAR II BEGINS.

(Curfew for Jews is instituted: 9 P.M. in summer, 8 P.M. in winter.)

September 21, 1939   Pogroms against Jews in Poland.

September 23, 1939   All Jews must hand in their radios to the police.

October 12, 1939	Austrian Jews are beginning to be deported to Poland.
October 19, 1939	"Reparations" for German Jews are increased to 1.25 billion Reichsmarks and are now payable by November 15, 1939.
November 23, 1939	Polish Jews must now wear yellow stars of David.

(1940)

February 6, 1940	Unlike the rest of the German people, Jews do not receive clothing coupons.
February 12, 1940	German Jews begin to be taken into "protective custody," that is, deported to concentration camps.
July 29, 1940	Jews may no longer have telephones.
December 24, 1940	Jews to pay special income tax.

(1941)

June 12, 1941	Jews must designate themselves as "unbelievers."
July 31, 1941	Beginning of the "final solution."
September 1, 1941	Every Jew in Germany must also wear a star of David. Jews may no longer leave their places of residence without permission of the police.
October 14, 1941	The large-scale deportation of Jews to concentration camps begins.
October 24, 1941	Friendly relations with Jews prohibited.
December 26, 1941	Jews may no longer use public telephones.

(1942)

January 1, 1942	Approximately 130,000 Jews now live in the Third Reich.
January 10, 1942	Jews must hand in any woolen and fur clothing still in their possession.
February 17, 1942	Jews may no longer subscribe to newspapers or magazines.
April 17, 1942	A Jewish apartment must be identified as such with a star of David beside the name plate.
April 24, 1942	Jews are forbidden the use of public transportation.
May 15, 1942	Jews are forbidden to keep dogs, cats, birds, etc.
May 29, 1942	Jews are no longer permitted to visit barber shops.
June 9, 1942	Jews must hand over all "spare" clothing.
June 11, 1942	Jews no longer receive smoking coupons.
June 19, 1942	Jews must hand over all electrical and optical equipment, as well as typewriters and bicycles.
June 20, 1942	All Jewish schools are closed.
July 17, 1942	Blind or deaf Jews may no longer wear armbands identifying their condition in traffic.
September 9, 1942	Jews not permitted to institute civil suits.
September 18, 1942	Jews can no longer buy meat, eggs, or milk.
October 4, 1942	All Jews still in concentration camps in Germany are to be transferred to (extermination camp) Auschwitz.

(1943)

April 21, 1943	Jews found guilty of crimes are to be conveyed to extermination camps in Auschwitz or Lublin after serving their sentences.
July 1, 1943	Property of Jew to be confiscated after his death.

(1944)

September 1, 1944	Approximately 15,000 Jews now live in the Third Reich.

(1945)

January 17, 1945	Soviet troops liberate Warsaw.
February 4-11, 1945	Yalta Conference in the Crimea.
March 5, 1945	American troops reach the Rhine River.
April 11, 1945	American troops liberate Buchenwald death camp.
April 15, 1945	British troops liberate Bergen-Belsen death camp.
April 25, 1945	American and Soviet troops meet at the Elbe River.
April 30, 1945	Hitler commits suicide.
May 7, 1945	Germany surrenders unconditionally. End of the war in Europe.
August 15, 1945	Japan surrenders unconditionally. End of World War II.
November 22, 1945	Nuremberg War Crimes Tribunal commences.

The Nuremberg Trials concluded on October 1, 1946, which happened to be the Day of Atonement (Yom Kippur), with a judgment in which 12

defendants were sentenced to
death, three to life imprisonment, four to various prison
terms, and three acquitted.

———————————

Between the years 1933 and 1938, some
280,000 Jews, or a little more than half the
Jewish population of Germany, managed to
leave the country, despite enormous difficulties
in gaining permission to enter other countries.
An American woman here recounts her own
family's experiences when Hitler came to power. This family was one of the fortunate ones.
The article appeared originally in *Scholastic
Search*, May 2, 1974.

Catherine Hanf Noren is the author of
The Camera of My Family, a 100-year album
of a German-Jewish family.

10. We Escaped From Hitler's Germany

Catherine Noren

I am a member of a very large German family.
On my mother's side alone, there are 30 first cousins.
(Her mother was one of eight children. Her father was
one of 10 children.) My mother's family name is Wallach. The Wallachs in Germany have been traced back
to the 14th century.

There are almost no members of my family left in
Germany now. They were all driven out by Adolf
Hitler and the Nazis before the Second World War.
Those that did not escape from Germany died in concentration camps. The camps were part of Hitler's
"final solution"—his plan to murder all the Jews in
every land he took over.

Many members of my family did escape. They now live all over the world—in the U.S., Africa, South America, Israel, France, and other nations. For nine years after we left Germany, my parents, my sister, and I lived in Australia.

Hitler Moves to Our Town

In 1918, Adolf Hitler was 29 years old. That year, he moved to Munich. Munich was the home of my grandparents and their four children—my mother, my aunt, and my two uncles.

Germany was in a real mess. World War I had just ended. The German government was all in confusion. The people were hungry. The land had been ruined by the war. Even if you had money, there was little to buy. It was the perfect time for a strong man to step in and take over the country.

When Hitler started the Nazi Party in Munich in 1920, it had only seven members. If they were alive today, they would be thought of as the worst kind of vagrants. Hitler himself was a school dropout. He spent his teenage years wandering the streets of Vienna, Austria. He slept in flophouses and did odd jobs from time to time. Once in a while, he sold a painting or two. (He thought of himself as an artist, but he had little talent.)

Hitler, with his tiny Nazi Party, had dreams of power. He decided to try to take over the government of the state of Bavaria in 1923. His idea was to capture 50 important businessmen and city leaders as hostages. He would threaten them with death if the government was not handed over to him.

My grandfather was to be taken as one of Hitler's hostages. My Uncle Rolf remembers that day very clearly. This is how he described it to me recently:

"It was November 8, 1923. First the Nazis took one of the Bavarian leaders at gunpoint. They made him agree to work with them in the new government they were setting up. At nine in the morning, they sent out groups of men to capture the 50 hostages. They knew exactly who they wanted, and they sent three or four men to capture each one.

"I was in school that day—high school. They let the whole school out at 11. We were told not to go into the city, but to go straight home. When I got home, a Nazi storm trooper opened the door for me. He had our maid and the mailman in the kitchen. Anybody who came to the door was put into the kitchen so they couldn't warn my father. They had sent people to our apartment and to our father's business.

"After about 15 minutes, the phone rang. The storm trooper took the call. After a while, he told us we could go. They had captured my father at his business. Mother and a friend of hers were walking down the street. They saw people being taken away. They didn't know what was going on. They didn't know that Father had been captured until they got home.

"After the Nazis had all their hostages, they marched into the city. There they were met by the police. The police gave orders to halt, but the Nazis didn't halt. Shots rang out and 19 people—13 Nazis, three policemen, three bystanders—were killed. Hitler threw himself to the ground when the shooting started, and then escaped. The police then went and released the hostages. Father was home again by five o'clock. What would have happened if Hitler was successful? I don't know. But as it was, the whole thing lasted only half a day."

Two days later, Hitler was found hiding in a cupboard at a friend's home. He was arrested and sent to prison. While Hitler was in jail, he wrote a book called *Mein Kampf—My Struggle*. In it, he wrote of his plans to take over the whole German government. He wrote about his hatred of democracy and his hatred of the Jews. He wrote that the Aryans (white, non-Jewish people) were the master race of the world. He wrote that he would lead Germany and make it the greatest empire in the world.

Hitler was released from jail in 1924. The Nazi

Party grew larger and stronger. In 1933, less than 10 years after his first takeover attempt, Hitler was named chancellor of all of Germany. As soon as he became chancellor, he started to introduce some of the things he had written about in *Mein Kampf.*

Only Half a Block Away

My grandparents and their four children lived only half a block from Hitler in Munich. My Aunt Annelise, one of the four children, told me: "I used to walk home from school. Every once in a while, Hitler and a group of his people passed by in their car. They would honk the horn. Everybody on the sidewalk would stop and salute. Of course, I wouldn't do that. It was quite uncomfortable living so close to him."

Annelise was in junior high during the early 1930s. I asked her whether the hatred of the Jews could be found in the schools as well as in the government. She said that it depended which school you went to and who the teachers were.

"I had only one bad experience," she told me. "It was with my gym teacher who was a real Nazi. I had a friend in that class who was also Jewish. She and I were the best in the gym class. And the teacher was always yelling at the rest of the class, saying, 'You lazy girls! How can you let these two Jew girls be better than you!' "

One of the Nazi laws was that Aryans were not allowed to date Jews. When Annelise was in high school, she had a non-Jewish boyfriend. Wherever they went, they were always scared that they would be caught.

One day, as they were crossing a big square near my grandparents' house, a policeman called her over. "Oh, this is it!" she thought. "Now they've got me."

She walked up to the policeman. "You shouldn't walk on the grass," he said. "You should walk around the square."

A Storm Trooper Knocks

Hitler and the Nazis began to make things very rough for the Jews. My grandfather was also in trouble because of the work he did.

My grandfather was born in a small town in the north of Germany. As he and his brother grew up, they saw that many of the peasant folk traditions of Germany were dying out. As women left their homes and went to work in city factories, they threw away their peasant costumes. Every area of Germany had its own native dress. But this clothing was being forgotten as people wanted to look more modern and sophisticated.

My grandfather and his brother decided to try to save these dying traditions. They opened a folk museum in Munich. The museum had 42 rooms. Each room was designed and decorated with traditional native furniture and folk art of a different area.

Because of this museum, my grandfather was a target for the Nazis. Hitler also wanted to bring back the clothes, furniture, and art of the past. He hated the idea of Jewish people owning this museum. So, the Nazis wanted to get their hands on my grandfather's business. They wanted his collections, his furniture, and his art.

One day in 1937, a Nazi storm trooper knocked on my grandparents' door. My grandmother answered and asked him what he wanted. "I am here to take away all of your cultural objects," he said. "Is there anything that you would like to keep? Is there anything that you particularly love that you would like to save?"

"Yes," my grandmother said. "I want to save these antique pewter containers. I'm saving them for my son Rolf."

The pewter containers were the first thing that the Nazi took. He had just wanted to find out what my grandmother treasured the most, so he could be sure and take them. He took a great many other things as well.

My grandparents were among hundreds of thousands of people robbed by the Nazis. During the war, the Nazis stole art treasures from all over Europe. They stashed their loot away in caves and other hiding places. They planned to unpack and enjoy them once they had won the war.

After the war, U.S. and Allied soldiers found these hidden treasures. One of the crates they found was labeled with my grandfather's name—Wallach. They wrote to my grandfather and asked him to list everything the Nazis had taken from him. He sent them the list. All of the stolen property was in the crate, including the pewter containers. My Uncle Rolf got the containers, after all. They are now in his living room in Connecticut. I photographed them a few weeks ago.

Crystal Night

In the late 1930s, the Nazis started to take over all businesses owned by Jewish people. In 1937, an antique dealer named Witte came to see my grandfather. He offered to buy my grandfather's business. But my grandfather said no. The next year, Mr. Witte came again. This time his offer was not an offer at all—it was a threat. Things had changed.

This is what had happened: On November 8, a German embassy worker was shot and killed by a Jewish man who hated the Nazis. As revenge, during the next three days, the windows of Jewish stores and synagogues all over Germany were smashed. Thousands of Jewish men and boys were rounded up and thrown into concentration camps. Hitler now had the excuse he needed to start what he called "the final solution" —the murder of all Jews in Germany.

This incident is known as Crystal Night. That's because of the sound of broken glass that was heard throughout the whole country that night. My father was one of the men thrown into jail that night. But he was lucky. He had some money on him. He used it to bribe the guard to let him out of his cell.

A few days after Crystal Night, Witte came back to see my grandfather. He told my grandfather that if he didn't sell, he would be thrown into a concentration camp. So my grandfather sold his business to Witte for a very small sum of money. He put the money in the bank. A few days later, the money was taken by the government. They said it was a tax for being able to leave the country.

Getting Out

Many Jewish people had already left Germany. My Uncle Rolf had left, but the rest of my family was still there.

On Crystal Night, right after he was let out of his cell, my father went to the police. He told them that our family had visas to leave the country. He asked if we could go. (I was a tiny baby at that time, and my sister Brigitte was four.) We were given 10 days to get out of the country. Ten days later, we were on a boat to Australia.

My grandparents did not have visas to leave. You had to have a visa from the country to which you wanted to go. They were not easy to get. Hundreds of thousands of people were trying to get out of Europe at that time.

But my Uncle Rolf had come to the U.S. in 1928. He was already a U.S. citizen. And he was able to get visas for my grandparents.

Rolf had come to the U.S. because he was angry. He was 18 in 1928. He had been invited to sit in on my grandfather's business meetings. At his very first meeting, he opened his mouth to say something, and my grandfather told him to be quiet.

Rolf sat silently until the meeting was over. Then he walked out of the room and went to the American Consulate. He applied for a visa to the U.S. A few weeks later, he sailed to America.

Rolf's falling-out with my grandfather turned out to be very lucky. By 1938, he was a U.S. citizen. And he had enough money to be able to sponsor my grand-parents, my Uncle Fritz, my Aunt Annelise, and six other members of the family.

Some of my grandparents' sisters and brothers could not get out, though. They couldn't find a sponsor (Rolf was allowed to sponsor only 10 people). And they didn't have enough money to buy their way out. These people—some of my great aunts and uncles and some of their children—died in Hitler's concentration camps. This has been one of the great sadnesses of my family's life.

A New Life

If my grandfather had been paid fairly for his business, he would have been able to get the rest of the family out of Germany. But he was not. He and my grandmother arrived in New York in 1939 with 10 marks—$2.50 in U.S. money—in their pockets.

My grandparents were starting a new life in New York. And my parents, my sister, and I were doing the same thing in Australia. For the last year of our stay in Australia, I went to public school in Melbourne. The school was very old-fashioned. If you did something wrong or didn't do your homework, the teachers would hit you. The girls were hit with a ruler, the boys got the strap. We used to get rapped over the knuckles for every spelling word we got wrong. To this day, I'm a very good speller!

I loved to draw, and I was always drawing in class. The teacher warned me several times to stop. But one day, a friend asked me to draw a picture of her. Needless to say, I was caught.

The teacher called me up to the front of the class. I was hit 10 times across the back of my knees with a ruler. Then I was sent to stand in the corner with a dunce cap on my head. I stood there, facing the wall, and the tears dripped down my face.

All over the world, the war was going on and people were suffering and dying. But this day in class

in Melbourne is one of my most vivid memories from
that time.

I will also never forget how happy we all were the
day the war ended. We were all set to sail for the U.S.
It was very exciting. The journey from Melbourne to
New York took six weeks. When we finally arrived,
there at the pier waiting for us were my grandparents,
my Uncle Rolf, my Uncle Fritz, and my Aunt Annelise.

We were a family again.

In 1943, Elie Wiesel was a boy living in
the village of Sighet, in a mountainous region
of Hungary. The war had barely touched this
remote settlement; the radio was their sole
source of information about the fighting. In his
novel, *Night*, Wiesel relates how one day all
non-Hungarians were expelled from the town.
His beloved teacher, Moche the Beadle, was
among those rounded up and deported.

11. "Listen to Me!"

Elie Wiesel

Several days passed. Several weeks. Several
months. Life had returned to normal. A wind of calm-
ness and reassurance blew through our houses. The
traders were doing good business, the students lived
buried in their books, and the children played in the
streets.

One day, as I was just going into the synagogue, I
saw, sitting on a bench near the door, Moché the Beadle.

He told his story and that of his companions. The
train full of deportees had crossed the Hungarian
frontier and on Polish territory had been taken in
charge by the Gestapo. There it had stopped. The Jews
had to get out and climb into lorries. The lorries drove

toward a forest. The Jews were made to get out. They were made to dig huge graves. And when they had finished their work, the Gestapo began theirs. Without passion, without haste, they slaughtered their prisoners. Each one had to go up to the hole and present his neck. Babies were thrown into the air and the machine gunners used them as targets. This was in the forest of Galicia, near Kolomaye. How had Moché the Beadle escaped? Miraculously. He was wounded in the leg and taken for dead. . . .

Through long days and nights, he went from one Jewish house to another, telling the story of Malka, the young girl who had taken three days to die, and of Tobias, the tailor, who had begged to be killed before his sons. . . .

Moché had changed. There was no longer any joy in his eyes. He no longer sang. He no longer talked to me of God or the cabbala, but only of what he had seen. People refused not only to believe his stories, but even to listen to them.

"He's just trying to make us pity him. What an imagination he has!" they said. Or even: "Poor fellow. He's gone mad."

And as for Moché, he wept.

"Jews, listen to me. It's all I ask of you. I don't want money or pity. Only listen to me," he would cry between prayers at dusk and the evening prayers.

I did not believe him myself. I would often sit with him in the evening after the service, listening to his stories and trying my hardest to understand his grief. I felt only pity for him.

"They take me for a madman," he would whisper, and tears, like drops of wax, flowed from his eyes.

Once, I asked him this question:

"Why are you so anxious that people should believe what you say? In your place, I shouldn't care whether they believed me or not. . . ."

He closed his eyes, as though to escape time.

"You don't understand," he said in despair. "You can't understand. I have been saved miraculously. I managed to get back here. Where did I get the strength from? I wanted to come back to Sighet to tell you the story of my death. So that you could prepare yourselves while there was still time. To live? I don't attach any importance to my life any more. I'm alone. No, I wanted to come back, and to warn you. And see how it is, no one will listen to me. . . ."

That was toward the end of 1942. Afterward life returned to normal. The London radio, which we listened to every evening, gave us heartening news: the daily bombardment of Germany; Stalingrad; preparation for the second front. And we, the Jews of Sighet, were waiting for better days, which would not be long in coming now.

I continued to devote myself to my studies. By day, the Talmud, at night, the cabbala. My father was occupied with his business and the doings of the community. My grandfather had come to celebrate the New Year with us, so that he could attend the services of the famous rabbi of Borsche. My mother began to think that it was high time to find a suitable young man for Hilda.

Thus the year 1943 passed by.

Spring 1944. Good news from the Russian front. No doubt could remain now of Germany's defeat. It was only a question of time—of months or weeks perhaps.

The trees were in blossom. This was a year like any other, with its springtime, its betrothals, its weddings and births.

People said: "The Russian army's making gigantic strides forward . . . Hitler won't be able to do us any harm, even if he wants to."

Yes, we even doubted that he wanted to exterminate us.

Was he going to wipe out a whole people? Could he exterminate a population scattered throughout so many countries? So many millions! What methods could he use? And in the middle of the twentieth century!

Besides, people were interested in everything—in strategy, in diplomacy, in politics, in Zionism—but not in their own fate.

Even Moché the Beadle was silent. He was weary of speaking. He wandered in the synagogue or in the streets, with his eyes down, his back bent, avoiding people's eyes.

At that time, it was still possible to obtain emigration permits for Palestine. I had asked my father to sell out, liquidate his business, and leave.

"I'm too old, my son," he replied. "I'm too old to start a new life. I'm too old to start from scratch again in a country so far away. . . ."

The Budapest radio announced that the Fascist party had come into power. Horthy had been forced to ask one of the leaders of the Nyilas party to form a new government.

Still this was not enough to worry us. Of course we had heard about the Fascists, but they were still just an abstraction to us. This was only a change in the administration.

The following day, there was more disturbing news: with government permission, German troops had entered Hungarian territory.

Here and there, anxiety was aroused. One of our friends, Berkovitz, who had just returned from the capital, told us:

"The Jews in Budapest are living in an atmosphere of fear and terror. There are anti-Semitic incidents every day, in the streets, in the trains. The Fascists are attacking Jewish shops and synagogues. The situation is getting very serious."

This news spread like wildfire through Sighet. Soon it was on everyone's lips. But not for long. Optimism soon revived.

"The Germans won't get as far as this. They'll stay in Budapest. There are strategic and political reasons. . . ."

Before three days had passed, German army cars had appeared in our streets.

Anguish. German soldiers—with their steel helmets and their emblem, the death's head.

However, our first impressions of the Germans were most reassuring. The officers were billeted in private houses, even in the homes of Jews. Their attitude toward their hosts was distant, but polite. They never demanded the impossible, made no unpleasant comments, and even smiled occasionally at the mistress of the house. One German officer lived in the house opposite ours. He had a room with the Kahn family. They said he was a charming man—calm, likable, polite, and sympathetic. Three days after he moved in he brought Madame Kahn a box of chocolates. The optimists rejoiced.

"Well, there you are, you see! What did we tell you? You wouldn't believe us. There they are *your* Germans! What do you think of them? Where is their famous cruelty?"

The Germans were already in the town, the Fascists were already in power, the verdict had already been pronounced, yet the Jews of Sighet continued to smile.

——————

Like the Jews, the Gypsies were outside the Christian churches' universe of obligation. They have been repeatedly persecuted in Europe since they appeared there. Although the Gypsies are believed to have migrated from India, a homeland of Aryan languages, they were defined in Nazi Germany as non-Aryan and further labelled as asocial. Thus, they could not be assimilated into the race "of pure blood"—the mythical Aryans—which Hitler and Himmler dreamed of creating. And thus, they became legitimate targets for extinction and were the next victims of genocide.

The following passages are taken from *Accounting for Genocide: National Responses*

and Jewish Victimization During the Holocaust
by Helen Fein (New York: The Free Press, 1978).

12. Extermination of the Gypsies
Helen Fein

The Jews were not the only group in Germany
stigmatized as alien, but they were the only stigmatized
group of political significance whose elimination had
been promised publicly by Hitler twenty years before it
began. The Gypsies were also designated for destruction, although scarcely any publicity was devoted to the
"Gypsy problem."

Although Gypsies have not played a symbolic
role similar to that of the Jews—they cannot be labeled a "middleman minority"—they have been accused of crime and corruption since their entry into
Europe, charged with assistance at the Crucifixion, un-
natural copulation, cannibalism, necrophiliac activity,
and spreading filth and disease. The first response of
European states from the fifteenth to the eighteenth
century was to expel them: 148 such laws were passed
by German states alone between 1416 and 1774. Violence was commonly employed for enforcement and
deterrence. As late as the nineteenth century, Gypsy
hunts (like fox hunts) occurred in Denmark. Only after
drives for expulsion and extermination had failed did
states attempt to assimilate them, denying the right of
Gypsies to live together, by encouraging settlement and
criminalizing the nomads' life. By 1933 police in
France, Baden, and Prussia already had files with finger-
printed identification of Gypsies there.

Gypsies were officially defined as non-Aryan by
the Nuremberg laws of 1935, which also first defined
Jews; both groups were forbidden to marry Germans.
Gypsies were later labeled as asocials by the 1937 Laws
against Crime, regardless of whether they had been
charged with any unlawful acts. Two hundred Gypsy

men were then selected by quota and incarcerated in Buchenwald concentration camp. By May 1938, SS Reichsführer Himmler established the Central Office for Fighting the Gypsy Menace, which defined the question as "a matter of race," discriminating pure Gypsies from part Gypsies as Jews were discriminated, and ordering their registration. In 1939, resettlement of Gypsies was put under Eichmann's jurisdiction along with that of the Jews. Gypsies were forbidden to move freely and were concentrated in encampments within Germany in 1939, later (1941) transformed into fenced ghettos, from which they would be seized for transport by the crime police (aided by dogs) and dispatched to Auschwitz in February 1943.

The legal status of Gypsies and Jews, determined irrevocably by the agreement between Justice Minister Thierack and SS Reichsführer Himmler on 18 September 1942, removing both groups from the jurisdiction of any German court, confirmed their fate. Thierack wrote, "I envisage transferring all criminal proceedings concerning [these people] to Himmler. I do this because I realize that the courts can only feebly contribute to the extermination of these people."

The Citizenship Law of 1943 omitted any mention of Gypsies since they were not expected to exist much longer. Himmler decreed the transport of Gypsies to Auschwitz on 16 December 1942, but he did not authorize their extermination until 1944. Most died there and in other camps of starvation, diseases, and torture from abuse as live experimental subjects. By the end of the war, 15,000 of the 20,000 Gypsies who had been in Germany in 1938 had died.

The largest single group of people killed by the Nazis were six million European Jews. This number represented one-third of the entire Jewish population of the world at that time. In 1976, the world Jewish population stood at

14,500,000. In addition to the six million Jews, the Nazis destroyed an equal number of non-Jews, of various nationalities, during the course of the war.

The chart is reprinted from *Keeping Posted*.

13. Estimates of Jewish Losses 1939–45

COUNTRY	ESTIMATED PRE-FINAL SOLUTION POPULATION	ESTIMATED JEWISH POPULATION ANNIHILATED	
		Number	Percent
Poland	3,300,000	3,000,000	90
Baltic countries	253,000	228,000	90
Germany/Austria	240,000	210,000	90
Bohemia/Moravia	90,000	80,000	89
Slovakia	90,000	75,000	83
Greece	70,000	54,000	77
The Netherlands	140,000	105,000	75
Hungary	650,000	450,000	70
SSR White Russia	375,000	245,000	65
SSR Ukraine*	1,500,000	900,000	60
Belgium	65,000	40,000	60
Yugoslavia	43,000	26,000	60
Rumania	600,000	300,000	50
Norway	1,800	900	50
France	350,000	90,000	26
Bulgaria	64,000	14,000	22
Italy	40,000	8,000	20
Luxembourg	5,000	1,000	20
Russia (RSFSR)*	975,000	107,000	11
Denmark	8,000	—	—
Finland	2,000	—	—
Total	8,861,800	5,933,900	67

*The Germans did not occupy all the territory of this republic.

THE NATURE OF MAN

We now turn our attention away from the history of the Holocaust, and begin to seek answers to the questions that arise, inescapably, from the foregoing readings. How could this immense tragedy have happened? How could civilized, religious, educated Germans commit acts of such unspeakable bestiality? Were the Nazis unique—or could anyone, we ourselves perhaps, be capable of the same?

The five readings that follow present different perspectives on the nature of man by well-known philosophers and scientists from the 15th century to the present. Though some of the readings are difficult, each makes reasonably clear its author's beliefs about whether people are fundamentally good or bad.

Niccolo Machiavelli (1469–1527) ("The Prince") was an Italian statesman and writer who is regarded as the first political philosopher of modern times. Among his writings are: *The Prince* and *The Art of War*. He believed in government by the people but felt that the Italians of his day were unfit to rule themselves. He is concerned with the use and abuse of power.

14. The Prince

Niccolo Machiavelli

This, then, gives rise to the question "whether it be better to be beloved than feared, or to be feared than beloved." It will naturally be answered that it would be desirable to be both the one and the other; but as it is difficult to be both at the same time, it is much more safe to be feared than to be loved when you have to choose between the two. For it may be said of men in general that they are ungrateful and fickle, dissemblers, avoiders of danger, and greedy of gain. So long as you shower benefits upon them, they are all yours; they offer you their blood, their substance, their lives, and their children, provided the necessity for it is far off; but when it is near at hand, then they revolt. And the prince who relies upon their words, without having otherwise provided for his security, is ruined; for friendships that are won by rewards, and not by greatness and nobility of soul, although deserved, yet are not real, and cannot be depended upon in time of adversity.

Besides, men have less hesitation in offending one who makes himself beloved than one who makes himself feared; for love holds by a bond of obligation which, as mankind is bad, is broken on every occasion whenever it is for the interest of the obliged party to break it. But fear holds by the apprehension of punishment, which never leaves men.

It being necessary then for a prince to know well how to employ the nature of the beasts, he should be able to assume both that of the fox and that of the lion; for while the latter cannot escape the traps laid for him, the former cannot defend himself against the wolves. A prince should be a fox, to know the traps and snares; and a lion, to be able to frighten the wolves; for those who simply hold to the nature of the lion do not understand their business.

A sagacious prince then cannot and should not fulfill his pledges when their observance is contrary to his interest, and when the causes that induced him to pledge his faith no longer exist. If men were all good, then indeed this precept would be bad; but as men are naturally bad, and will not observe their faith toward you, you must, in the same way, not observe yours to them; and no prince ever yet lacked legitimate reasons with which to color his want of good faith. Innumerable modern examples could be given of this; and it could easily be shown how many treaties of peace, and how many engagements, have been made null and void by the faithlessness of princes; and he who has best known how to play the fox has ever been the most successful.

Thomas Hobbes (1588–1679) ("Man Is Evil and Warlike") was an English political philosopher whose critical and negative perceptions of man were often unpopular. In his famous work *Leviathan* he was so critical of his government that this work was condemned by the British House of Commons in 1666 and *Behemoth* was censored. He also wrote *The Elements of Law, Natural and Politic.*

15. Man Is Evil and Warlike
Thomas Hobbes

From this equality of ability arises equality of hope in the attaining of our ends. And therefore if any two men desire the same thing, which nevertheless they cannot both enjoy, they become enemies, and in the way to their end, which is principally their own conservation, and sometimes their delectation only, en-

deavor to destroy or subdue one another. And from
hence it comes to pass that where an invader has no
more to fear than another man's single power, if one
plant, sow, build, or possess a convenient seat, others
may probably be expected to come prepared with
forces united to dispossess and deprive him, not only
of the fruit of his labor, but also of his life or liberty.
And the invader again is in the like danger of another.

And from this diffidence of one another there is
no way for any man to secure himself so reasonable
as anticipation—that is, by force or wiles to master the
persons of all men he can, so long till he see no other
power great enough to endanger him; and this is no
more than his own conservation requires, and is generally allowed. Also, because there be some that take
pleasure in contemplating their own power in the acts
of conquest, which they pursue farther than their security requires, if others that otherwise would be glad
to be at ease within modest bounds should not by invasion increase their power, they would not be able,
long time, by standing only on their defense, to subsist.
And by consequence, such augmentation of dominion
over men being necessary to a man's conservation, it
ought to be allowed him.

Again, men have no pleasure, but on the contrary
a great deal of grief, in keeping company where there
is no power able to overawe them all. For every man
looks that his companion should value him at the same
rate he sets upon himself; and upon all signs of contempt or undervaluing naturally endeavors, as far as
he dares (which among them that have no common
power to keep them in quiet is far enough to make
them destroy each other), to extort a greater value from
his contemners by damage and from others by the
example.

So that in the nature of man we find three principal causes of quarrel: first, competition; secondly, diffidence; thirdly, glory.

The first makes men invade for gain, the second

for safety, and the third for reputation. The first use violence to make themselves masters of other men's persons, wives, children, and cattle; the second, to defend them; the third, for trifles, as a word, a smile, a different opinion, and any other sign of undervalue, either direct in their persons or by reflection in their kindred, their friends, their nation, their profession, or their name.

Hereby it is manifest that, during the time men live without a common power to keep them all in awe, they are in that condition which is called war, and such a war as is of every man against every man.

John Locke (1632–1704) ("Man Is Rational") was an English philosopher who believed in civil liberty, religious tolerance, the power of reason, and the value of experience. His works include: *Essay Concerning Human Understanding; Two Treatises on Civil Government* and *Essays on the Law of Nature.*

16. Man Is Rational

John Locke

The state of nature has a law of nature to govern it, which obliges every one, and reason, which is that law, teaches all mankind, who will but consult it, that being all equal and independent, no one ought to harm another in his life, health, liberty or possessions.

Men living together according to reason without a common superior on earth, with authority to judge between them, are properly in the state of nature.

Robert Ardrey (b. 1908) ("Man Is Innately Aggressive") is a lecturer in the natural sciences and on anthropology. He is also a dramatist or playwright. In 1955 he began his African travels and studies and wrote *African Genesis* (1961), a personal investigation into the Animal Origins and Nature of Man.

17. Man Is Innately Aggressive
Robert Ardrey

In the past 30 years a revolution has been taking place in the natural sciences. It is a revolution in our understanding of animal behavior, and of our link to the animal world. In sum, therefore, the revolution concerns that most absorbing of human entertainments, man's understanding of man. Yet not even science, as a whole, is aware of the philosophical reappraisal which must proceed from its specialists' doings.

Assumptions concerning the nature of man, today unquestioned by education, by psychiatry, by politics, by art, or even by science itself, are being eroded by the tiny streams set loose from obscure scientific springs. And few of us, scientists or laymen, know.

That the contemporary revolution in the natural sciences has proceeded thus far in almost total silence must not be regarded as too great a wonder. Other and noisier revolutions have overwhelmed our unquiet time. As compared with the fortunes of the totalitarian state, of nuclear physics, of antibiotics or the longplaying record, the fortunes of the palaeontologist may seem remote from our daily life. And the work of the revolution has been accomplished by such extreme specialists that it has been recorded only in such inaccessible pages as those of the *American Journal of Anthropology* or the *Biological Symposia*. Such heralds gain few hearers in the modern marketplace.

Still more important than the obscurity or specialization of the revolution has been its suddenness. When in 1930 I emerged from a respectable American university as a respectably well-educated young man, no hint had reached me that private property was other than a human institution evolved by the human brain. If I and my young contemporaries throughout the following years wasted much of our fire on social propositions involving the abolition of private ownership, then we did so in perfect faith that such a course would free mankind of many a frustration. No part of the curriculum of our psychology, sociology, or anthropology departments had presented us with the information that territoriality—the drive to gain, maintain, and defend the exclusive right to a piece of property —is an animal instinct approximately as ancient and powerful as sex.

The role of territory in general animal behavior lies today beyond scientific controversy; then it was unknown. We of the Class of 1930 had to emerge into a world of tumultuous evaluation without benefit of this most salient observation. Similarly, we could not know, as we bemused ourselves with the attractions of the classless state, that hierarchy is an institution among all social animals and the drive to dominate one's fellows an instinct three or four hundred million years old. . . .

We, the approximate Class of 1930, today furnish trusted and vital leadership to world thought, world politics, world society and to whatever may exist of world hope. But we do not know that the human drive to acquire possession is the simple expression of an animal instinct many hundreds of times older than the human race itself. We do not know that the roots of nationalism are dug firmly into the social territoriality of almost every species in our related primate family. We do not know that the status-seekers are responding to animal instincts equally characteristic of baboons, jackdaws, rock cod, and men. Responsible though we may be for the fate of summit conferences, disarmament agreements, juvenile delinquents and new African states, we do not know that the first man was an armed killer, or that evolutionary survival from his mutant instant depended upon the use, the development, and the contest of weapons.

We do not know these things, since they are conclusions to be drawn from the contemporary revolution in the natural sciences. We should know, however, that acquired characteristics cannot be inherited, and that within a species every member is born in the essential image of the first of its kind. No child of ours, born in the middle twentieth century, can differ at birth in significant measure from the earliest of Homo sapiens. No instinct, whether physiological or cultural, that constituted a part of the original human bundle can ever in the history of the species be permanently suppressed or abandoned.

B. F. Skinner (b. 1904) ("Man Is a Product of His Environment") is a professor of psychology at Harvard and a researcher who has won several awards for his contributions in the area of human behavior. He is the author of Walden Two, Science and Human Behavior, Verbal Behavior, and Beyond Freedom & Dignity.

18. Man Is a Product of His Environment

B. F. Skinner

Q: Suppose that people who read your book, and take its message seriously, realize that they are controlled. Will they lose their feelings of freedom?

Skinner: I don't know. I certainly believe that my own behavior is entirely a function of three things—my genetic endowment, my past history as an individual (my family, my religious experience, my government, my schooling, the physical environment in which I have lived, and so on), and the present situation. I am absolutely sure that that is all there is in the determination of what I'm going to do at this very moment. But I don't feel discouraged or unhappy about it at all.

Q: You don't feel like a puppet?

Skinner: I don't feel the least bit like a puppet. Operant conditioning is not pulling strings to make a person dance. It is arranging a world in which a person does things that affect that world, which in turn affects him.

Q: When you come into the classroom and make children want to come to school, would you be controlling their behavior?

Skinner: That's right. A girl who teaches in a Kentucky sixth grade told me of a good example. Her students were not doing their homework; they would not sit down and study; they ran around the room and talked a great deal. She decided to try some operant conditioning. Every Friday afternoon she held a lottery, and the child whose name was drawn out of a jar got a prize. Every Monday morning she would put the week's prize on the wall. One week it was a Halloween costume, another a transistor radio. Whenever a pupil brought in his homework, he could write his name on a ticket and drop it in the jar. Whenever he finished an assignment in class, he could do the same. The system changed the girl's life as a teacher completely. Her pupils did all their homework; they sat quietly and listened to her, because something she said might be just the thing they could use to get another ticket with their name in the jar.

Q: A number of your attackers charge that behavior modification is being used in China today, and they are horrified at the very thought that we might apply it that way in this country.

Skinner: Yes, it is said that the word "fascism" surfaces frequently in discussions of my book. The critics are usually good enough to say that I am not fascist, but that I give aid and comfort to fascism. But every fascist state I've heard of uses aversive control. Its citizens behave as the government dictates because they are afraid not to do so. I've spent my life looking for alternatives to punitive control and arguing in their favor. I oppose standard totalitarian techniques and I want people to feel free and enjoy what they're doing. But it may be true that I give aid and comfort to those who want to make any way of life more effective. What worries me is that in some curious way the struggle for freedom and dignity has made it impossible for us to take advantage of what we're discovering about human behavior. If that proves to be the case, there has been a lethal mutation in our culture that may bring it to an end. A fascist way of life might then gain an advantage, but I'm doing what I can to prevent it.

———————

II

VICTIMS
AND VICTIMIZERS

"And we must not forget that the hate
and terror directed against the Jews were
greater than against any other group (except, possibly, the Gypsies, who were also
marked for genocide). The truth is that
quantitative terms like greater, more, additional are irrelevant here; the hostility toward the Jews was different in kind and
not in degree. It was abysma, 'irrational,'
groundless in the plain meaning of the word
as having no sense, as being beyond sense,
not as mere non-sense, for its consequences
were dire and dismal, but as non-sense, as
having no warrant and no ascertainable
'frame-of-reference.' "

—JACOB GLATSTEIN
Anthology of Holocaust Literature

THE JEWS OF EUROPE

One of the striking and puzzling features of the Holocaust is the singling out of the Jews as the main target of hostility. What made them so vulnerable to attack? The next two readings provide some answers to this question. In the first selection, historian Uriel Tal explains that while Jews won equal rights in Germany at the end of the last century, they could never fully integrate into German society. One reason was that the German people believed "German" and "Christian" to be synonymous; a Jew, therefore, could never be considered a "true" German. The selection is from the book *Christians and Jews of the Second Reich, 1870–1914,* by Uriel Tal.

19. Christians and Jews in Germany 1870–1914

Uriel Tal

We began our study with a discussion of the double aspiration of the Jews in the Second Reich to integrate into the dominant society and at the same time retain their Jewish identity. This endeavor on the part of German Jews was part of a larger struggle of men to achieve freedom in modern society without forfeiting individuality. This struggle gave rise to a number of concomitant questions: how was this Jewish aspiration regarded by the German Christian society of that day; how did it affect the relations between Jews and Christians on the one hand and the Jew's conception of his role in the modern world on the other; what can we learn from this historical attempt of German Jewry to become an integral part of German society and still retain its Jewish identity, that is, achieve equality without surrendering its freedom; and, finally, what conclusions can we draw from this study concerning the interrelationship between modern Jewish history and the history of mankind or between Judaism and Christianity in the modern era and between the Second and the Third Reich.

Friedrich Paulsen explained in his *System of Ethics,* if one is proud of the fact that he is a Jew and not a German, he has no right to complain that the German people do not accept him as a judge or as a teacher of German children: "To remain a complete Jew and a complete German is impossible." When we recall that Paulsen was a prominent liberal and humanist and an outspoken opponent of anti-Semitism, his words take on added significance as a reflection of Germany's determination not to acknowledge the claims of German Jewry to civil equality while retaining its Jewish identity.

In the Second Reich, as well, religion, albeit in its secular form, occupied an important place. Contrary to the expectations of the Jews and the liberals, religion had not become a private matter limited to the sphere of the individual, nor was it cleansed of its irrational elements in accordance with the principles of the Enlightenment. On the contrary, as a result of the process of religious secularization, Christian and especially Protestant patterns of thought and behavior were impressed on the cultural, social, and political life of the Second Reich. The national movement, the political parties, the social and economic organizations, and some of the principal scientific societies—all of which were an integral part of Germany's rapid process of industrialization—defined themselves explicitly as Christian in essence. The Conservative Protestants and an increasing number of Catholics wished to establish the Second Reich on the principle of a Christian state as it had been formulated in conservative ideology throughout the greater part of the 19th century.

German nationality, contrary to the expectations of the Jews, was not acquired by conscious selection or subjective feelings of the citizen but (according to the romantic school of thought) by belonging to a historic community whose roots went back to ancient tribal and pagan sources or in the more recent past to Lutheran Christian culture or (according to the anthropological school of thought) by belonging to a community whose roots went back to groups of different ethnic, cultural, and even religious origins which, through intermarriage and mutual biological assimilation, had come to constitute the present German nation.

Neither of these two views was favorable to German Jewry in its determined effort to integrate into the dominant society while retaining its identity, the first view because of its exclusive conception of German nationality according to which it was not the conscious acknowledgment of belonging to the nation that determined German nationality, but the objective fact of belonging to an organic ethnic group whose roots went back to the pagan Germanic tribes and to the Germans who became Christians and lived under a feudal system in principalities, duchies, and other traditional social forms in the historical German states, the second view because of its inclusive conception of German nationality according to which the determining factor in nationality was not membership in the nation, but the religious and biological fusion of the various ethnic components of the nation that left no room for particularistic internal groups. This second view was the one accepted by a considerable number of intellectual liberals, including many of the leading opponents of modern anti-Semitism, such as Rudolf von Gneist and

Theodor Mommsen, who urged the complete assimilation of Jews into German society and argued that the addition of the Jewish heritage and the personal talents of the Jews would constitute an immense contribution, culturally and biologically, to the growing German nation and would at the same time strengthen the cause of the liberal intellectuals in their struggle against the irrational and pagan elements in German romanticism, potent ingredients in the anti-Semitic ideology of this movement.

Against the background of these conflicting ideologies and political parties within the Second Reich the Jews endeavored to achieve their double goal of complete integration into the social environment without surrendering their identity. Political and racial anti-Semitism during this period failed to exert any appreciable public influence, and whatever effectiveness it had was limited to short intervals and restricted regions. The members of this movement were for the most part recruited from the unstable lower middle class, that is, from marginal groups within the liberal professions, workers who had migrated from rural to urban areas where they led a precarious existence, and city dwellers of the proletarian working class. Only a small number among these social classes turned to the racial-political anti-Semitic movement, most of them being represented in Christian or socialist political and economic organizations.

As a result of this policy of social reform, in which anti-Jewish propaganda had little part, the anti-Semites in 1893, the year when they first became politically significant, received 263,861 votes in the Reichstag election or 3.4 percent of the total vote of 7,673,973. In 1898 they reached the high point of their political success when they received 284,250 votes or 3.7 percent of the total vote of 7,752,693. It is therefore obvious that even in the heyday of their political activity the anti-Semites could not muster enough votes to endorse their policy among their own rank-and-file supporters, who voted instead for the Conservative Protestant and Catholic parties on the one hand and the socialists on the other. This trend continued until the election of 1907 which was preceded by an intensive anti-Semitic campaign in which the anti-Semites sought to strengthen their image as the party of the "small man." The resolutions adopted at the conventions held in Erfurt (1895), in Halle (1896), in Cassel (1898), and in Berlin (1903) reiterated this policy of social reform in favor of the lower middle class, the impoverished farmer, the underprivileged economically and socially, and the embittered and frustrated elements in the large urban centers.

After World War I and during the Weimar Republic the mythological, non-Christian, and anti-Christian character of anti-Semitism grew stronger, thus removing one of the main obstacles to the spread of racial anti-Semitism during the Second Reich and its acceptance by growing masses of the population.

Christian anti-Semitism was not as virulent as racial anti-Semitism. It stigmatized Jewish perfidy, but it permitted the Jew to exist (though not flourish) as the living witness to the truth of Christianity. The Jew must remain to act out his preordained ignominious role as villain in the drama of salvation, at the end of which he would be crowned with glory. But he was always free to abrogate his covenant with Jehovah and accept the benevolent efforts of the church to redeem him. According to racial theory, however, baptism could not penetrate the tainted Jewish seed; the deep stain could only be removed by destroying the source of infection and its bearer, the physical Jew. The Jew must not only be excoriated but eliminated. Christianity, insofar as it had succumbed to Jewish influences, was also culpable since Christian agape, love and pity, like Jewish logos, law and reason, had alienated man from nature and weakened him in his struggle for existence. However, the Jewish stain could be removed from the Christian cloth, so to speak, by fumigation without destroying the cloth itself.

In the days of the Second Reich these racial theories were not accepted by the great majority of the German people. After World War I and in the period of the Weimar Republic, however, they became increasingly popular, thus removing one of the chief obstacles in the path of the Nazi rise to power. The source of this ideology at the beginning of the Second Reich could be found in the teachings of Naudh-Nordmann, E. Dühring, C. Radenhausen, A. Wahrmund, F. Lange, and P. Förster, which were then transmitted by Theodor Fritsch, H. S. Chamberlain, and members of the anti-intellectualist Rembrandt movement to the leading Nazi ideologists, to such figures as Alfred Rosenberg on the one hand and to the heads of the Deutsche-Christen movement on the other.

Animated by this aggressive mood that sought to deprive the Enlightenment of all its gains, the racial anti-Semites put their faith in the efficacy of blood, the mysterious fountain from which all life flows and which determines the hierarchy of powers that shape history. Apriorism, whether in theology or in critical rational thought, was done away with and blood became the epistemological model whose uniqueness, contrary to the logical structure of rational thought, was that it comprehends both form and content, symbol and reality, the concept and that which is expressed by the concept. Blood became an absolute value because it erases the distinction between the symbol and that which is symbolized, between theory and practice; it attempts to create a total identity between the particular and the general, between the individual sphere and the public domain, between society and the state. It was felt that man's life must be rescued from the anemic ideals of Christianity and restored to its root and anchor in blood. Truth is not within reach of the pretentious intellect nor the reward of holiness, for both remove man from the deep sources of life. When the world demands a courageous response and genuine sacrifice, religion covers its face, unable to sustain the bravest efforts, and the untrustworthy intellect betrays man with its spurious profundities. It is then that blood clamors to be heard, and truth, long repressed, emerges through its cleansing filter. Evangelical Christianity with its morality of humility, selflessness, and excessive self-contempt, reinforced in modern times by democratic social altruism, thus constituted for the racial anti-Semites one of the principal obstructions to man's natural development. By placing spirit above matter, conscience above intuition, and speculative thought above the experience of blood, Christianity poisoned the noblest instincts in man and removed him from his natural roots. The cross is the Christian symbol for the crucifixion of the body and its vital instincts.

It would seem then that racial anti-Semitism and traditional Christianity, although starting from opposite poles and with no discernible principle of reconciliation, were moved by a common impulse directed either to the conversion or to the extermination of Jews. Thus we find that the racial anti-Semites appropriated basic Christian ideas even while reprobating them and adapted them for their own purposes. The Christian doctrine of the Incarnation, for example, whereby God became man, was interpreted by them not in the evangelical sense (John 1:14) nor in the Pauline sense (Colossians 2:9), nor even in Nietzsche's purely mythological sense, but in an empirically political and racial sense. According to the Christian Heilsgeschichte the Jews were the theological means to correct evil by acknowledging the principle (John 1:14): "And the Word became flesh and dwelt among us, full of grace and truth; we have beheld his glory, glory as of the only Son from the Father", and hence the Jews as the children of promise were eligible for salvation "in order that God's purpose of election might continue" (Romans 9:11). According to the racial anti-Semites, however, the Jews could not be the means to correct evil for they themselves were the essence of evil, evil incarnate, and must therefore be exterminated not only in the spirit (as Christianity) but also in the flesh.

When we recall the traditional Christian bias against the Jews—the collective guilt of deicide and the eternal curse of the world that rests upon them because of their unpardonable defection (Matthew 27:22, 25; I Thessalonians 2:15), the official policy of the church as formulated in such councils as the Synod of Elvira in 306, Clermont in 535, Toledo in 681, or the Third Lateran in 1179 and the Fourth Lateran in 1215, the preachments of Martin Luther against the Jews and his incitement to violence, especially after 1543 when he was disillusioned in his efforts to convert them, the blood libels and accusations in which the persecuted wandering Jew became the symbol of sin and abomination—when we recall all this, we see how Christianity created the patterns of prejudice, hatred, and calumny that could readily provide a rationale to justify organized violence. The anti-Christian elements of racial anti-Semitism were interpreted in such a way that the traditional theological concepts of Christianity were not completely rejected; only their meanings were changed by using a pseudoscientific jargon and applied to the historical realities of that day, without the salutary correction of Christian discipline and belief.

Racial anti-Semitism and the subsequent Nazi movement were not the result of mass hysteria or the work of single propagandists. The racial anti-Semites, despite their antagonism toward traditional Christianity, learned much from it, and succeeded in producing a well-prepared, systematic ideology with a logic of its own that reached its culmination in the Third Reich.

Enormous economic upheavals in Europe, both before and after World War I, served both to weaken the position of Jews and to intensify anti-Jewish feeling, as explained in this reading, excerpted from *The Jewish Catastrophe in Europe*, edited by Judah Pilch. The conditions of Jewish life—social, political, and cultural—in various countries, are also described here. Jews were urbanites and villagers, professors and peasants, religious and secularists, rich and poor.

20. Jewish Life in Europe Between the Two World Wars (1919–1939)
Judah Pilch

General Economic and Political Conditions

1. *Regions of Jewish Settlement*

The economic and political conditions of Jewish life in continental Europe varied with each geographic division between East and West. This was the result mainly of the relocation of populations within new boundaries after World War I, when the old empires broke up and many new and old states gained national independence. For purposes of our discussion, Europe will be divided into four geographical regions, as follows:

a. *Eastern Europe:* Poland, Hungary, Rumania; the Baltic countries—Lithuania, Latvia, Estonia, Finland; and the Balkan countries—Yugoslavia, Bulgaria, Greece, and Albania;
b. *The Soviet Union:* White Russia, the Ukraine, the Crimea, and northwest Russia;
c. *Central Europe:* Germany, Austria, and Czechoslovakia;
d. *Western Europe:* France, Luxemburg, Belgium, Holland, Denmark, Norway, and Italy; and those

countries that remained neutral in the second world war—Switzerland, Sweden, Spain and Portugal.

2. Distribution of the Jewish Population by Region

Both in their actual numbers and in their proportion to the general population, European Jews were more concentrated in the east than in the west. The largest portion lived in Poland—over 3,000,000; the next largest in southwestern Soviet Russia—over 2,000,000; and the third largest in Rumania—some 900,000. Germany's 525,000 constituted almost half of the Jews in central Europe. France's 240,000 and Holland's 157,000 Jews were the bulk of western European Jewry.

In proportion to the general population, too, the five million Jews in eastern Europe (outside Soviet Russia) constituted almost 5 percent of the total population; in the Soviet Union, the Jews made up 1.7 percent of the total, but in the southwestern region, which had two-thirds of Russian Jewry, the figure was over 5 percent of the total. In central Europe the Jewish proportion was 1.8 percent, while in the West it was only 0.5 percent. In the whole of continental Europe the Jews, numbering 9 million, constituted only 2 percent of the total population.

3. The Jews as Major City Dwellers:
Regional Contrasts

The Jews of Europe in modern times have been living mostly in cities rather than in rural areas. By the end of the 19th century they were already concentrated in the metropolitan complexes. In many of the large urban centers, Jews stood out as an ethnic and economic group, and many businesses, professions and other occupations were identified as specifically Jewish. This was not so noticeable in western Europe, where the Jewish population was small in proportion to the general population, even though three-fifths of Western European Jewry lived in 10 of the largest cities. Similarly, in central Europe, while almost all of Austrian Jewry lived in Vienna and half of the German Jews resided in Berlin, their proportion to the general urban population in those two cities and other large centers in western Europe was only 4.5 percent.

The picture changed quite radically in the large cities of eastern Europe and of the Soviet Union. In Polish cities like Warsaw, Lodz, Lublin, Cracow, and Wilno, the Jews comprised between one-fourth and one-half of the inhabitants. . . .

4. Effects of Increased Urbanization
a. Changes in Economic Positions before World War I

As a result of their rapid urbanization in the second half of the 19th century, the Jews gained new and stronger positions than heretofore in the general national economies. In central Europe, notably in Germany, they grew from small shopkeepers and village peddlers (60 percent of their occupations) to big merchants and department store owners, and occupied important places in the professions, the sciences, literature and the press. They also developed a white-collar working class, which had not been in existence before. The small-town peddler and tradesman had practically disappeared by the beginning of the 20th century.

In eastern Europe, too, the Jews moved into the middle and higher urban positions of commerce and industry, having occupied in some areas complete fields of production. Thus, in Lodz in 1900, the textile factories were predominantly in Jewish hands (68 percent)—Jews being owners, technicians and workers. In tsarist Russia they developed export, import, sugar, and petroleum industries and took an active part in railroad building and some in banking. A large Jewish working class occupied posts in small shops and factories, particularly those producing leather, brush, and confectionary products. In the western countries, where they constituted a small proportion of the general population, the Jews had long occupied positions in com-

merce and industry and were not dominant in any
particular branch of the national economy as a whole,
or in any urban occupations as such.

b. Changes in Economic Positions after World War I

In the West, economic positions acquired by Jews
during the preceding century remained practically unchanged, but in central and eastern Europe they under-
went drastic changes. Two main factors contributed to
this change: 1) the rising urbanization of the non-
Jewish population, and 2) the breakup of the Russian
and Austrian empires after the First World War.

In tsarist Russia, as well as in the Austrian Empire, most Jews lived in compact masses among the
minority peoples, who were themselves subjugated by
the dominant Great-Russians under the tsars, and by the
Germans and Hungarians in Austria-Hungary under the
Habsburg emperors. Toward the end of the 19th and
the beginning of the 20th centuries, these minority
peoples, who were predominantly peasants, began to
leave the rural areas in search of new economic opportunities in the cities. There they encountered the
already established Jewish merchants, shopowners and
professionals with whom they began to compete in their
striving to enter the middle and upper economic strata.
As long as the central governments were in the hands of
the dominant nationalities, the minorities were handled
without bias, none receiving any substantial government help. Competition remained on purely economic
grounds, and the Jews, more experienced and skilled in
the higher occupations, were able to meet the rivalry.
Dissatisfaction grew among the subjected minority
groups, especially among the Poles, the Ukrainians,
and the White Russians, and there was considerable
agitation against their Jewish neighbors. In tsarist
Russia these anti-Jewish sentiments were often utilized
by the central government to instigate pogroms
(massacres) and thus to divert the attention of the
disgruntled peasants, workers and small merchants
from its own failure to meet their needs.

The situation took a drastic turn for the worse at the end of the First World War, when the western provinces of Russia and the entire Austro-Hungarian Empire were carved up into a number of independent states. Former minority peoples, among whom the Jews had dwelt as just another minority, now became the majorities, dominant nationalities with governmental powers in their own hands. The urban occupations to which they had aspired were now opened to them with the full support of their own governments, and the Jews in those occupations received one heavy blow after another through legislative and financial restrictions or through other economic devices contrived by the ruling authorities.

In Germany and Austria the process of dislodging the Jews from the social and economic status they had achieved had gained great momentum even before the Nazis came to power, and assumed a legal form after they gained control of the government. In Poland, where the Jews had played a determining role in the national economy, the government proceeded more cautiously, for fear of crippling the economic welfare of the country. Similar caution, but to an even greater extent, was exercised in the Baltic states and in Rumania. In Czechoslovakia under President Thomas G. Masaryk (1918–1935), on the other hand, liberal political conditions allowed the Jews to hold on to their own. In the Soviet Union, after the Communist Revolution of October 1917, the economic positions held by the Jews under the tsars were swept away in the general transformation of the social and economic order. Finding their place in the economy of the new system involved more hardship and took longer than it did for the non-Jewish population. In other respects their condition resembled that of other Soviet citizens who became employees of the state-owned enterprises. A considerable proportion of the Jewish population of the small towns resettled in the large cities of the Soviet Union, and a large number of them engaged in professional and managerial occupations.

5. Emigration

As indicated above, the economic conditions of the Jews in central and eastern Europe began to weaken at the beginning of the 20th century and reached a critical stage during the interwar period. In their struggle to retain what they could of their hard-earned status or to make readjustments within the controlled national economies, they encountered ever-increasing obstacles. The general depression, shrinking markets and inflation in the 1920s and 30s, added greatly to their difficulties. While American Jewry, through its Joint Distribution Committee and the ORT, rendered substantial aid in direct relief and in financing and retraining Jews for new occupations, the odds against them in central and eastern Europe were too great. Their impoverishment went steadily from bad to worse. Unable to readjust within their native lands, they chose emigration.

Beginning with the turn of the century, when overseas lands were still wide open to newcomers of every nationality, large numbers of Jews from tsarist Russia (including Poland), Rumania, Austria-Hungary and the Baltic areas, streamed across the Atlantic to the United States; some fled to Canada and Latin America. The period of 1899–1914 witnessed the greatest movement of Jews from eastern Europe to the United States, totalling 1,448,226; of these 70 percent came from Russia and Rumania. Emigration to Palestine was promoted by the emerging Zionist movement which, in the words of Basel Program, adopted by the first Congress of the World Zionist Organization at Basel, Switzerland, in 1897, aimed "at establishing for the Jewish people a publicly and legally secured home in Palestine."

After 1922, American immigration laws sharply reduced Jewish immigration. Average annual immigration of Jews to the United States dropped to 50,000 in 1922–24 and to 11,280 in 1925–30. Many Jews of the former Russian provinces found a haven of refuge in Central and Western Europe, in Germany, Austria, France, Belgium, the Netherlands, and Great Britain, where they succeeded in establishing themselves as permanent residents or citizens. The Zionist Organization directed thousands of Jews to Palestine, especially after the Conference of the Great Powers at San Remo, Italy, in 1920, when Great Britain accepted the Mandate over Palestine with specific responsibility for "the establishment in Palestine of a national home for the Jewish people."

With the advent of Nazi rule in Germany in 1933, the enactment of the notorious Nuremberg Laws in 1935, the annexation of Austria to Germany and the dismemberment of Czechoslovakia in 1938, Jewish emigration from Central Europe turned into flight. Unfortunately, the Western Hemisphere was not open widely enough to welcome the surviving masses of refugees. From 1933 to 1937, the United States admitted only some 30,000 Jewish refugees; Argentina, 63,500; Brazil 64,000; and South Africa, 26,000. The Jewish community of Palestine absorbed 175,000 additional Jews during that period. Up to 1939 a special rescue operation, known as "Youth Aliyah," succeeded in bringing to Palestine 4,635 Jewish children from Germany. Numerous other Jewish refugee families were stranded in various countries of the continent, where they later suffered the same fate as the rest of European Jewry. . . .

6. *Political Emancipation*
a. Individual and Collective Emancipation

"Emancipation" as used in modern Jewish history entails the right of individuals to participate in every phase of political, social-cultural and economic activities, subject only to the laws governing all citizens of a given country without distinction of race, color or creed. Specifically, emancipation means the right to reside anywhere in the country, to own property, engage in any legal occupation of one's choice, to receive education in any school or academic institution in the land, to participate in governmental functions that may be available to all citizens, to serve in the armed forces in any rank attainable on merit, and to share in the duties and responsibilities of citizenship on an equal basis with the rest of the inhabitants.

In more than 1500 years of their sojourn on European soil, Jews did not enjoy these rights as individuals until they were formally emancipated, first in western, then in central, and last in eastern Europe. This does not mean that prior to emancipation they were unable to engage in social-cultural, economic or even political activities. On the contrary, official emancipation came in most instances as the last stage of their cultural and economic integration in the general community: in France and Holland in the 18th century, in other countries of western and central Europe in the 19th century, and in eastern Europe after World War I. But before they were granted political freedom, they did not have a legal right, like all the other inhabitants, to their occupations and positions. The Jews were engaged in varied, yet limited, occupations, holding many positions only by sanction of the ruling authorities, who could grant, withhold or rescind their "privileges" at will or, as one autocrat expressed it, according to "the interests of the exchequer."

Political emancipation, however, also entails not only individual rights but also the rights of groups who constitute an ethnic or national minority within a given country. Such are the rights of minority groups to cultivate their religious and cultural traditions, to educate their children in the ancestral heritage, and generally to form communal associations for the purpose of perpetuating their distinctive form of life and modes of expression. Before emancipation, the Jewish people, as a minority group, enjoyed this "internal freedom" within their own communities in every country in which they lived. Even at times when the ruling authorities sharply curtailed the free exercise of Jewish religious and cultural practices, the restrictions were applied only to the group as a whole rather than to the individual. The individual Jew identified himself with his people, as a body, in suffering as well as in joy. The inner structure of the Jewish community remained intact and continued to be governed by its own traditional laws and customs, and it was thus able to overcome external pressures by reorganizing its inner forces or by emigrating to more friendly lands.

This dual position of Jews as individuals within their own community and as an organized body in relation to the general population and to the government changed radically with the advent of their political emancipation. Basically, the political freedom that was granted to them in various stages of the emancipation period meant their right as individuals to participate in the life of the country like all other individual citizens. The freedom of the individual Jew as a citizen also brought with it his freedom to reduce his association with the Jewish community, to sever his relations with it entirely, and to blend or assimilate completely with the non-Jewish majority. This did not take place with the same intensity or speed in every country, for Jewish leaders, concerned with the preservation of Jewish traditional life, resisted political emancipation in the early stage, as for example in the eighteenth century in Alsace and Holland. What they really sought was not to prevent political freedom as such, but to obtain certain provisions in the acts of emancipation that would guarantee the survival of the Jews as a distinct community and to save them from disappearing within the general population. These guarantees, when achieved, assumed various forms, legal and voluntary, in different countries, depending on the political structure and the general cultural climate of each state. . . .

Communal, Cultural and Religious Life

While the internal Jewish "life style" differed from country to country, we present here a picture of the communal, cultural and religious life of Polish Jewry which in 1939 numbered 3,300,000. Eighty-five percent were to be killed by the Nazis.

After World War I, the newly established state of
Poland had a Jewish community of 3,300,000, the
largest and one of the oldest in Europe and the second
largest in the world. It was organized as a *Kehillah,*
with power of owning all communal property, such as
synagogues, cemeteries, hospitals, and the like, and with
authority to direct the communal educational, religious
and social-cultural institutions. Each town, large and
small, was represented on a Council which was elected
by direct, secret ballot. The various organizations
found their interests reflected in the bodies of the
Kehillah through proportional representation.

The greatest achievement of Polish Jewry was its
educational system maintained at its own cost. Here,
too, the different Jewish ideological and religious
groups maintained their respective types of schools,
each with its own language of instruction in Hebrew,
Yiddish, Polish, or bilingual. Of the total Jewish school
population of 425,000 some 340,000 attended these
schools. The Jewish community also maintained teacher training schools, rabbinical academies, trade schools
and other cultural institutions, such as museums, li-
braries, and adult study courses.

In higher general education, Jewish students were
greatly handicapped because of discrimination against
them by the universities. As many as half of the Jewish
trainees in various professions had to seek admission
to foreign universities. When they returned home they
had great difficulty in gaining permits to practice their
professions.

Jewish cultural life of a religious and secular
character flourished throughout Poland. There was a
large output of books, magazines, dailies and other
publications. In higher institutions of Jewish learning,
such as the famous *Yeshivoth* of Lublin and Mir, the
Yiddish Scientific Institute (in Vilna), the Institute
for the Science of Judaism (in Warsaw), scholars produced many volumes on Jewish subjects and trained
students who later spread Jewish knowledge through-

out the world. In the Jewish museums of Warsaw, Vilna, and Cracow one could find treasures of the past as well as creations of such contemporary artists as Marc Chagall, Henryk Glicenstein, and Arthur Szyk. A vibrant religious life, centering around thousands of synagogues, courts of hasidic rabbis, and individual homes, endowed the Jews with the strength and courage to live a traditional Jewish life in a non-Jewish world, frequently hostile. The Sabbaths and the holidays, all rites and customs were observed in an atmosphere that glowed with joy and piety.

Jewish communal life also abounded with a variety of political, social, philanthropic, and mutual aid organizations and institutions which helped the Jew to cope with the complexity of problems calling for action. There were organizations aiming to restore to the Jew individual human rights and freedom as well as collective autonomy, and to defend these rights along political lines. Numerous Zionist organizations helped in the rebuilding of Palestine. Agencies were established for health work, as well as a net of philanthropic institutions and youth organizations (upholding divergent religious, secular, Zionist, Yiddishist, and socialist ideologies), most of them aiming at a strong, living Jewish people.

Jews also contributed their full measure to the general culture of Poland in science, art, literature, and music. Among others, Julian Tuwim was considered the foremost contemporary poet of the Polish language, Bruno Winawer was prominent in literature, Bronislaw Huberman in music, and Szymon Ashkenazi in historiography.

The Jewish community of Poland functioned under tremendous hardships of financial limitations and governmental discrimination, which drove large Jewish masses into poverty and migration. The anti-Semitic attitudes of the government and the masses produced economic boycotts and outbreaks of violence against Jews. Nevertheless, the Jews fought their battle for survival with all possible means through internal efforts and with the aid of American Jewry, and they maintained their communal life on a high level to the very end of the interwar period, when the German army overran the country in September 1939.

PREJUDICE AND SCAPEGOATING

Prejudice . . . an important word, a word about feelings and attitudes, a word that has frightening implications. "The Germans were prejudiced against the Jews." That's one explanation for Nazi behavior. But how did they get that way? Were the Nazis born prejudiced? Why are people prejudiced? The next three readings, taken from the book *Prejudice: The Invisible Wall*, by William Goodykoontz, helps to increase our understanding of this complex subject—as it relates directly to our own lives.

21. The Greenies
William Goodykoontz

John Doe, Jr., is not born with prejudice against people who have green hair. But from the time he is a small child, he is warned against them. He is not supposed to play with green-haired children. He is told not to talk with them. His parents say, "Stay with your own kind. You'll be bad, John, if you mix with green-haired children."

As John grows older, he learns that his parents, their friends, and neighbors do not want people with green hair to:

attend his church

live in his neighborhood

go to his school, or playground, or camp.

John believes what the adults around him say. And they say that green-haired people should go to church elsewhere, live elsewhere, and go to other schools. As a child, John does not see many people with green hair.

At home, John often listens to his father talk. John Doe, Sr., started out in life with high hopes. But somewhere along the way, John Doe, Sr., did not get the job he wanted or the raise he hoped for. He began to believe that a certain group of people were the cause of his failure and that these people are to blame for everything that is wrong in life. Naturally, the bad ones are the Greenies—the people with green hair!

John Doe, Sr., talks against the people with green hair everywhere he goes—in public and in private. At home, especially, he talks about how dirty, dumb, poor, and evil the people with green hair are. Day after day, he makes jokes about them. He says that they should be thrown out of the community or that they are turning the country over to the enemy. And he always says that no Greenies will ever move into his neighborhood. Complaining about the green-haired people makes John Doe, Sr., forget that he himself is something of a failure. And when he is reminded of his failure, he can easily blame it on the green-haired people.

John Doe, Jr., begins to believe that his father is right. And anyhow he doesn't often talk with green-haired people to see what they're really like. Sometimes he reads about them in newspapers. But since newspapers play up crime, he usually reads about green-haired people who have gotten into trouble with the law. Again John believes his parents are right. Green-haired people do bad things. Even the newspapers say so.

John Doe, Jr., becomes a man. He believes the things he has learned about people with green hair. Then he marries Jane Roe, who has learned the same prejudices against people with green hair. Later they have children. And what do they teach their children? "Don't play with children with green hair. You are bad if you do."

So John Doe, Jr., carries over his prejudices to his children. And his children, too, become infected with the disease called prejudice.

---

22. What Is the Difference Between a Prejudice and a Misconception?
William Goodykoontz

Herb: Say, did you know that new math teacher is an Armenian?

Lucius: An Armenian! Man, that's terrible. I got him for fourth period. I'm gonna get my schedule changed.

Herb: Take it easy, Lucius. You don't know what he'll be like.

Lucius: What you mean I don't know? He's Armenian. That's enough for me.

Herb: What's wrong with Armenians?

Lucius: Man, are you dumb! I got an uncle knew some Armenians once. He told me all about 'em. All I need to know. (Whispers.) You know what Armenians do? They take people's heads and cut 'em off and shrink 'em real small. And then they wear 'em on watch-chains. Man, they're headshrinkers for real.

Herb: Sure you're talking about Armenians?

Lucius: Sure I'm sure. (Pauses.) Well—it was one of those jungle tribes from down there in South America, anyway.

Herb: Armenians don't come from South America.

Lucius: They don't?

Herb: And they aren't a tribe of headhunters, either. You must have them mixed up with somebody else.

Lucius: You sure?

Herb: If you don't believe me, let's go look up Armenians in the library. (They go to the library and read about Armenians in an encyclopedia.)

Lucius: Man, they don't sound so bad. That uncle of mine! He don't know from nothing.

Herb: Maybe you got him wrong.

Lucius: Well—maybe. Anyway, I'm glad I don't have to get my schedule changed!

---

23. What Should I Do?
William Goodykoontz

I'm 16. A boy who has a lot of money has asked me out on a date. I'm ashamed of my family and the poor neighborhood that we live in. How can I go out with him and still not have him know what my family life is like?

There's this one boy who has an ugly face. I like him very much. But I don't know if I *really* like him or if I just feel sorry for him. My friends tell me to quit him. Should I?

We are in a special preparation class. It is not graded the way classes are graded in regular high schools. We don't know what to say when our friends ask us what grade we are in. The grade doesn't really make any difference. It's just the way people act when we say we are in "spec." It takes a lot of courage for us to tell people the kind of class we are in. Can you tell us what to do?

In this excerpt from the book *Hey, White Girl!* by Susan Gregory, the reader feels acutely the distress of a girl who finds herself a distinct minority of one. Try to think of situations in which you have experienced similar emotions. Here the girl is self-conscious about "being different" and unsure, perhaps fearful, of what might happen.

24. Hey, White Girl!

Susan Gregory

"Hey, white girl!" Daddy and I were standing on the curb waiting to cross Jackson when I heard the voice. For a moment I felt a tight knot form in my stomach. But I fought to relax my muscles, look straight ahead, and ignore him. The light changed, and the street became clear. Trying not to feel the eyes I knew were looking me over, I stepped over broken glass and paper. I couldn't help comparing this walk to school with the drive Daddy and I used to take when we lived in Wilmette. For three years, each school day we drove past stately mansions and carefully manicured lawns. We went down Sheridan Road along Lake Michigan. We parked near the school tennis courts and football field. But now we were two pale figures in a sea of black, kicking cans and bottles along the sidewalk like everyone else. And instead of mansions, the streets were lined with squalid tenements, liquor stores, and an occasional empty lot.

John Marshall High School faced an empty lot littered with trash and dressed with one large stand-up billboard advertising the latest thing in Chevrolets. The school's tired red brick walls had a foreboding, prison-like quality as I stood among the students milling outside the locked front entrance, waiting for the bell on that first day of the fall term.

All new students from outside the Chicago public school system were to meet in Room 129. Never had I seen a quieter group of people. I was the only white student present. Sue, now you'll know, I thought. You'll know what it was like for every Negro who ever integrated a white school alone. As that Negro represented all Negroes to his white fellow students, so you will represent all whites to the Negroes around you. You're on trial now. Yes, really on trial. . . .

There were 5,000 black students, and I had never had contact with so many people before. I was constantly alert to where I was and who I was with and what others' eyes were telling me. I felt most self-conscious in the hall. I tried not to let anyone's glance unnerve me. But sometimes I felt so alone. I couldn't wait to get home, close myself off in our small apartment, get something to eat, and turn on the radio. . . .

Lunch was by far my most difficult ordeal. There was no one to eat with, and I felt tight. I became accustomed to the stares. But was it curiosity or resentment I saw in the eyes of my fellow students? Boys approached me constantly. "Do you feel rich today?" one asked. He wants to borrow money, I thought. He thinks I'm an easy pushover because I'm new and white. "No, never," I shook my head. "What's the matter with everybody? Nobody feels rich. . . ," he walked off sadly. . . .

I got lost on the way home that first day. I took a wrong turn and had no idea where I was. I tried to read street signs and watch out for strange people at the same time. I was wary of everyone. By the large Chicago Transit Authority barn I ran into a group of boys. "Hey, girl . . . Hey, white girl . . ." There it was again. I crossed the street as quickly as I could. But there I faced several Puerto Ricans. "Oooooo—I wonder where she goes to school?" I heard one whistle.

The next three excerpts are from *The Nature of Prejudice*, a major work on this subject by psychologist Gordon Allport. Allport has contributed enormously to our understanding of the mechanisms of prejudice. According to his theory, prejudice grows out of personal *frustration*, which in turn generates aggressive feelings. When this *aggression* cannot be directed against the real cause of the frustration, the aggression is *displaced* onto relatively defenseless "scapegoats." This displaced hostility is then rationalized and justified by blaming, projecting, and stereotyping.

As you read the first two sections, which explain the terms "scapegoat" and "prejudice," think of examples from your own life of scapegoating, stereotyping, and projecting.

25. The Meaning of Scapegoat
Gordon Allport

The term "scapegoat" originated in the famous ritual of the Hebrews, described in the Book of Leviticus (16:20–22). On the Day of Atonement a live goat was chosen by lot. The high priest, robed in linen garments, laid both his hands on the goat's head, and confessed over it the iniquities of the children of Israel. The sins of the people thus symbolically transferred to the beast, it was taken out into the wilderness and let go. The people felt purged, and for the time being, guiltless.

The type of thinking here involved is not uncommon. From earliest times the notion has persisted that guilt and misfortune can be shifted from one man's back to another. Animistic thinking confuses what is mental with what is physical. If a load of wood can be shifted, why not a load of sorrow or a load of guilt?

Nowadays we are likely to label this mental process *projection*. In other people we see the fear, anger, lust that reside primarily in ourselves. It is not we our-

selves who are responsible for our misfortunes, but
other people. In our common speech we recognize this
failing in such phrases as "whipping-boy," "taking it
out on the dog," or "scapegoat. . . ."

Yankees in a conservative Maine community may
discriminate socially against the Italians or French-Ca-
nadians who live there—but the snobbery is relatively
mild, and one can seldom see evidences of actual
aggression (true scapegoating). On the other hand, a
much more serious problem of antagonism exists in
the case of other minorities (Jews, Negroes, Orientals, Mexicans) to whom the dominant majority has
said, "We shall never accept you as one of us."

Just as it is impossible to tell clearly when a group
is a scapegoat and when it is not, so too we cannot
find a clear formula that will cover the selection of
scapegoats. The essence of the matter seems to be that
different groups are singled out for different reasons.
We have already noted the contrast between the accusations made against Negroes and Jews, and have
discussed the theory which states that each of these
two scapegoats "take away" different *kinds* of guilt.

There seems to be no such thing as an "all-duty
scapegoat" although some groups come nearer to this
objective than others. Perhaps today Jews and Negroes
are blamed for the widest variety of evils. We note
that these are *inclusive* social groups consisting of both
sexes (and their children), which transmit social values
and cultural traits. They are more or less permanent,
definite, and stable. By contrast one finds many *ad hoc*
scapegoats who are blamed for quite specific things.
The American Medical Association or the Soft Coal
Miners Union may be much hated by certain portions
of society, being blamed for evils in health policy,
labor policy, high prices, or some particular inconve-
nience for which they may or may not be partly responsible. (Scapegoats need not be lily-white in their
innocence, but they always attract more blame, more
animosity, more stereotyped judgment than can be ra-
tionally justified.) . . .

One reason for the popularity of the scapegoat theory is that it is easy to understand. Probably this fact is also an argument for its validity, for the ease of understanding must be related in some way to the commonness of the experience. A storybook for seven-year-olds contains a clear example of the scapegoating theme. The tale runs as follows:

> An enterprising pig with some ducks as companions is aloft in a rudderless balloon. A farmer with evil intentions is trying to capture the balloon, but the alert piglet pelts the farmer with cans of tomato soup. The farmer is spattered by the soup and thoroughly angry. A dirty-faced boy comes out of the barn to help him wipe off the soup. But the farmer cuffs the little boy good. He does this for three reasons: first, because the balloon had got away; and second, because he would now have to take a bath to get the sticky soup off him; and, third, because it seemed like a pretty good thing to do anyway.

The following case shows how a blend of home and school frustration may lead to prejudice. A college student writes:

> I had honors all the way through school and one double promotion, but I did not have a straight "A" record. I was not happy. My father boasted that he had had only an A and A-plus record when he was in college, and at the same time held down a full-time job. He never let me forget it, and berated me for doing less well than he. I felt utterly frustrated. I wanted to please him but could not succeed. Finally I found comfort in telling myself and other people that it was only the Jewish grinds and cheats who did me out of the top position. (In thinking the matter over I realize that I do not know for a fact that the boys who excelled me in scholarship were Jews, or that they cheated.)

26. Prejudice

Gordon Allport

The word "prejudice," derived from the Latin noun *praejudicium,* has, like most words, undergone a change of meaning since classical times. There are three stages in the transformation.

(1) To the ancients, *praejudicium* meant a *precedent*—a judgment based on previous decisions and experiences.

(2) Later, the term, in English, acquired the meaning of a judgment formed before due examination and consideration of the facts —a premature or hasty judgment.

(3) Finally the term acquired also its present emotional flavor of favorableness or unfavorableness that accompanies such a prior and unsupported judgment.

The wording offered by the New English Dictionary recognizes positive as well as negative prejudice: "A feeling, favorable or unfavorable, toward a person or thing, prior to, or not based on, actual experience." While it is important to bear in mind that biases may be *pro* as well as *con,* it is none the less true that *ethnic* prejudice is mostly negative. . . .

It is not easy to say how much fact is required in order to justify a judgment. A prejudiced person will almost certainly claim that he has sufficient warrant for his views. He will tell of bitter experiences he has had with refugees, Catholics, or Orientals. . . .

No one can possibly know *all* refugees, Catholics, or Orientals.

Therefore, any negative judgment of these groups must be based on characteristics that an individual has assumed that all members of an ethnic group possesses. These generalities are known as *stereotypes*.

Why were the Jews the main butt of Hitler's fanatic hatred? Why have Jews been the object of prejudice throughout much of history? Allport suggests five explanations for the Jew's selection as an object of hostility.

27. The Jew as Scapegoat
Gordon Allport

Anti-Semitism is thought to reach back at least to the fall of Judea in 586 B.C. When the Jews were dispersed, they took with them their relatively rigid and unbending customs. Dietary laws prohibited them from eating with others; intermarriage was forbidden. They were even by their own prophet Jeremiah considered "stiff-necked." Wherever they went their orthodoxy presented a problem.

In Greece and Rome—to mention only two of their new homelands—new ideas were welcomed. The Jews were received as interesting strangers. But the cosmopolitan cultures which they entered could not understand why Jews did not reciprocate the meals, games, and gaiety of their own pagan life. Jehovah could easily be fitted into the galaxy of gods who were worshipped. Why could not the Jews accept the pantheon? Judaism seemed too absolute in its theology, ethnic customs, and rites.

Yet in Ancient Rome it is fairly certain that Christians were persecuted more vigorously than Jews. Tertullian gives a terse record of the scapegoating of Christians. Until the fourth century when Christianity became the officially dominant religion under Constantine, it is probable that the Jews fared relatively better than the Christians. But after that time the Sabbaths were separated, and the Jews became a highly visible group marked off from the Christians.

Since the early Christians were themselves Jews, it took the first two or three centuries of the Christian era for this fact to be forgotten. Then only did the accusation arise that the Jews (as a group) were responsible for the Crucifixion. Subsequently, for centuries it seems that to a large number of people the epithet "Christ killer" was a sufficient cause for scapegoating the Jew on any and all occasions. Certain it is that by the time of St. John Chrysostom (fourth century) elaborate anti-Semitic homilies were preached, accusing Jews not only of the Crucifixion but of all other conceivable crimes as well.

Some support for anti-Semitism is drawn from straight Christian theological reasoning. Since the Bible explicitly asserts that the Jews are God's chosen people, they must be hounded until they acknowledge their Messiah. God will punish them until they do so. Thus their persecution by Christians is ordained. It is true that no modern theologian would interpret this situation to mean that an individual Christian is justified in acting unfairly or uncharitably toward any individual Jew. Yet the fact remains that God acts in mysterious ways, and apparently His concern is to bring recalcitrant Jews, His chosen people, to acknowledge the New Testament as well as the Old. While modern anti-Semites are certainly not aware that they are punishing the Jews for this particular reason, from the theological point of view their conduct is understandable in terms of God's long-range design.

It is necessary to stress these religious factors in anti-Semitism, for the Jews are above all else a religious group. It may be rightly objected that many (perhaps most) Jews today are not religious. While orthodoxy has declined, there has been no decrease in persecution. Further, it may be objected that in present-day anti-Semitism the sins of the Jews are said to be moral, financial, social; religious deviance is seldom mentioned. All this is true—and yet the vestiges of the religious issue certainly persist. The Jewish religious holidays make for visibility; so too the imposing synagogues in Jewish residential districts.

Still, many people today are indifferent to the specifically religious quarrel between Judaism and Christianity. Many more are able in their own minds to transcend it, realizing well the essential unity of the Judeo-Christian tradition. But, according to a broader interpretation of the matter, each one of us is still affected by the epic quality of spiritual ferment in Jewish culture. Jacques Maritain, the Catholic scholar, expresses the matter thus:

> Israel . . . is to be found at the very heart of the world's structure, stimulating it, exasperating it, moving it. Like an alien body, like an activating ferment injected into the mass, it gives the world no peace. . . . it teaches the world to be discontent and restless as long as the world has not God, it stimulates the movement of history.

A Jewish scholar continues the argument: the Jews as a group are no larger than certain unheard-of tribes in Africa. Yet they have provided continuous spiritual ferment. They insist upon monotheism; upon ethics; upon moral responsibility. They insist upon high scholarship; upon closely knit home life. They themselves aspire to high ideals, are restless, and ridden by conscience. Throughout the ages they have made mankind aware of God, of ethics, of high standards of attainment. Thus—though imperfect in themselves—they have been the mentors of the world's conscience.

On the one hand people admire and revere these standards. On the other hand they rebel and protest. Anti-Semitism arises because people are irritated by their own consciences. Jews are symbolically their superego, and no one likes to be ridden so hard by his superego. Ethical conduct is insisted upon by Judaism, relentlessly, immediately, hauntingly. People who dis-like this insistence, along with the self-discipline and acts of charity implied, are likely to justify their rejection by discrediting the whole race that produced such high ethical ideals.

Jews, partly at least because of their religious deviance, were excluded in many countries for long periods of time from owning land. Only transient and fringe occupations were open to them. When the Crusaders needed money, they could not borrow from Christians (whose code did not allow usury). Jews became the moneylenders. In so doing they invited customers but also contempt. Excluded not only from landowning but also from handicraft guilds, Jewish families were forced to develop mercantile habits. Only moneylending, trading, and other stigmatized occupations were open to them.

This pattern has to some extent persisted. Occupational traditions of the European Jews transferred to new lands when Jews emigrated. To some extent the same discrimination barred them from conservative occupations. They were again obliged to develop the fringe activities where risk, shrewdness, enterprise were required. We have seen how this factor led large numbers of Jewish people, especially in New York City, into retailing, theatrical ventures, and professions. This somewhat uneven distribution on the economic checkerboard of the nation made the Jewish group conspicuous; it also intensified the stereotype that they work too hard, make lots of money, and engage in shady dealings in the less stable occupations.

Looking backward once more over the historical course of events, we find another consideration of importance. Lacking a homeland, the Jews were regarded by some as parasites upon the body politic. They had certain attributes of a nation (ethnic coherence plus a tradition of nationhood). But they were, in fact, the only nation on earth without a home. People who distrusted "bi-loyalty" accused them of being less patriotic, less honorable within their adopted land than they should be.

A further factor to be noted is that the insistence upon scholarship and intellectual attainment is a long-standing mark of Jewish culture. Jewish intellectualism calls to mind one's own defects of ignorance and laziness. The Jews once more symbolize our conscience, against whose pricks we protest.

Surveying such a welter of historico-psychological factors, one naturally wonders whether there is a leading motif that would sum them all up. The nearest approach would seem to be the concept of "fringe of conservative values." The expression, however, must be understood to cover not only deviance in religion, occupation, nationhood, but likewise departure from conservative mediocrity: conscience pricking, intellectual aspiration, spiritual ferment. One might put the matter this way: the Jews are regarded as just far enough *off center* (slightly above, slightly below, slightly outside) to disturb non-Jews in many different ways. The "fringe" is perceived by conservative people to represent a threat. The differences are not great; indeed, the fact that they are relatively slight may make them all the more effectively disturbing. Again we cite "the narcissism of slight differences."

This analysis of anti-Semitism, historically considered, is far from complete. It is intended only to demonstrate that, without historical perspective, we cannot tell why one group rather than another is the object of hostility. The Jews are a scapegoat of great antiquity, and only the long arm of history, aided by psychological insights, can reconstruct the story.

The problem is exceedingly complex, but it will never be solved unless there is at every stage scrupulous regard for factual evidence, concerning both the traits of the Jewish group and the psychodynamic processes of anti-Semites.

ON RESISTANCE

Our attention to this point has been
focused largely on the Nazi aggressors—the
unprecedented crimes they committed, and possible explanations of their behavior. Now we
turn to the victims, and an analysis of the ways
in which Jews responded to their fate. In this
selection a survivor of the Holocaust, Abraham
Foxman, shows why armed resistance, though
heroic instances of it did occur, was ultimately
impossible to carry out. Far from being totally
passive, however, many Jews resisted in countless small ways, which, while largely ineffectual
against the enemy, served to keep self-respect
and hope alive in the victims. Finally, in con-
sidering the whole question of resistance, ask
yourself this: if others at the time who possessed armies and weapons could not halt the
madman's progress, what should a defenseless
minority have done?

28. On Resistance

Abraham Foxman

During the past 30 years, hundreds of books,
periodicals and research papers have been published
dealing with the Jewish catastrophe of 1939–1945.
While the majority of these works focused upon the

martyrdom of the European Jews, only recently have historians and researchers begun to examine the resistance aspect. Where earlier works had concentrated upon recording the fact of destruction, primarily in subjective terms, the more recent ones attempted to invoke objective value judgments. For example, Raul Hilberg, in *The Destruction of the European Jews,* submitted that the Jews actually aided the Germans in achieving their genocidal aims by "going like sheep to the slaughter"; Bruno Bettelheim, in *The Informed Heart,* concluded that the Jewish inmates of the concentration camps had lost their "will to live," thereby espousing a "death wish," and Hannah Arendt, in *Eichmann in Jerusalem,* said that the Jews were, to a great extent, responsible for their own death, claiming that they collaborated with the Germans.

Such judgments are a tortured analysis of historical fact and a misunderstanding of the conditions that existed in the ghettos and concentration camps of Europe. To the frequently asked question of whether there was Jewish resistance, the answer is yes!

Not only did Jews take part in every phase of the general resistance movements in the occupied countries, but there was a specific Jewish resistance which manifested itself in most surprising and unusual ways. This was so not only in countries such as Poland, the Baltic States, Czechoslovakia, Hungary and Rumania, where there were large, cohesive Jewish communities, but also in countries where Jews were a very small percent of the population.

The word "resistance" usually connotes an organized, armed, collective action, carried out according to the rules of military strategy. But resistance is a concept which includes persons who resisted passively, who participated in uprisings in ghettos and concentration camps, who fought in partisan units in the forests, who participated in general underground movements. It also includes Jews who fought, knowing that certain death awaited them, but wanted to demonstrate the courage of the Jewish people and were willing to die for *K'vod Ha-am,* the honor of the nation. It includes still others who sacrificed their lives to rescue others, those who committed any act plainly against the laws of the German authorities or the goals of "the final solution."

Attempting to stay alive another day was resistance. Escaping from the ghetto or hiding in a bunker was resistance. So was giving birth to a child, praying in congregation, singing, studying the Bible or the Talmud, bringing flowers into the ghetto, keeping archives, writing humor under the shadow of death, rescuing Torah scrolls left lying in the streets.

One of the most brilliant aspects of Jewish life under these horrendous circumstances was in the area of spiritual resistance. Vilna, for example, which had for generations been a great Jewish cultural center called "The Jerusalem of Lithuania," became during the Holocaust "The Jerusalem of the Ghettos," a symbol of spiritual resistance against German authority. Aid for the needy was provided by organized social-aid groups, a hospital and infirmary were established, free food centers were provided, schools and youth clubs were set up, theaters and choirs gave performances—all in the shadow of death. Jewish cultural life remained vital and creative. This, too, was resistance.

While the Warsaw Ghetto uprising was a symbolic high point, it was not the only place where Jews took positions and fought their oppressors with firearms and bare hands. Organized battles and skirmishes took place in ghettos, concentration camps and work camps—among them, Vilna, Bialystok, Krakow, Auschwitz, Treblinka, Chêlmo.

The decision to participate in an underground movement and resist the Germans by force was not based solely on courage, although that was important. There were other factors.

One of the strongest drives in a human being is his will to survive. No man wants to believe that he is about to be killed. He will hang on to any straw of hope, even to the point of self-delusion. When the infamous Nuremberg Laws were passed, the German Jews minimized their importance, allowing themselves to believe that these laws were only temporary measures. When Hitler announced his plan to destroy the Jewish people, very few believed it to be more than propaganda. Transports of Jewish children were taken away from their parents, on the pretext that they were being sent to a "summer camp"; the children were even forced to write postcards home. When eyewitnesses told the parents that their children were no longer alive, the parents produced the postcards and refused to believe the truth.

The same desire to live manifested itself in the "normalization" of ghetto life—writing, singing, reading and other amenities of civilized living. The archivist of the Vilna Ghetto, for example, noted that on the morrow of an *Aktion* which took 5,000 Jews to their doom, a line of 400 people stood outside the library doors. It was this stubborn faith in a brighter tomorrow that led many to their death.

The Jews maintained belief in the goodness of the human being and in the justice of mankind, and hoped that any day salvation would come. How can the world stand idly by, they asked themselves. How long can such events continue? Why risk losing redemption and freedom by taking up arms against the foe—the Allied Forces would surely raise their voices, destroy the ovens of Auschwitz, any day . . . after all, this was the 20th century and they lived in a Christian society. A poem found in the rubble of the destroyed Warsaw Ghetto, written by a 12-year-old boy named Motele, is a perfect example of naive hope:

> *From tomorrow on, I shall be sad—*
> *From tomorrow on!*
> *Today I will be gay.*
> *What is the use of sadness—tell me that?*
> *Because the evil winds begin to blow?*
> *Why should I grieve for tomorrow—*
> *today?*
> *Tomorrow may be so good, so sunny.*

Tomorrow the sun may shine for us
*   again;*
We shall no longer need to be sad.
From tomorrow on, I shall be sad—
*   From tomorrow on!*
Not today; No! today I will be glad.
And every day, no matter how bitter it
*   be, I will say;*
From tomorrow on, I shall be sad—Not
*   today.*

In the case of Orthodox Jewry, the concept of heroism was interwoven with the idea of spiritual courage, of sacrifice for the sake of religion, known as *Kiddush Hashem,* Sanctification of God's Name. It was resistance stemming from religious inspiration and contained a deeply rooted ancestral heritage epitomized by the saying "not by force but by the strength of spirit." Their attitude was that world evil should not be fought and cannot be defeated by physical force because the struggle between good and evil will be decided by Divine Providence. They believed the recital of a chapter of the Psalms would do more to affect the course of events than killing Germans.

The Orthodox Jews were also opposed to physical resistance from the *Halachic* (Law) point of view. Any act of open and active resistance was equivalent to suicide, which Judaism strongly opposes.

The Jewish underground and resistance movements, wherever they existed, were isolated from the outside world, and, in fact, were refused aid by national resistance movements which existed in most occupied countries. Most of the native population, where there was a long record of anti-Semitism, was openly hostile to the Jews. In many instances they volunteered to aid in "the final solution."

In several countries, the Nazi troops were met as liberators and not as conquerors. The Lithuanian population welcomed the German Army with flowers and cheers. In the streets of Vilna, the Nazi flag, the swastika, was flown next to the Lithuanian flag.

Ukrainians, Letts, Estonians and others volunteered to help the Germans exterminate the Jews. Any active military resistance would have had to be done alone, without any support, moral or physical. Escape was in many cases futile, for the natives would only turn the escapee over to the Germans.

Thus, any attempt of resistance was an implicit act of suicide, the only objective *K'vod Ha-Am*. The religious leaders considered such an act sinful. Still, there were Orthodox Jews who fought, resisted and actively participated in the underground.

The Germans used the concept of collective responsibility to discourage the growth of resistance movements, as well as individual acts of resistance. For any such disorder, not only the individual would be punished by death, but the whole ghetto population.

Despite these obstacles, there were acts of resistance in every section of Nazi-occupied Europe. Unfortunately, however, the complete record of martyrdom and heroism will never be written. For most of the participants and witnesses did not survive.

HOW AND WHY?

III

HOW AND WHY?

"I also want to speak very frankly about an extremely important subject. Among ourselves we will discuss it openly; in public, however, we must never mention it. . . .

"I mean the evacuation of the Jews, the extermination of the Jewish people. This is something that is easy to talk about. 'The Jewish people will be exterminated,' says every member of the party, 'this is clear, this is in our program: the elimination, the extermination of the Jews: we will do this.' And then they come to you—80 million good Germans—and each one has his 'decent' Jew. Naturally, all the rest are pigs, but this particular Jew is first-rate. Not one of those who talk this way has seen the bodies, not one has been on the spot. Most of you know what it is to see a pile of one hundred or five hundred or one thousand bodies. To have stuck it out and at the same time, barring exceptions caused by human weakness, to have remained decent: this is what has made us tough. . . .

"This is a glorious page in our history which never has and never will be written."

—SS REICHSFÜHRER HEINRICH HIMMLER Speech to a meeting of SS generals in Posen on October 4, 1943

THE THIRD REICH

This brief history examines the reasons for the failure of democracy in Germany, and describes the means by which Hitler came to power. As you read, note these key concepts which help to explain why Germany was fertile ground for a dictatorship: extreme nationalism, idealization of the military, little experience of democracy, humiliating defeat in World War I, economic depression, unemployment.

The selection is from *The Third Reich in Perspective* by Gertrude Noar.

29.   The Third Reich in Perspective
Gertrude Noar

Modern German history is the history of the failure of German democracy. The roots of Nazism lie in that history of failure.

Until late into the 19th century, long after most western peoples were united, the word "Germany" did not refer to a single nation, but to a Central European patchwork of over 100 German states ranging in size from miniscule to middling. Each was more or less independent and under the autocratic rule of a petty prince or—in the case of larger ones like Prussia and Bavaria—a king. In the Middle Ages every attempt to impose a central authority upon the German lands had proved abortive, the Holy Roman Empire being more a fiction than a fact. In the 16th century, the Lutheran Reformation had tremendous effects which still affect our lives today, but it too failed to bring about the unification of Germany.

The world-shaking French Revolution, at the end of the 18th century, with its ideals of liberty, equality, and fraternity expressed politically in rule by Parliament, failed to inspire the German people to similar effort. The aristocracy and landed gentry fought all attempts to establish a parliament based on democratic suffrage. When a great wave of revolution swept Europe in 1848, democratic uprisings also took place in Berlin, the capital of Prussia, and in other German states. The German liberals, supported by most of the middle class and peasantry, came to power for the first time. But they lacked resolution and compromised with the Prussian military autocracy and the German princes. In the end many were forced to flee Germany for England or America.

Until 1848 democracy and nationalism had more or less gone hand in hand in Germany, as they had in western Europe and America. But after the failure to institute liberal reforms in 1848, this situation changed. Prussia—the strongest of the German states, thanks to a powerful army commanded by a military elite— set about uniting Germany under its own rule. Prussia's Prime Minister, Otto von Bismarck, used a policy of intimidation and conquest to bring about the unification.

The union was completed on January 18, 1871, when the Prussian King was proclaimed Kaiser of the German Reich (Emperor of the German Empire) after the defeat of France in the Franco-Prussian War. Thus Germany did not unite voluntarily on the basis of a democratic parliamentary system, which was the pattern in Western Europe and America; rather did Prussia unite the German people by conquering them. From the alliance between German nationalism and Prussian militarism there followed all those sinister events of modern German history which culminated in the catastrophe of Nazism.

William L. Shirer writes: "Bismarck's unique

creation is the Germany we have known in our time . . . in which first this remarkable man and then Kaiser Wilhelm II and finally Hitler, aided by a military caste, . . . succeeded in inculcating a lust for power and domination, a passion for unbridled militarism, a contempt for democracy and individual freedom and a longing for authority. . . ."

Bismarck announced the future course of Prussian Germany in 1862 by declaring: "The great questions of the day will not be settled by resolutions and majority votes—that was the mistake of the men of 1848 —but by blood and iron."

The policy of blood and iron, of war and conquest and empire, led Imperial Germany into World War I, which, after years of enormous slaughter, ended with her ignominious surrender and the abdication and flight of Kaiser Wilhelm II. The revolution that broke out in November 1918 again presented Germany with an opportunity to reconstruct herself on democratic foundations, and again she failed, although the failure did not become apparent at once.

The Weimar Republic proclaimed by the Social Democrats at the end of 1918 was established quite half-heartedly, as it were, by default. It was born out of defeat in war and not out of a triumph of democratic sentiment. And indeed the old Junker landowning and military class remained very much alive and powerful. Although the Weimar Constitution was a model liberal and democratic *document,* the Republic rested on shaky foundations so long as it failed to disarm and defeat all those hostile classes and groups which were biding their time and merely tolerating a democratic regime: the feudal Junker landlords and upper castes, the General Staff and military caste, the industrial magnates, and the heads of the Prussian bureaucracy.

The Social Democrats, or Labor party, who were the largest single political organization, vacillated. Instead of moving energetically to destroy these hostile elements, they compromised with them, just as German liberalism had compromised with the autocracy in the

19th century. Later these same reactionary elements, in spite of their dislike for Hitler as a vulgar demagogue, would finally install him in power.

The Weimar period from 1918 to 1933 was just such a time of turmoil and disorder as was needed to spawn the Nazi movement. Almost immediately after the end of the war, reactionary groups began to clamor that the army had not been defeated by the Allies at the front, but had been "stabbed in the back" at home by democrats and socialists. They said this even though they knew the General Staff had compelled the Imperial government to sue for an armistice long before there was any revolutionary disturbance, by informing it that the army could not carry on the war any longer.

Armed bands of terrorists and freebooters assassinated liberals, democrats and socialists, and supported attempts to overthrow the government. The humiliating Versailles Treaty was laid at the door of the Weimar democrats. The mark began to fall. By 1923 it was worth 4 billion to the American dollar. The savings of the middle class, the principal depositors, were wiped out and there was general impoverishment and desperation.

When the crash of 1929 ushered in the worldwide depression, factory production declined drastically, businesses closed, and millions were thrown out of work. Conditions bred fear and despair, which in turn, bred violent hatreds. Adolf Hitler knew how to play on these feelings and enlist them in the service of nationalist delirium, hatred of democracy, and the drive for military domination and conquest—which, for all his talk of a Nazi "revolution," were the more or less traditional features of Prussian Germanism.

Adolf Hitler was born on April 20, 1889, in the Austrian town of Braunau-on-the-Inn across the border from Bavaria. Austria was then a part of the Austro-Hungarian Empire. The Austrians spoke German and many, like Hitler, thought of themselves as German and looked with contempt on the other, mostly Slavic, nationalities that made up the Empire. The youthful Hitler wished passionately to become an artist, but was rejected by the Vienna Academy of Fine Arts as lacking talent. He spent four crucial years, 1909–13, in Vienna, most of the time as a down-and-out tramp shunning regular employment. During these years, Hitler crystallized his own brooding hatreds and resentments into a philosophy. Its cornerstones were: glorification of war and conquest; exaltation of the Germans as the Master Race; hatred of the Jews; contempt for democracy.

In 1913 Hitler went to Munich and when World War I broke out enlisted in the German army. After the war he stayed in the army and was assigned to spy on political parties in Munich which the military considered dangerous. One such party was the tiny German Workers party, which turned out to be violently nationalist. Hitler, instead of reporting it to the authorities, was the seventh man to join it, in 1919. The name of this party was changed to the National Socialist German Workers party in 1920 ("Nazi" is an abbreviation of the first part of the German title). Under Hitler's frenzied leadership it grew from a tiny group to a mass organization with millions of members. Eventually it became the only political party in Germany.

Hitler built the Nazi party in frank emulation of the mass party of the Social Democrats; in Vienna he had been impressed by the great demonstrations of Viennese Social working men, their popular press, and their oratory. But the Social Democratic party was democratic—what did Hitler see in it to serve his dictatorial purpose? Hitler had appreciated very early that in the modern age, German militarism and nationalism could no longer rule by means of the traditional aristocratic minorities and elites, but required the support of the "masses."

To win the mass support of unemployed factory workers, small farmers lacking land, threadbare and underfed office clerks and civil servants, shopkeepers on the verge of ruin, and disinherited middle class people, to whom the Communist party was also appealing, the Nazis needed to promise more than anti-Semitism and anti-Communism, nationalism and militarism. They needed to pretend that they would carry out a social revolution. (Hence the word "Socialist" in the party name. The Nazi "social" aims were dropped soon after the party came to power.)

At the very first public meeting of the Nazi party in 1920, Hitler's talents as a demagogue and orator had marked effect. His pounding fists, burning eyes, hoarse cries and hysterics aroused his audience to a fever pitch. He outlined a 25-point program, which became the party's official platform, that promised everything to everybody. Among other things he promised a larger "living space" (i.e., more territory) for Germany; full citizenship only for people of "German blood"; confiscation of war profits; old age pensions; low rentals to small businessmen; anti-Communism and abolition of interest on land and mortgages.

By 1923 the party membership had grown from the handful of 1920 to some 17,000, most of it concentrated in and around Munich. In November of that year, Hitler enlisted the support of General Erich von Ludendorf and attempted to carry out what has since come to be known as the "Beer Hall Putsch": he proclaimed the outbreak of the "national revolution" in a Munich beer hall and announced that the Bavarian and Reich governments were dissolved. A few shots fired by the authorities sufficed to rout the Nazi "revolutionaries." The Nazi party was banned. He was released after less than a year, at the end of 1924— the Weimar judges, for the most part the old judiciary of Kaiser Wilhelm days, being always tolerant of treason when committed by nationalists. Hitler seemed defeated and discredited.

After completing his autobiography, *Mein Kampf* (My Battle), which openly revealed his sinister political intentions, Hitler set out to rebuild the National Socialist party. No more "putsches" from now on; he had learned his lesson. Now he would capture power legally. "We shall have to hold our noses and go into the Reichstag," he said.

In the years from 1925 to the end of 1928, the

Nazi membership was scarcely more than 100,000, in spite of active campaigning. But in 1929 the depression struck Germany. In the hunger, despair and chaos that it brought, Hitler at last found his chance; millions of Germans began to listen to the promises and threats he vociferated daily. Where the Nazis had polled 810,000 votes in 1928, in the fall of 1930 they polled six-and-a-half million, increasing their seats in the Reichstag from 12 to 107. They were now second only to the Social Democrats.

Meanwhile the Nazi party had grown into a vast apparatus organized down to the street and block level, and complete with special sections for children, youth, women, professional groups and labor organizations. It published innumerable newspapers and magazines. The party itself was organized like the government and became a state within a state. The brown-shirted Storm Troopers (*Sturm Abteilungen*—SA), the Nazi armed force, were bands of thugs who conquered the streets for Hitler by beating and killing opponents and breaking up their meetings. Everywhere the Nazi emblem of the swastika, the crooked cross which so perfectly expressed the sinister spirit of Hitlerism, was in evidence.

With a powerful mass organization and an electoral following of millions, Hitler now began to look to the top. In the spring of 1932, he ran for president (head of the state; the chancellor was head of the government) against the incumbent, Field Marshal Paul von Hindenburg. He failed, and Hindenburg was re-elected, but the Nazi party had increased its vote to thirteen-and-a-half million. In two Reichstag elections in 1932 Hitler tried to win a majority of Germans to his party so as to become chancellor and form a government of his own. The Nazis won nearly 14 million votes in the first, and became the largest German party, but still they fell short of a majority. In the second election the Nazi vote fell off by 2 million.

At this point a union of the anti-Nazi forces could have stopped Hitler. But the Communists were attacking the Social Democrats as "social fascists" and looking to the victory of Hitler as a stage along the

way to their own capture of power. They denounced
the Weimar Republic as violently as the Nazis.

The conservative and reactionary groups, the
ever-powerful Prussian Junkers, army and big business, who had only tolerated the Republic, were now
prepared to bury it. Using Hitler as their tool, they
hoped to eventually restore the Hohenzollern monarchy.
Through Franz von Papen they made a deal with Hitler agreeing to back him for chancellor. In return for
this they would retain the preponderance of power for
themselves, including the vice-chancellorship and most
of the cabinet posts. On January 30, 1933, President
von Hindenburg appointed Adolf Hitler Chancellor of
Germany.

The Nazi leader had no intention of serving as the
Junkers' tool. In only a few months he became dicta-
tor. He used the occasion of the Reichstag fire in February 1933, which the Nazis almost certainly started
themselves but which they blamed on the Communists,
to attack and drive out of existence not only the Communist party but the democratic anti-Nazi parties.

In spite of the Nazi reign of terror which was now
backed up by the power of the state, Hitler still failed
to capture a majority of the vote in the last free elections in March 1933. At this point the Nazis simply
refused to seat the Communist delegates who had
been elected, threatened other delegates with the same
fate, and thus secured the two-thirds majority by
which the Constitution was amended, to place all legislative functions in Hitler's hands. Now he and he
alone made the laws, as well as executed them.

By the summer of 1933 the Nazis were the only
party in Germany. They proceeded to nazify German
life completely (their word for this process was *Gleich-
schaltung*), bringing it under the total domination of
the political religion (ideology) of National Socialism.
They nazified the Christian churches as well, and even
made efforts to replace them with an outright pagan
racist ("Nordic") ritual. "Totalitarianism" is the term
we have coined to describe the total control of a nation's life by a mass political movement. Concentration

camps, that dreadful invention of the 20th century, were set up in which to lock up opponents of the regime: liberals, radicals, Jews, religious leaders and intellectuals.

These descriptions of individual Germans, what their lives were like, and their feelings, breathe life into the dry facts of history. The vignettes reveal Germans, in the year 1930, in every stratum of society, suffering the consequences of the Treaty of Versailles, which imposed harsh terms on the German vanquished. The mood of the country was one of growing bitterness and dissatisfaction.

This material is reprinted from *The Shaping of Western Society* by Edwin Fenton and John Goode.

30. Seven Case Studies
Edwin Fenton and John Goode

Case 1

Hermann Struts, a lieutenant in the German army, has been a lieutenant since World War I when he fought bravely on the western front. Coming from a long line of military officers and having graduated from the German military academy, Hermann is proud of Germany's military tradition. His pride is personal, because his family had been part of that tradition, and it is general, because Germany had always boasted a fine army that had secured the nation's well-being and leadership.

Yet Hermann has not been promoted for more than ten years. Because the German army had been so drastically reduced by the Treaty of Versailles, there have been relatively few promotions. In the old army, Hermann would have been at least a captain by now, because he is a resourceful officer. He probably would have been a major. Hermann resents the Versailles Treaty, which forced Germany to give up its military tradition. He believes this has forever injured Germany's honor, and his honor as a soldier. He feels that if the present government had vetoed the treaty and allowed the German army to resist it, neither Germany nor he would be in their present position.

Case 2

Karin Hauptmann works in a textile factory in Berlin. Although her trade union has actively worked for better conditions and higher wages, it has not made many gains, primarily because the 1923 inflation and the present depression have weakened the entire economy. However, Karin believes that the union would succeed if the economy were stable. As it is, the union has kept her employed. When many of her friends were laid off, Karin's union persuaded the company managers to keep the senior employees. Factories where unions are weak kept only the younger employees, because the company managers say they are more productive.

Karin has been worried by the ideas many of her fellow workers have expressed recently. They have said that the greediness of the factory owners causes business cycles and that when the owners are forced to cut back production, they take it out on the workers. These fellow workers think the only way to end the depression is to let the workers control the factories and the government. Karin still believes that the workers get fair treatment as long as there are strong unions. Moreover, she thinks that managing the factories and the government should be left to people who understand these complicated jobs.

Case 3

Eric von Ronheim, chief executive of an electric motor factory in Frankfurt, is extremely concerned about the present economic depression. Reduced production means lower profits for his company. If Germany had not been treated so harshly at Versailles, the nation would have enough resources to produce goods for consumption, and conditions would be far better. But the government had had to impose heavy taxes in order to pay the reparations the Allies had demanded. Indeed, much of his own profits are going into these taxes. Moreover, the overtaxed Germans have little money to spend on German goods, and so demand is dangerously low. Since other countries are also suffering from depressions, there is almost no foreign market for German goods. Even if Germany were to come out of the depression, Eric knows taxes would be increased to finish paying the reparations.

Eric is also worried about the menacing number of Communists in Germany who wish to organize the same kind of government as the Soviet Union has. If the Communists succeed, the capitalists would receive no mercy from the workers. And Germany would be controlled by its old enemy, the Soviet Union.

Case 4

Karl Schmidt is a steelworker in the rich steel-producing Ruhr Valley. But like so many people in the Ruhr, he is out of work. The depression has forced many steel mills to shut down until there is a market for their goods. On the day Karl's mill closed, the owners announced that shrinking profits made it impossible to keep the workers on their jobs. Yet, Karl reasons, the owners still live in big houses and drive expensive automobiles. Why are the owners protected from this economic slump while the workers suffer? The government is helping the workers somewhat with unemployment compensation, but the payments are hardly enough to support Karl, his wife Anna, and their two children. Moreover, the government has declared that it has little money left, and it cannot continue the payments much longer.

As far as Karl understands, if the government would stop paying the reparations, perhaps it could help Germany recover. But Karl also knows that if the government stops its payments, the French might again occupy the Ruhr Valley, as they had in 1923. What is needed, Karl believes, is a government that listens to the workers—perhaps even one that is run by the workers, as some of his friends argue. And he feels Germany needs a government that can deny France and the other nations the reparation payments.

Case 5

Lotte von Kohler, a prominent attorney who attended the University of Bonn, has a strong sense of the German cultural, literary, and historical traditions. She believes that the great gifts her people have contributed to western civilization have been ignored. Lotte dreams of a newly created republic uniting all the German democratic traditions and leading the way to a totally democratic Europe. She is upset by the unfortunate methods the Weimar Republic often uses to repress the parties of the extreme left more cruelly than those of the extreme right.

However, Lotte's sense of justice is more outraged by the demeaning attitude with which the Allies, particularly the French, view the German republic. She, and others like her who believe in Germany and human dignity, would like to prove to these countries that the Germans are a great race.

Case 6

Wilhelm Schultz is a peasant who works with his parents on their farm in East Prussia. His aunt and uncle live just a few miles away, in the area of East Prussia that the Versailles Treaty had sectioned off as the Polish Corridor. They send reports describing how the Poles mistreat the Germans. Wilhelm's grandparents live nearby in Danzig, but their relatives never visit them. Going to Danzig means crossing into Poland which has many travel restrictions. Wilhelm's schooling had taught him great love for the German heroes like Siegfried, and he was dismayed that his government had signed a treaty that put many Germans, like his aunt and uncle, under Polish rule. Then again, he watches people who violate basic Prussian values rise to respected positions in the government. He sees that these people are often drunk and rowdy. This is not the way Prussians should behave, Wilhelm thinks.

Wilhelm and his parents are finding times hard. The thriving port of Danzig had once been the market for his parents' goods. Now it is difficult to ship goods there because they have to cross the Polish Corridor. Besides, the Poles have opened a rival port to take business away from Danzig. Moreover, the Depression does not make things easier. Finally, the Communists nearby in the Soviet Union are a constant threat to Wilhelm and his parents because they support the end of private property. Wilhelm and his parents are proud to call their land their own, for this gives them an added dignity. Communists want to take this land and this dignity from them—the last rewards the world seems to offer.

Case 7

Gerda Munchen is the owner of a small Munich grocery store started by her parents. For years her parents had saved to send her to the university. But Gerda chose not to go to the university, and the money stayed in the bank. In 1923 Gerda had had a good use for it. Her two daughters were both brilliant; one wanted to be a doctor, and the other hoped to be a lawyer. The money in the bank would have paid for their education. But that same year inflation had hit Germany because the government had printed so much money to pay the reparations. Since the money was not backed by anything economically solid, it had become nearly worthless. Two weeks before her older daughter was to leave for the university, the bank had called to say that her savings were worth only enough to buy three postage stamps. This was certainly a blow to Gerda, but it was more of a blow to her daughters whose futures hung in the balance. They asked her what kind of faith they could put in a system that ruined hardworking people.

Now in 1930, there seems little to be done to regain the losses. People are not making any money and, therefore, cannot buy as many groceries as they had before. And the competition from the big department and chain stores makes it difficult for Gerda to compete. Again Gerda's economic difficulties are not her fault. Her daughters once more question the system that has brought these hardships to their mother and to them.

The Communists offered one answer for Germany's problems, but most Germans rejected it. Hitler gave them what they were most hungry for—pride in being German, as well as hope for economic improvement. This is explained by Herr Damm, an "ordinary" German, to Milton Mayer, from whose book *They Thought They Were Free* the selection is taken.

Note how freely Herr Damm speaks of his anti-Semitism. Try to relate what you read earlier about prejudice, and about anti-Semitism in particular, to Herr Damm's reasons for his dislike of Jews.

31. Herr Damm

Milton Mayer

". . . I was a tobacco salesman," said Herr Damm, who had risen to be officer manager of the Party headquarters in Kronenberg, "but I was let out when the state tobacco tax was raised 100 percent in 1930. I reported to the Labor Office immediately and wrote applications for every job, but I got no work. At first I drew unemployment compensation, but then, since I was still single, I was told I could go back home to the village and live on my father's farm, which, when my father died, my oldest brother would get. That's the way it was in the spring of 1932, when the National Socialists from Kronenberg held a recruiting evening in the village *Bierstube*. Only one member of each household was allowed to sign up, and my family all agreed that I was the one. I agreed, too. Why not? And, by the way, Herr Professor, it was the *only* political party that had ever held a recruiting meeting in our village as far back as anyone could remember. . . .

"Hitler was a simple soldier, like millions of others, only he had a *feeling* for masses of people, and he could speak with passion. The people didn't pay any attention to the Party program as such. They went to the meetings just to hear something new, anything new. They were desperate about the economic situation, 'a new Germany' sounded good to them; but from a deep or broad point of view they saw nothing at all. Hitler talked always against the government, against the lost war, against the peace treaty, against unemployment. All that, people liked. By the time the intellectuals asked, 'What is this?' it had a solid basis in the common people. It was the *Arbeiter, Sozialist* Party, the Party of *workers controlling the social order;* it was not for intellectuals.

"The situation in Germany got worse and worse. What lay underneath people's daily lives, the real root, was gone. Look at the suicides; look at the immorality. People wanted something *radical*, a real change. This want took the form of more and more Communism, especially in middle Germany, in the industrial area, and in the cities of the north. *That* was no invention of Hitler; *that* was real. In countries like America there is no Communism because there is no desire for *radical* change.

"Hitlerism had to answer Communism with something just as radical. Communism always used force; Hitlerism answered it with force. The really absolute enemy of Communism, always clear, always strong in the popular mind, was National Socialism, the *only* enemy that answered Communism in kind. If you wanted to save Germany from Communism—to be *sure* of doing it—you went to National Socialism. The Nazi slogan in 1932 was, 'If you want your country to go Bolshevik, vote Communist; if you want to remain free Germans, vote Nazi.'

"The middle parties, between the two millstones, played no role at all between the two radicalisms. Their adherents were basically the *Bürger,* the bourgeois, the 'nice' people who decide things by parliamentary procedure; and the politically indifferent; and the people who wanted to keep or, at worst, only modify the status quo. . . ."

All 10 of my friends, including the sophisticated Hildebrandt, were affected by this sense of what the Germans call *Bewegung,* movement, a swelling of the human sea, something supraparty and suprapolitical, a surge of the sort that does not, at the time, evoke analysis or, afterward, yield to it. These men were victims of the "Bolshevik" rabies, to be sure. They were equally victims of economic hardship and, still worse, of economic hopelessness, a hopelessness that they suffered more easily by identifying it with their country's. But they were seekers, too, and affirmers— agents, not just patients.

Their country was torn to pieces from without, of course, but still more cruelly from within. Germans had been at one another's throats since 1918, and dissension grew shriller and more bitter all the time. In the course of the decomposition, the principle of *being German,* so newly won under Bismarck and so preciously held for fear of its slipping away, was indeed being lost. The uniting of the country, of all of its people, was possible only on this one principle of *being German,* and my 10 friends, even including the old fanatic Schwenke, onlookers at the disruptive struggles of the old parties and the old party politicians, at the process of shredding the mystical fabric which supported this principle, asked, "Where is Germany?" Nazism—Hitler, rather—knew this and knew that

nothing else mattered to my friends so much as this, the
identification of this Germany, the community again,
in which one might know he belonged and, belonging,
identify himself. This was the movement which any
non-German might see at once for what it was; and
this was the movement which restored my friends as the
sight of home restores the lost child; or as the sight of
the Lorelei Maiden, seen sitting high above the Rhine,
combing her golden hair with a golden comb in the
surprising late sunshine, bewitches the sailor, who
overlooks the rocks beneath the river.

National Socialism was a revulsion by my friends
against parliamentary politics, parliamentary debate,
parliamentary government—against all the higgling and
the haggling of the parties and the splinter parties, their
coalitions, their confusions, and their conniving. It was
the final fruit of the common man's repudiation of "the
rascals." Its motif was, "Throw them all out."

My friends wanted Germany purified. They wanted
it purified of the politicians, of *all* the politicians. They
wanted a representative leader in place of unrepresen-
tative representatives.

Against "the whole pack," "the whole kaboodle,"
"the whole business," against *all* the parliamentary
politicians and *all* the parliamentary parties, my
friends evoked Hitlerism, and Hitlerism overthrew them
all. . . .

"Yes," said Herr Damm, "our family were always
great anti-Semites. My father and grandfather were followers of Dr. Böckel, who founded the Anti-Semitic
Party in Hesse, way back in the eighties. We used to
have the Party flag, with the anti-Semitic inscription
on it, 'Freedom from Jewry,' but the Americans took
it away."

"Did you ever have any dealings with Jews?" I
said.

"Always," he said. "We had to, in the country.
Before the farmers' credit union was founded by Dr.
Böckel—it was anti-Semitic, to save the farmers

from the Jews—we were at the mercy of the cattle dealers. They were all Jews, and they all worked together."

"How do you know that they all worked together, Herr Damm?"

"They always do. They held us in the palm of their hand. Do you know what one of them once did? He bought a calf from my father and took it to town and sold it to my father's cousin, *at a profit*."

"Yes," I said, "but that is just the profit system. You believe in the profit system, don't you? You're certainly no Communist!"

"Of course," he said, "but only think—to my father's own cousin! If my father had known his cousin wanted the calf, he could have sold it to him himself, without the Jew."

"Well—" I said.

"Look, Herr Professor, a Jew buys a cow. When he buys it, it's terrible, everything's wrong with it, he wouldn't have it for a gift. So he pays a few marks for it. Then he goes to the next farmer with it, to sell it, and it's the most wonderful cow in the world. Do you see what I mean?"

"I think so," I said, wreathed, internally, with a smile as I thought of "the American Way," "but don't Germans," that is, non-Jews, "buy as low and sell as high as possible?"

"Yes, but that's just it. Look, Herr Professor," he went on, patiently, "Germans couldn't trade with one another. There was always a Jew between them. All Jews are *Händler*, traders, never workers or farmers. Every child knows this. All trade was in the hands of the Jews. What could we poor Germans"—he was speaking of what Hitler calls, in *Mein Kampf*, the "genius-race"—"do?"

I liked Herr Damm. He was a professional clodhopper—he had been used for Party work among the farmers, whose "language," that is, whose mind, he spoke—but he was still a clodhopper. On another occasion, he was visiting me in town; or, rather, since it was to be our last talk together, I was his host at a one-dollar de luxe dinner at Kronenberg's best restaurant. I brought the talk back to one of our first conversations, in which he had told me that he was the only Kreisamtsleiter in our whole *Gau* who had refused to leave the Church. "I told them I was born in the Church," he had said, "and I would die in it, and not in the 'German Church,' but the Christian Church."

"Now," I said, as we were lighting up after dinner, "what many Christians in America cannot understand is how you Christians in Germany could accept the persecution of the Jews, no matter how bad they were. How could you accept it as *Christians?*"

It was the first time I had taken the initiative on the subject. "The Jews?"—he said—"but the Jews were the *enemies* of the Christian religion. Others might have other reasons for destroying them, but we Christians had the *Christian duty* to. Surely, Herr Professor, you know how the Jews betrayed our Lord?"

These excerpts from William Allen's *The Nazi Seizure of Power* shed further light on German willingness to follow Hitler. The author provides information about some of the ingenious means by which the Nazis won support.

The Hitler Youth movement was formed for the express purpose of creating loyal subjects to the state. By 1935, over 3 million boys and girls aged 10 and older were enrolled. "We are born to die for Germany" was one of their popular slogans. In addition to a strenuous physical fitness program, they received training in the use of weapons and heard lectures on Nazi ideology.

32. Why I Joined the Hitler Youth
William Allen

There was no pressure put on me by my father or anyone else to join the Hitler Youth—I decided to join it independently simply because I wanted to be in a boy's club where I could strive towards a nationalistic ideal. The Hitler Youth had camping, hikes, and group meetings. I was number nine in the Thalburg group when I joined in 1930. There were boys from all classes of families though mainly middle class and workers. There were no social or class distinctions, which I approved of very much. There was no direct or obvious political indoctrination until later —after Hitler came to power. Without really trying to get new members, the Thalburg Hitler Youth grew rapidly. I think most of the other boys joined for the same reason I did. They were looking for a place where they could get together with other boys in exciting activities. It was also a depression time and there were many such influences abroad from which decent boys wished to escape. In any event, I don't think the political factor was the main reason boys joined. We did march in parades and hated the SPD, but that was all general, not specific—it was all a part of it. We weren't fully conscious of what we were doing, but we enjoyed ourselves and also felt important.

33. A Town Goes Nazi
William Allen

The factors that brought Thalburg to the brink of the Third Reich with a three-fifths Nazi majority (almost double the national average) were not numerous, but they were complexly interrelated. Paramount among them was the Depression. Though only the working class suffered physically in the three-year crisis, the town's middle class was more decisively affected through fears that an ultimate catastrophe would thrust upon it the same fate as the "shelterless," or that social revolution would destroy its status. More important than the actual misery caused by the depression was the constant flow of news items stressing that misery.

There were only 17 bankruptcies in Thalburg in the entire Depression era, 11 of which befell small, marginal shopowners, and the other six for causes dissociated from the Depression. But the bankruptcies were strung out over a long period of time and each involved lengthy and dolorous legal proceedings, all faithfully reported in the press. At the high point of unemployment, in April, 1932, only 8 percent of the townspeople were unemployed, but the constant protests, fights, demonstrations, and the endless stream of gray-faced workers coming to the District Employment Office kept unemployment uppermost in the minds of the town's middle class. Nazi agitation drew upon this mood and intensified the unsettled atmosphere.

Thalburg was a nationalistic town long before 1930, though as the Depression wore on, commitment to nationalism and militarism increased. Outside forces contributed to this, as did Nazi propaganda, but by manipulating the symbols of patriotism the NSDAP in Thalburg associated itself with an important tradition. The same applied to the Nazis' exploitation of religious feelings, especially their use of Lutheran pastors as speakers in Thalburg.

A further factor which aided the rise of Nazism in Thalburg was politicalization. The yearnings and needs created by the Depression, class antagonisms, and resurgent nationalism all seemed capable of political solution. Constant elections meant constant campaigning and each campaign spurred bitterness and radicalism. From the local elections of November, 1929, to the Reichstag elections of November, 1932, there were nine major campaigns, five in 1932 alone. Thalburgers voted heavily in all of these. This followed the pattern of the whole electoral district, which had the second highest voting participation record of Germany's 35 electoral districts. In Thalburg, between 94 percent and 97 percent of those eligible voted in each of the major elections. Since registration was automatic, only the sick and feeble-minded stayed home. The rest were involved in politics, which is to say that political passion pervaded almost all areas of human existence in Thalburg.

Nazi propaganda efforts in Thalburg went beyond pure activism. Persistent, imaginative, and driving effort was coupled with a shrewd appreciation of what was specifically suitable for Thalburg, and for each element in the town. Aside from general speeches on nationalism, Jews, and "Marxists," there were meetings devoted to artisans, businessmen, civil servants, pensioners, and workmen. Thalburg's local peculiarities were taken into account; there was little real anti-Semitism in the town, hence this was soft-pedaled. But the townspeople were strongly religious and this was exploited to the hilt. When there was no specific group to be appealed to, the Nazis relied on pageantry, "evenings of entertainment," film showings, plays, acrobatic acts, lotteries, dances, sport exhibitions, military displays, recitals by children, and other expedients from a seemingly inexhaustible bag of tricks. They drew the tortured masses into the mammoth meetings where one could submerge oneself in the sense of participating in a dynamic and all-encompassing movement geared towards radical action in fulfillment of every need. The enemy was defined in similar terms: he was the Jew, the Socialist, the godless one, or, if one preferred amorphous generalities, the System which was to blame for everything from the collapse of the Enterprise Bank to the Treaty of Versailles.

IN THEIR OWN WORDS

What motivated the Nazis themselves, especially those in the SS and the Gestapo who organized the transports, ran the camps, and participated in the mass slaughter? Four Nazis, two of them near the top of the hierarchy, two of them rank-and-file secret police, offer explanations of their behavior. Rudolf Hoess was commandant of Auschwitz; Albert Speer was the Minister for Armament and War Production.

These selections are taken from the following sources: *Commander of Auschwitz* by Rudolf Hoess; *Nuremberg Diary* by G. M. Gilbert; *Auschwitz* by Bernd Naumann.

34. Rudolf Hoess, Commander of Auschwitz

My task was not an easy one. In the shortest possible time I had to construct a transit camp for 10,000 prisoners, using the existing complex of buildings which, though well-constructed, had been completely neglected, and were swarming with vermin. . . .

It was clear to me from the very beginning that Auschwitz could be made into a useful camp only through the hard and untiring efforts of everyone, from the commandant down to the lowest prisoner.

If I wanted to get good and useful work out of the prisoners, they must be given better treatment. . . .

I had complete confidence in these assumptions.

Nevertheless, within a few months, I might even say during the first weeks, I became bitterly aware that all goodwill and all the best intentions were doomed to be dashed to pieces against the human inadequacy and sheer stupidity of most of the officers and men posted to me. . . .

I must emphasize here that I have never personally hated the Jews. It is true that I looked upon them as the enemies of our people. But just because of this I saw no difference between them and the other prisoners, and I treated them all in the same way. I never drew any distinctions. In any event the emotion of hatred is foreign to my nature. But I know what hate is, and what it looks like. I have seen it and I have suffered it myself. . . .

When in the summer of 1941 Himmler gave me the order to prepare installations at Auschwitz where mass exterminations could take place, and personally to carry out these exterminations, I did not have the slightest idea of their scale or consequences. It was certainly an extraordinary and monstrous order. Nevertheless the reasons behind the extermination program seemed to me right. I did not reflect on it at the time. I had been given an order, and I had to carry it out. Whether this mass extermination of the Jews was necessary or not was something on which I could not allow myself to form an opinion, for I lacked the necessary breadth of view.

35. Hoess Explains Why He Killed The Jews

I asked him if he had ever considered whether the Jews whom he had murdered were guilty or had in any way deserved such a fate. Again he tried patiently to explain that there was something unrealistic about such questions because he had been living in an entirely different world. "Don't you see, we SS men were not supposed to think about these things; it never even occurred to us.—And besides, it was something already taken for granted that the Jews were to blame for everything." I pressed him for some explanation of why it was taken for granted. "Well, we just never heard anything else. It was not just newspapers like the *Stürmer* but it was everything we ever heard. Even our military and ideological training took for granted that we had to protect Germany from the Jews. . . . It only started to occur to me after the collapse that maybe it was not quite right, after I heard what everybody was saying.—But nobody had ever said these things before; at least we never heard of it. Now I wonder if Himmler really believed all that himself or just gave me an excuse to justify what he wanted me to do.— But anyway, that really didn't matter. We were all so trained to obey orders without even thinking that the thought of disobeying an order would simply never have occurred to anybody and somebody else would have done just as well if I hadn't. . . . Himmler was so strict about little things, and executed SS men for such small offenses, that we naturally took it for granted that he was acting according to a strict code of honor. . . . You can be sure that it was not always a pleasure to see those mountains of corpses and smell the continual burning.—But Himmler had ordered it and had even explained the necessity and I really never gave much thought to whether it was wrong. It just seemed a necessity."

36. Other Gestapo Men Explain

WILHELM BOGER, former member of the camp Gestapo:

During the reign of National Socialism I knew only one mode of conduct: to carry out the orders of superiors without reservation. I did not ask to be stationed in Auschwitz. Today I realize that the idea I believed in spelled disaster and that it was wrong. It has been said here that I conducted rigorous interrogations as ordered. But what I saw at the time was not Auschwitz as a terrible extermination site of European Jewry but the fight against the Polish resistance movement and Bolshevism.

HANS STARK, former member of the camp Gestapo:

I took part in the murder of many people. I often asked myself after the war whether I had become a criminal because, being a dedicated National Socialist, I had murdered men, and I found no answer. I believed in the Führer; I wanted to serve my people. Today I know that this idea was false. I regret the mistakes of my past, but I cannot undo them.

37. Albert Speer Speaks

I should have and actually did realize it sooner, but kept playing at this hypocritical game until it was too late—well, because it was easier. . . .

That was the kind of weakness and hypocrisy I accuse myself of, because I had begun to realize even then that Hitler was playing havoc with German lives and resources; but I put the thought away. It was too dangerous. It is easy to rationalize things—patriotism in war, and all that. That is my guilt, and I don't deny it.

HITLER'S THEORIES

Hitler's system of beliefs and ideas was articulated in his book *Mein Kampf* ("My Struggle") in 1923, 10 years before he came to power. Part autobiography and part manifesto, it was written when he was in his mid-30s, and just beginning his political activity. Accepting and building on theories of innate differences between "races" which were current at that time, Hitler preached the superiority of the Aryan (Indo-European) races, specifically the German people. The Jews, in Hitler's view, were members of a distinct "race," all having the same blood. Not only was this race inferior, it was the antithesis of everything noble and enlightened that distinguished the German "master race."

The first two selections are from *Mein Kampf*; the third is from *The War Against the Jews* by Lucy Dawidowicz.

38. On the Aryan

Adolf Hitler

All the human culture, all the results of art, science and technology that we see before us today, are almost exclusively the creative product of the Aryan. This very fact admits of the not unfounded inference that he alone was the founder of all higher humanity, therefore representing the prototype of all that we understand by the word "man." He is the Prometheus of mankind from whose shining brow the divine spark of genius has sprung at all times. . . .

Thus, for the formation of higher cultures the existence of lower human types was one of the most essential preconditions. . . . It is certain that the first culture of humanity was based less on the tamed animal than on the use of lower human beings. Only after the enslavement of subject races did the same fate strike beasts. For first the conquered warrior drew the plow—and only after him the horse. Hence it is no accident that the first cultures arose in places where the Aryan, in his encounters with lower peoples, subjugated them and bent them to his will. . . . As long as he ruthlessly upheld the master attitude, not only did he remain master, but also the preserver and increaser of culture.

39. About the Jew

Adolf Hitler

The Jewish people, despite all apparent intellectual qualities, is without any true culture, and especially without any culture of its own. For what sham culture the Jew today possesses is the property of other peoples, and for the most part it is ruined in his hands.

Thus, the Jew lacks those qualities which distinguish the races that are creative and hence culturally blessed.

The Jew never possessed a state with definite territorial limits and therefore never called a culture his own. . . .

He is, and remains, the typical parasite, a sponger who like a noxious bacillus keeps spreading as soon as a favorable medium invites him. And the effect of his existence is also like that of spongers: wherever he appears, the host people dies out after a shorter or longer period.

Thus, the Jew of all times has lived in the states of other peoples, and there formed his own state, which, to be sure, habitually sailed under the disguise of "religious community" as long as outward circumstances made a complete revelation of his nature seem inadvisable. But as soon as he felt strong enough to do without the protective cloak, he always dropped the veil and suddenly became what so many of the others previously did not want to believe and see: the Jew.

40. The Jews in Hitler's Mental World
Lucy Dawidowicz

The Jews inhabited Hitler's mind. He believed that they were the source of all evil, misfortune, and tragedy, the single factor that, like some inexorable law of nature, explained the workings of the universe. The irregularities of war and famine, financial distress and sudden death, defeat and sinfulness—all could be explained by the presence of that single factor in the universe, a miscreation that disturbed the world's steady ascent toward well-being, affluence, success, victory. A savior was needed to come forth and slay the loathsome monster. In Hitler's obsessed mind, as in the delusive imaginings of the medieval millenarian sectarians, the Jews were the demonic hosts whom he had been given a divine mission to destroy.

All his life Hitler was seized by this obsession with the Jews. Even after he had murdered the Jews, he had still not exorcised his Jewish demons. At 4:00 A.M. on April 29, 1945, the last day of his life in the Berlin bunker, he finished dictating his political testament. His last words to the German people were: "Above all I charge the leaders of the nation and those under them to scrupulous observance of the laws of race and to merciless opposition to the universal poisoner of all peoples, international Jewry."

THE NAZI PROGRAM

The concepts of racial and national superiority were given practical expression in the very first Nazi party platform, adopted in 1920. Though the party did not come to power for another 13 years, many of the proposals remained unchanged and were eventually put into effect. The "socialist" planks, however, were essentially propaganda aimed at winning the support of the workers, and were never taken seriously by party leaders.

The document is reprinted from *National Socialism*, published by the U.S. Department of State.

41. The Nazi Program

The National Socialist German Workers' Party at a great mass meeting on February 25th, 1920, in the Hofbrauhaus-Festsaal in Munich announced their Program to the world.

In section 2 of the Constitution of Our Party this Program is declared to be inalterable.

The Program of the German Workers' Party is limited as to period. The leaders have no intention, once the aims announced in it have been achieved, of setting up fresh ones, merely in order to increase the discontent of the masses artificially, and so ensure the continued existence of the Party.

1. We demand the union of Germans to form a

Great Germany on the basis of the right of the self-determination enjoyed by nations.

2. We demand equality of rights for the German People in its dealings with other nations, and abolition of the Peace Treaties of Versailles and St. Germain.

3. We demand land and territory [colonies] for the nourishment of our people and for settling our superfluous population.

4. None but members of the nation may be citizens of the State. None but those of German blood, whatever their creed, may be members of the nation. No Jew, therefore, may be a member of the nation.

5. Anyone who is not a citizen of the State may live in Germany only as a guest and must be regarded as being subject to foreign laws.

6. The right of voting on the State's government and legislation is to be enjoyed by the citizen of the State alone. We demand therefore that all official appointments, of whatever kind, whether in the Reich, in the country, or in the smaller localities, shall be granted to citizens of the State alone.

We oppose the corrupting custom of Parliament of filling posts merely with a view to party considerations, and without reference to character or capability.

7. We demand that the State shall make it its first duty to promote the industry and livelihood of citizens of the State. If it is not possible to nourish the entire population of the State, foreign nationals [non-citizens of the State] must be excluded from the Reich.

8. All non-German immigration must be prevented. We demand that all non-Germans, who entered Germany subsequent to August 2nd, 1914, shall be required forthwith to depart from the Reich.

9. All citizens of the State shall be equal as regards rights and duties.

10. It must be the first duty of each citizen of the State to work with his mind or with his body. The activities of the individual may not clash with the interests of the whole, but must proceed within the frame of the community and be for the general good.

We demand therefore:

11. Abolition of incomes unearned by work.

12. In view of the enormous sacrifice of life and property demanded of a nation by every war, personal enrichment due to a war must be regarded as a crime against the nation. We demand therefore ruthless confiscation of all war gains.

13. We demand nationalization of all businesses which have been up to the present formed into companies [Trusts].

14. We demand that the profits from wholesale trade shall be shared out.

15. We demand extensive development of provision for old age.

16. We demand creation and maintenance of a healthy middle class, immediate communalization of wholesale business premises, and their lease at a cheap rate to small traders, and that extreme consideration shall be shown to all small purveyors to the State, district authorities and smaller localities.

17. We demand land-reform suitable to our national requirements, passing of a law for confiscation without compensation of land for communal purposes; abolition of interest on land loans, and prevention of all speculation in land.

18. We demand ruthless prosecution of those whose activities are injurious to the common interest. Sordid criminals against the nation, usurers, profiteers, etc., must be punished with death, whatever their creed or race.

19. We demand that the Roman Law, which serves the materialistic world order, shall be replaced by a legal system for all Germany.

20. With the aim of opening to every capable and industrious German the possibility of higher education and of thus obtaining advancement, the State must consider a thorough reconstruction of our national system of education. The curriculum of all educational establishments must be brought into line with the requirements of practical life. Comprehension of the State idea [State sociology] must be the school objective, beginning with the first dawn of intelligence

in the pupil. We demand development of the gifted children of poor parents, whatever their class or occupation, at the expense of the State.

21. The State must see to raising the standard of health in the nation by protecting mothers and infants, prohibiting child labor, increasing bodily efficiency by obligatory gymnastics and sports laid down by law, and by extensive support of clubs engaged in the bodily development of the young.

22. We demand abolition of a paid army and formation of a national army.

23. We demand legal warfare against conscious political lying and its dissemination in the Press. In order to facilitate creation of a German national Press we demand:

(a) that all editors of newspapers and their assistants, employing the German language, must be members of the nation;

(b) that special permission from the State shall be necessary before non-German newspapers may appear. These are not necessarily printed in the German language;

(c) that non-Germans shall be prohibited by law from participating financially in or influencing German newspapers, and that the penalty for contravention of the law shall be suppression of any such newspaper, and immediate deportation of the non-German concerned in it.

It must be forbidden to publish papers which do not conduce to the national welfare. We demand legal prosecution of all tendencies in art and literature of a kind likely to disintegrate our life as a nation, and the suppression of institutions which militate against the requirements above-mentioned.

24. We demand liberty for religious denominations in the State, so far as they are not a danger to it and do not militate against the moral feelings of the German race.

The Party, as such, stands for positive Christianity, but does not bind itself in the matter of creed to any particular confession. It combats the Jewish-materialist

spirit within us and without us, and is convinced that
our nation can only achieve permanent health from
within on the principle: THE COMMON INTEREST
BEFORE SELF.

25. That all the foregoing may be realized we
demand the creation of a strong central power of the
State. Unquestioned authority of the politically cen-
tralized Parliament over the entire Reich and its organizations; and formation of Chambers for classes and
occupations for the purpose of carrying out the general
laws promulgated by the Reich in the various States of
the confederation.

The leaders of the Party swear to go straight forward—if necessary to sacrifice their lives—in securing
fulfilment of the foregoing Points.

A logical extension of the Nazi racial
philosophy was the two-pronged movement to
improve the German stock: on the one hand, to
add as many "pure" Germans as possible to
the population, and, on the other, to rid the
German people of undesirable elements. How
these goals were implemented, with characteristic efficiency, is described in these selections
from the book *Hitler's SS* by Richard Grun-
berger. It is important to note here that protests against euthanasia succeeded in bringing the program to a halt.

42. The Lebensborn Movement
Richard Grunberger

All the pieces in Himmler's eugenic jigsaw—in-
fertile couples, Germanized Slavs, "procreation assistants," unmarried mothers—were moved into place by
"Lebensborn" (Fountain of Life), as SS foundling hos-
pital-cum-adoption society established in 1936. Ac-

cording to the Lebensborn report for 1938, "eight hundred thirty-two valuable German women decided despite their single state and the sacrifice entailed, to eschew abortion and present the nation with a child." Assessing each German's life contribution to the economy at 100,000 Reichsmark, Lebensborn claimed to have enriched the country by 83 million Reichsmark.

Eventually thousands of Lebensborn wards were placed with childless Nazi couples; more importantly, in wartime the original objective—delivering and fostering illegitimate German children—was superseded by the genetic spoliation of Eastern Europe.

During his first inspection tour of occupied Poland Himmler had been deeply stirred by the Nordic appearance of many Slav children and this may have started a train of thought culminating in his war aim "to enlarge Germany's existing blood basis of 90 million to 120 million." Kidnapped children—snatched from orphanages or alleged resistance families—were taken to Lebensborn homes dotted across occupied Europe; after a processing period during which the bewildered children were drilled in rudimentary German and denied any contact with their compatriots, they went off to the Reich already bearing the names of their designated foster parents.

Germanization was by no means confined to children nor were all Germanized Slavs necessarily outright victims of force. In Poland, where Poles and Germans had long intermarried, Polish nationals of part-German ancestry could apply for Reich citizenship which—given the situation of Poles under Nazi occupation—many were quite eager to do.

But volunteers could never meet Himmler's need for genetic reinforcements, and two special SS agencies—the Volksdeutsche Liaison Office and the Race and Settlement Office—scoured Europe to select human specimens considered suitable for Germanization. Besides abduction, the tasks of RUSHA, the Race and Settlement Office, ranged from conscription of slave labor, the infliction of (frequently capital) punishment on East Europeans guilty of intimacy with German women, to the clearance of Slavs from regions earmarked for German settlement.

One such region was the Warthegau in western Poland. The Warthegau "plantation" involved clearing one and a half million Poles and Jews out of a large area to make room for half a million *Volksdeutsche* from eastern Poland, Rumania and the Baltic States. Himmler, newly styled "Reich Commissioner for the consolidation of German folkdom," ordered the clearance during the Arctic winter of 1939–40, and thus caused a heavier death toll than resulted from Hitler's concurrent directive to decapitate the Polish nation by liquidating its intellectuals and priests.

---

43. Euthanasia

Richard Grunberger

A related aim—that of purifying the gene pool of the German race—lay behind the Euthanasia Campaign of 1940–41. In September 1939 Hitler ordered the "mercy-killing" of the feebleminded and incurables throughout the Reich—on grounds both of eugenics and wartime economy in food, accommodation and medical personnel. The first liquidation center became operational before the end of the year; another five, one of them situated at the well-known psychiatric clinic of Hadamar, came into operation early in 1940. The man placed in overall charge of the program was Christian Wirth, the former superintendent of the Criminal Investigation Department in Stuttgart.

Wirth initially disposed of his victims by shooting them in the neck. After some time he switched over to gassing them in specially constructed chambers—and thus qualifies as co-originator of the mass-extermination methods subsequently used in the so-called "Final Solution of the Jewish Question."

In each euthanasia establishment a room camouflaged as a shower room was hermetically sealed. This was connected by a system of pipes to cylinders of carbon monoxide. The patients, before being taken in groups of 10 or 15 into this gas chamber, were generally made drowsy with the aid of morphine (or scopolamine) injections or drugged with soporifics. Each center housed a crematorium; families were informed of patients' deaths on preprinted forms attributing death to heart failure or pneumonia.

The steep increase in fatalities, reported under conditions of ill-concealed secrecy—palls of smoke above the crematoria were visible for miles, and at Hadamar the village children would greet incoming hospital buses with cries of "here come some more to be gassed"—prompted mounting disquiet in the country. Among many rumors in circulation was one which alleged that even badly wounded soldiers were being "mercy-killed" at military hospitals.

In August 1941 the Catholic Bishop Galen denounced the euthanasia killings in a sermon from the pulpit of his cathedral at Münster, Westphalia. This turned out to be the most successful single act of resistance ever undertaken in the Third Reich: the systematic killing of institution inmates (which had thus far cost approximately 100,000 lives) ceased almost immediately.

Nor was any retaliatory action taken against the bishop, although the Gestapo soon afterward beheaded three parish priests who had distributed his sermon in leaflet form. Such glaring discrepancy of punishment was the fruit of Machiavellian calculation: while the death of anonymous parish priests would go unremarked in the surrounding welter of violence and confusion, persecution might have elevated the well-known prelate to the status of a national resistance figure.

IV

WHAT DOES THE HOLOCAUST REVEAL ABOUT THE INDIVIDUAL AND SOCIETY?

"Though the German people who gave active or passive support to Hitler must of necessity carry the *main burden of guilt* for what was done, there are many others who must share it with them: the men and women of other nations who joined the SS and helped to staff the camps; the countries, such as Rumania and Hungary, who in the end persecuted their Jews with a savagery no less possessed than that of the Nazis; in fact, when the truth of the matter was gradually revealed to the Allied nations and to the world outside Germany by those who risked their lives to bring the facts from the secret places of extermination, everyone who refused to take heed of this authenticated knowledge and made no attempt to prevent the further torture and death of these innocent people must, on however relative a scale, share in the great burden of guilt which still lies heavily on the conscience of us all."

—ROGER MANVELL AND HEINRICH FRAENKEL
The Incomparable Crime

Whenever a person finds himself in a situation of moral conflict, he must choose his course of action. Even if he is only a bystander, he will choose whether to look away—or to involve himself. Everyone whose life was touched in some way by the Nazis had to make a choice: to look away, to cooperate, or to resist. In the next four selections, we meet four individuals: two who were actively involved in killing prisoners in the camps; two who could have remained completely untouched, but who chose, freely and consciously, to involve themselves.

In this first selection taken from his memoir, *Auschwitz*, Dr. Miklos Nyiszli, a Jewish physician, is tortured by the memories of his participation in Nazi medical experiments.

44. A Doctor for the Nazis Remembers
Dr. Miklos Nyiszli

Sick at heart, and physically ill, I started my long voyage homeward. The trip was not a pleasant one: everywhere I looked I saw, where flourishing cities and towns had once stood, nothing but gutted ruins and the collective, white-crossed graves of the dead.

I dreaded the truth, fearing to return to an

empty, plundered home, a home where neither parents nor wife, daughter nor sister, would be waiting to greet me with warmth and affection. Persecution and sorrow, the horrors of the crematorium and funeral pyres, my eight months in the kommando of the living dead, had dulled my sense of good and evil.

I felt that I should rest, try to regain my strength. But, I kept asking myself, for what? On the one hand, illness racked my body; on the other, the bloody past froze my heart. My eyes had followed countless innocent souls to the gas chambers, witnessed the unbelievable spectacle of the funeral pyres. And I myself, carrying out the orders of a demented doctor, had dissected hundreds of bodies, so that a science based on false theories might benefit from the deaths of those millions of victims. I had cut the flesh of healthy young girls and prepared nourishment for the mad doctor's bacteriological cultures. I had immersed the bodies of dwarfs and cripples in calcium chloride, or had them boiled so that the carefully prepared skeletons might safely reach the Third Reich's museums to justify, for future generations, the destruction of an entire race. And even though all this was now past, I would still have to cope with it in my thoughts and dreams. I could never erase these memories from my mind.

At least twice I had felt the wings of death brush by me: once, prostrate on the ground, with a company of SS trained in the art of summary execution poised above me, I had escaped unharmed. But 3,000 of my friends, who had also known the terrible secrets of the crematoriums, had not been so lucky. I had marched for hundreds of kilometers through fields of snow, fighting the cold, hunger, and my own exhaustion, merely to reach another concentration camp. The road I had traveled had indeed been long.

Now, home again, nothing. I wandered aimlessly through silent rooms. Free, but not from my bloody past, nor from the deep-rooted grief that filled my mind and gnawed at my sanity. And the future seemed just as dark. I walked like my own ghost, a restless figure in the once familiar streets. The only times I managed to shake off my state of depression and lethargy was when, mistakenly, I thought for a fleeting second that someone I saw or briefly encountered on the street was a member of my family.

One afternoon, several weeks after my return, I felt chilly and sat down near the fireplace, hoping to derive a little comfort from the cheerful glow that filled the room. It grew late; dusk was falling. The doorbell roused me from my daydreams. Before I could get up to answer it my wife and daughter burst into the room!

They were in good health and had just been freed from Bergen-Belsen, one of the most notorious of the extermination camps. But that was as much as they were able to tell me before breaking down. For hours they sobbed uncontrollably. I was content just to hold them in my arms, while the flood of their grief flowed from their tortured minds and hearts. Their sobs, a language I was well familiar with, slowly subsided.

We had much to do, much to relate, much to rebuild. I knew it would take much time and infinite patience before we could resume any sort of really normal life. But all that mattered was that we were alive . . . and together again. Life suddenly became meaningful again. I would begin practicing, yes. . . . But I swore that as long as I lived I would never lift a scalpel again. . . .

This physician, not Jewish, at Auschwitz, appears to have been more concerned with the menu for lunch than with his activities in the camp. Hans Hermann Kremer joined the Nazi Party in 1932 and the armed SS in 1941. On August 29, 1942, he was ordered to Auschwitz to substitute for another physician who had fallen ill. The diary excerpts are reprinted from

Human Behavior in the Concentration Camp by Elie Cohen.

45. From a Doctor's Diary
Hans Hermann Kremer

September 2, 1942: First time present at a Sonderaktion. [The most spectacular of the mass atrocities were called *Sonderaktionen*. One of these, which was practiced particularly in Auschwitz, was the burning of live prisoners, especially children, in pits measuring 20 by 40 to 50 meters, on piles of gasoline-soaked wood.]

September 5, 1942: This afternoon present at a Sonderaktion from the female concentration camp (Muselmanner): The most horrible of horrors. Hschf. Thilo, doctor of the troops, is right when he told me this morning that we are at *anus mundi*. In the evening at approximately 9:00 hours again present at a Sonderaktion from the Netherlands. Men all want to take part in these actions because of the special rations they get then, consisting of a fifth of a liter of schnapps, five cigarettes, 100 gram sausage and bread. Today and tomorrow on duty.

September 6, 1942: Today, Sunday, excellent lunch: tomato soup, half a hen with potatoes and red cabbage (20 gram fat), sweets and marvelous vanilla ice. . . . In the evening at 8:00 hours a Sonderaktion.

September 9, 1942: This morning I got the most pleasant news from my lawyer Prof. Dr. Hallermann in Münster, that I got divorced from my wife on the first of this month (Note: I see colors again, a black curtain is drawn back from my life!). Later on, present as doctor at a corporal punishment of eight prisoners and an execution by shooting with small-calibre rifles. Got soap flakes and two pieces of soap. . . . In the evening present at a Sonderaktion, fourth time.

September 10, 1942: In the morning present at a Sonderaktion (fifth time).

September 20, 1942: Listened to a concert of the prisoners' band this afternoon in bright sunshine. Bandmaster: conductor of the Warschauer Staatsoper. Eighty musicians. For lunch we had pork. . . .

A young man who joined the resistance movement in Denmark was captured by the Nazis and sentenced to be executed. In this letter to his mother, he explains why he is glad he chose to live by his ideals. The selection is from *Dying We Live: The Final Messages and Records of the Resistance.*

46. Kim, Cabin Boy and Seaman
Kim Malthe-Bruun

Farewell Letter to His Mother

Western Prison, German Section, Cell 411
April 4, 1945

Dear Mother: Today, together with Jürgen, Nils, and Ludwig, I was arraigned before a military tribunal. We were condemned to death. I know that you are a courageous woman, and that you will bear this, but, hear me, it is not enough to bear it, you must also understand it. I am an insignificant thing, and my person will soon be forgotten, but the thought, the life, the inspiration that filled me will live on. You will meet them everywhere—in the trees at springtime, in people who cross your path, in a loving little smile. You will encounter that something which perhaps had value in me, you will cherish it, and you will not forget me. And so I shall have a chance to grow, to become large and mature. I shall be living with all of you whose hearts I once filled. And you will all live on, knowing that I have preceded you, and not, as perhaps you thought at first, dropped out behind you. You know what my dearest wish has always been, and what I hoped to become. Follow me, my dear mother, on my path, and do not stop before the end, but linger with some of the matters belonging to the last space of time allotted to me, and you will find something that may be of value both to my sweetheart and to you, my mother.

I traveled a road that I have never regretted. I have never evaded the dictate of my heart, and now things seem to fall into place. I am not old, I should not be dying, yet it seems so natural to me, so simple. It is only the abrupt manner of it that frightens us at first. The time is short, I cannot properly explain it, but my soul is perfectly at rest. . . .

When I come right down to it, how strange it is to be sitting here and writing this testament. Every word must stand, it can never be amended, erased, or changed. I have so many thoughts. Jorgen is sitting here before me writing his two-year-old daughter a letter for her confirmation. A document for life. He and I have lived together, and now we die together, two comrades. . . .

I see the course that things are taking in our country, and I know that Grandfather will prove to have been right, but remember—and all of you must remember this—that your dream must not be to return to the time before the war, but that all of you, young and old, should create conditions that are not arbitrary but that will bring to realization a genuinely human ideal, something that every person will see and feel to be an ideal for all of us. That is the great gift for which our country thirsts—something for which every humble peasant boy can yearn, and which he can joyously feel himself to have a part in and to be working for.

Finally, there is the girl whom I call mine. Make her realize that the stars still shine and that I have been only a milestone on her road. Help her on: she can still become very happy.

In haste—your eldest child and only son,

Kim

The press bureau of the chief of the SS and the police force in Denmark on Sunday, April 8, 1945, issued the following announcement:

> Condemned to death: Seaman Kim Malthe-Bruun, born July 8, 1923, in Saskatchewan, Canada, resident in Copenhagen, because, as a member of an illegal organization, he possessed himself of a revenue service boat and took it to Sweden. In addition he procured arms for his organization and took part in transporting arms. The death sentence was carried out by a firing squad.

A distinguished Berlin minister spent the final days of his life in prison because he dared to defy the Nazis by speaking out publicly against their policies. He died in 1943 as the Nazis were sending him to Dachau Concentration Camp on the grounds of "jeopardy to public order." This selection is from *Dying We Live: The Final Messages and Records of the Resistance.*

47. Bernhard Lichtenberg, Prelate

Bernhard Lichtenberg, born December 3, 1875, at Ohlau in Silesia, had been dean of the Cathedral of

St. Hedwig in Berlin since 1938. When the great trial of his life came to him, he was well advanced in years, a venerable priest whose body, consumed by long years of self-sacrificing pastoral service, continued to function only under compulsion of a fiery will. In him were combined the tenderness of the ardent worshipper and the hardihood of a crusader battling for injured justice. He was of those who hunger and thirst after righteousness. Thus a conflict with National Socialism was inevitable.

Even before the brown-shirted cohorts seized power, Father Lichtenberg was an object of hatred to them as a pacifist. And when in Germany terror was made a form of government, he could not and would not remain silent, because for a priest silence meant complicity. In October of 1941, the Party disseminated inflammatory pamphlets directed against the Jews; in answer to these, he had the following announcement read from the pulpits of all the churches of the diocese.

> ANNOUNCEMENT. An inflammatory pamphlet anonymously attacking the Jews is being disseminated among the houses of Berlin. It declares that any German who, because of allegedly false sentimentality, aids the Jews in any way, be it only through a friendly gesture, is guilty of betraying his people. Do not allow yourselves to be confused by this un-Christian attitude, but act according to the strict commandment of Jesus Christ: "Thou shalt love thy neighbor as thyself."

No one ever saw him raise his hand in the Hitler salute. When he was asked how he felt toward the Führer, he replied to the Gestapo commissioner: "I have only one Führer, Jesus Christ."

He was denounced for his public prayers on behalf of concentration camp prisoners and of Jews. On October 23, 1941, he was arrested, tried, and condemned to two years in prison. "I knew of the many priests who had been arrested," he admitted at the trial, "and even then surmised what I know today, because I have now been having a taste of it these last seven months and have been made to feel it in my own body how hard the fate of imprisonment is even for a priest, and how greatly, in such distress, even he stands in need of strength and consolation from God." . . .

The deprivation of freedom was synonymous with a death sentence. Dean Lichtenberg died November 5, 1943, in Hof, on the way to Dachau, where the Gestapo was sending him after the expiration of his term of imprisonment at Tegel, on the ground of "jeopardy to public order."

Could the Holocaust have been prevented? Quite possibly yes, but no one really tried. That is the chilling message of this harsh indictment of world indifference. Despite the seeming concern and good intentions of many people in western countries, little action was taken by their governments either to interfere with the Nazi program, or to provide refuge for fleeing Jews.

The selection is by Judah Pilch, from *The Jewish Catastrophe in Europe.*

48. The World Was Silent

Judah Pilch

The story of the Holocaust will not be complete unless some reference is made to the two basic questions which are uppermost in the minds of all students of the Tragedy. Why was the civilized world silent, and why did the Churches not raise their voices on behalf of the Jews? These are difficult questions to which there are no ready-made answers. Yet it is important to establish the truth that the civilized world

and the Churches knew of the tragedy but did not
bring pressure to bear on the Nazi leaders to halt
Jewish persecution.

The Inaction of the Governments

In the year 1933–39, when the German government was still mindful of the reaction of the rest of the
world, and during the years of the Holocaust (1939–
1945), when the slaughter was under way, the mild
protests of some statesmen, intellectuals, and clergy
notwithstanding, the enlightened world remained, on
the whole, silent. These are the facts: More than
2,000,000 Germans were directly connected with the
Nazi machinery of destruction, and many more millions profited from the pillage and loot. The masses of
the German and Austrian populations *knew* of the anti-
Jewish measures. Many were also aware of the ghettos
and concentration camps. For a number of years they
heard Hitler and his associates employ the terms
Ausrottung (annihilation) and *Vernichtung* (destruction) when they talked about the Jews. Yet the vast
majority of the Germans were silent. It is apparent
that the collective conscience of these people changed
radically in the 1930s. Nearly every person of German ancestry everywhere in the world became an apol-
ogist for the new Hitler policies, and the anti-Semites
among them became Nazi collaborators. Within the
Reich they were willing to conform to all Nazi plans.
The Nazi leadership, in unleashing a propaganda campaign laden with racialism and anti-Semitism, succeeded in fashioning a dehumanized "new Nazi man,"
who was ready to torture the Jew and wipe him off
the face of the earth. It is true that very small seg-
ments of the German community did oppose Nazi
theory and practice. Certain Church leaders were opposed to Hitlerian ideas and deplored the Nazi acts in
public. Here and there, some pastors made concerted
efforts to get Jews out of the country. Scattered groups
from among the professionals, working classes and

former aristocrats resisted Nazi brutality, but by and large the Germans as a people did not protest. For 10 years they heard the brownshirted fellow Germans singing: "Wenn das Judenblut vom Messer spritzt, dann geht's noch mal so gut" (When Jewish blood drips from the knife, then things are twice as good), but they did not condemn this bloody slogan of their compatriots. As Dr. Karl Jaspers, the German philosopher, put it at the meeting of the World Jewish Congress held in Brussels in August 1966: "When our Jewish friends were taken away, we did not go down into the street, we did not cry out until we, too, were exterminated. We preferred to remain alive, alleging—truthfully but weakly—that our death would not have made any difference."

As for the Poles, they, too, were indifferent to Jewish sufferings in the ghettos, and they were unmoved in the hour of Jewish deportations to the extermination centers. "They did not even express ordinary human compassion at the spectacle of our ordeal —let alone some manifestations of Christian charity. . . . While we bled and died, their attitude was at best indifference, and all too often it was 'friendly neutrality' toward the Germans ('let the Germans do this dirty job for us'). And there were far too many cases of willing, active enthusiastic Polish assistance to the Nazi murderers. There was a handful of noble Poles, of course, but nobody listened to them. Their voices never carried above the continual screams of hatred. Heroically, they managed to save individuals, but they could not bring about the slightest mitigation of Nazi ferocity."

The extent of Polish animosity to the Jew may best be illustrated by referring to the Kielce pogrom. After millions of Polish Jews had perished during the Nazi occupation, the Polish masses were still animated by hatred of the Jews. The Kielce pogrom of July 4, 1946, took the lives of 42 Jews in a massacre planned and perpetrated by bigots. This was done at a time when only remnants of Polish Jewry remained alive and sought to build their lives anew in their native country.

There were certainly acts of heroism on the part of individual Poles as well as some groups. Some of the leftist groups offered assistance to Jewish escapees. Some kindhearted and courageous individuals risked their lives to rescue Jews. However, the overwhelming majority of the Polish population manifested an apathy to the Jewish tragedy and, as already mentioned, substantial numbers of them collaborated with the Nazis in the persecution of the Jews.

It is apparently no accident that the Nazis chose Poland as the slaughterhouse of the Jews of Europe. Poland was the most "convenient" region for concentration camps because the centuries-old climate of anti-Semitism in that country was conducive to acts of terror against the Jews.

In the Ukraine, to the east of Poland, the attitude toward the Jewish Catastrophe seems to have been much the same. In the territory of the U.S.S.R. the extermination of the Jews by the Nazis did not take long. It was a sudden blow at the beginning of the occupation which caught the Jews in a state of total bewilderment. The native populations of the overrun regions—Letts, Lithuanians, Byelorussians, and especially Ukrainians—regarded the liquidation of the Jews calmly, and some with satisfaction. It is a matter of record that the Ukrainian collaboration with the German units in charge of the extermination program prompted the famous Russian poet, Yevgeny Yevtushenko, to write his "Babi Yar," a poem in which he deplored the participation of the civilian population in the mass killing of 40,000 Jews in the ravine of Babi Yar in the outskirts of Kiev. Ukrainians and White Russians also worked for the Nazis in the death camps, especially in Treblinka.

The attitude to the Holocaust in the occupied countries of the West differed radically. Compassion for the Jews was general throughout western, northern and southeastern Europe. In Belgium deportations were prevented until the summer of 1942. The greater part of the population was opposed to persecution of Jews. Some of the clergy offered refuge to Jewish children. Other citizens helped their Jewish friends. In France some Frenchmen in the nonoccupied part helped Jews to hide or to flee the country. The population of Denmark inscribed in its history a glorious page of heroism and self-sacrifice by a well-organized operation in transporting almost 7,000 Jews to Sweden. Other Scandinavian countries (Sweden in particular) made heroic efforts to rescue the harrassed Jews. In Italy, too, efforts were made to save the Jews from Nazi tyranny. Jews found a haven in Hungary until the occupation of the country by the Germans. In Bulgaria, the population as well as the clergy protested against deportation of Jews. In Greece clergymen in high office and many of the officials not only saved individual Jews but also voiced official protests against anti-Jewish measures. But sporadic acts of humanity and of compassion could not prevent the Holocaust.

Notwithstanding the good intentions of people from all walks of life who were shocked by the Nazi tyranny and tried to relieve the plight of the Jews, there was even in the West no organized and systematic rescue work, when rescue was still possible, and no mass action against Nazi brutalities. The civilized world remained officially content to consider the anti-Nazi measures of 1933–1939 as Germany's internal affair. Although the Racial Laws of September 1935 and the *Kristallnacht* of November 9, 1938, left no doubt as to the Nazi intentions, for, as a matter of fact, the Nazis themselves made no attempt to conceal them, the free world was still "minding its own business." James G. MacDonald, the American High Commissioner for Refugees, who had been appointed by the League of Nations to find havens for the multitudes of refugees streaming out of Germany, resigned from his post two years later because of his inability to find such asylum. In his letter of resignation he called the world's attention to the need either for bringing pressure to bear upon Germany to stop creating refugees, or else for opening the doors of new countries to them. His dramatic gesture proved fruitless.

It is true that President Roosevelt convened a conference, in July 1938, in Evian, at which the need for finding homes for the uprooted was discussed, but most participating countries were unable to find ways of admitting even part of the helpless refugees. America herself was not prepared to change the national quota system. The French insisted that they could not receive any more Jews. The Swiss complained against "the mass crossing of the borders by Jewish refugees." Britain and Australia admitted some refugees but were reluctant to do more. Admission of Jewish refugees to Palestine, the only country whose Jewish population was willing and ready to find room in their own community for unlimited numbers, was blocked by Britain, the Mandatory Power. The British White Paper of 1939 limited the number of Jewish immigrants to Palestine for the next five years to 15,000 per year.

A year and a half after the outbreak of World War II, reliable news of mass arrests, expulsions and massacres, concentration camps and gas chambers had already reached the governments of the civilized world, yet nothing was done. America was still unwilling to change its immigration laws. Britain was already engaged in the war and, anxious to please the Arabs, adhered to its White Paper of 1939 by refusing admission of Jewish refugees to Palestine. France and other western countries were struggling to keep alive, and the governments of the free world remained inactive. There was lip service but little action.

A concrete example of the free world's attitude to the Jewish refugee problem was the voyage of the ship *St. Louis* which sailed from Germany on May 13, 1939, with 930 refugees, all of whom had Cuban landing certificates. When they reached Havana, the Cuban authorities did not permit them to land. The American Government refused them admission although they held quota numbers which would have made it possible for them to enter the U.S. three months to three years after their arrival in Cuba. Only through the efforts of Jewish leaders were these refugees, still on the *St. Louis,* taking them back to Germany, finally admitted to Belgium, the Netherlands, Britain and France.

The *Struma,* packed far beyond capacity with 769 Rumanian Jews, sank in the Bosporus on February 24, 1943—its fate another indication of the inaction of the civilized world. The *Struma,* which sailed from Rumania toward Palestine, was at sea for 74 days, but no country was willing to admit the helpless victims of Nazi persecution. The agonized plea of its refugees reached the ears of all civilized people during that time, but not their hearts. The British refused to allow them entrance to Palestine; Turkey did not permit them to disembark. Its 769 men, women and children perished in the depths of the sea, just a few miles from Istanbul.

In 1942, both the U.S. Congress and the British House of Commons adopted resolutions condemning Nazi atrocities, but no word was heard about measures to rescue at least part of the doomed people.

Dr. Chaim Weizmann in London urged the bombing of extermination camps, but the Foreign Office replied that "the air staff was compelled, in view of the very great difficulties involved, to refrain from carrying out the proposal. Similar requests to destroy extermination factories were submitted in Washington and received similar treatment. Early in 1944 the Jewish Agency submitted a scheme to the British authorities for the dropping of hundreds of Palestinian Jews by parachute into Hungary. . . . But after it was approved by all the military authorities concerned and arrangements had been initiated to carry it out, the Foreign and Colonial Offices interfered and, for political reasons, instructed the military authorities to abandon the scheme."

Time and again, the question was asked: Why had these two great powers, Britain and the United States, done so little to halt the process of extermination? The answers varied. Some assumed that the great western powers did not want to threaten the Germans with retaliation lest they be suspected of waging a "Jewish" war. Others maintained that from the vantage point of diplomacy a defense of the Jews would have hindered the plans of invasion. But no sound answer was given to the question about the stubborn British refusal to open the gates of Palestine to Jewish escapees and about the Mandatory Government's practice of imprisoning in detention camps in Cyprus and in Palestine those who reached the shores of the Jewish National Home without bona fide certificates of immigration.

As for the United States, not only did the Government exercise great caution in dealing with Hitler, but it refused to enlarge the quota for Polish nationals in 1939 when Germany overran Poland. Keeping the status quo, insofar as the immigration law was concerned, meant that the doors of America remained locked and that appreciable numbers of either Polish Jews or Gentiles could find no refuge in this great country. When the Quakers campaigned in Congress (1939) to bring 20,000 children (Jewish and non-Jewish) to the U.S., the Administration's inaction was largely responsible for its failure. But when, after the fall of France, England was threatened with possible invasion of the Nazis, the U.S. Government quickly issued visas for 10,000 English children. When Jewish leaders negotiated with Rumania and Hungary about the emigration of their Jewish subjects with the view to bringing a considerable number of them to the U.S., the American Government refused to change its policy. As late as August 1, 1942, at a time when about one and a half million European Jews were already dead, the State Department insisted on verifying the reports submitted by Rabbi Stephen S. Wise, then president of the American Jewish Congress, to the effect that the Nazis were murdering Jews in Russia and in Poland. Checking the reports took more than three months. In the meantime more Jews perished. Finally, in November 1942, when the reports were confirmed, the U.S. Government joined the other Allied nations in a declaration entitled: "German Policy of Extermination of the Jewish Race," issued on December 17, 1942, which stated that the responsible perpetrators should not escape retribution. Although the framers of this declaration were in earnest and were no doubt eager to alleviate Jewish misery, the Nazis were hardly impressed with it. This manifestation of good will came too late. By the end of 1942, many more Jews had been liquidated by the Nazis. As Rabbi Wise put it in a letter to his friend, Rev. John H. Holmes, in 1943: "It appears to me that both authors, Eden [Foreign Minister of England] and Cordell Hull [Secretary of State], have been frozen into immobility." Nothing of any consequence was undertaken by these two great powers. There was a conference on refugees in Hamilton, Bermuda, on April 19, 1942. Yet neither Great Britain nor the U.S.A. was ready to admit the victims of Nazism. It was on June 12, 1944, almost five years after the launching of the extermination program, that the U.S. President Franklin Delano Roosevelt announced in a message to Congress "that America would bring to its shores 1,000 refugees, mostly women and children, who had escaped to Southern Italy." And once again Rabbi Stephen S. Wise

> worked out a secret plan (in 1944) for smuggling out Jews in exchange for bribes to be deposited in Switzerland. Seventy thousand lives could have been saved. Roosevelt gave the plan his full support and Morgenthau backed it immediately. But the State Department now held matters up for months. The British Ministry of Economic Warfare was informed and wrote back saying that "the British Foreign Office is concerned with the difficulty of disposing of any considerable number of Jews should they be released from enemy territory!"

. . . Ultimately, according to Stephen S. Wise, nothing was done owing to the shocking delay and sabotage . . . for five full months after the license had been approved by the President of the United States, the Secretary of State, and the Secretary of the Treasury.

Dr. Wise, one of the staunchest supporters of the Roosevelt administration, sums up the episode:

Let history, therefore, record for all time that were it not for the State Department and Foreign Office bungling and callousness, thousands of lives might have been saved and the Jewish catastrophe partially averted.

Dr. Wise's statements were substantiated in a recently published book, *While Six Million Died*. The author, Arthur D. Morse, examined the inaction of the American Government and came to the conclusion that the upright men in the administration of the humanitarian President Roosevelt knew of Hitler's order for the "final solution," knew of the mass executions, but were overcautious to do something about it. Mr. Morse indicts the Government's bureaucratic delays, refusal to try ransom and to revise immigration quotas. Thus, both America and England, through official procrastination, maintained their barriers against any serious rescue attempts.

Other great nations were also silent. The Russians were not concerned about the destruction of European Jewry. They signed a Soviet-Nazi pact during the short period of friendship between the Communists and the Nazis. The Russian press and radio ignored the existence of anti-Jewish measures in Greater Germany. As a matter of fact, Russian Jews remained unaware of what was in store for them when the German armies invaded Russia. During the German occupation of Russian territories, many Russians were employed by the Nazis to initiate pogroms and help in the process of extermination. It is also a known fact that during the

Warsaw Ghetto uprising the Red Army failed to send help to the courageous Jewish fighters.

The people of Afro-Asia and Latin America displayed an attitude of indifference to the Jewish tragedy. Although some refugees were admitted to certain Latin American countries, the population as a whole registered through its government no official protest against Nazi barbarities. In the Arab lands the political as well as religious leadership were favorably impressed with Nazi actions against the Jews. It is a fact that Haj Amin al Husseini, the Mufti of Jerusalem, a high dignitary of the religion of Islam, was an ardent Hitler collaborator.

It is therefore no surprise that many young people who study this period in world history charge the free world with complicity in the murder of 6 million Jews and that some contemporary writers maintain that the conscience of the world was destroyed with the destruction of millions of innocent people.

The Silence of the Churches

An even more painful question is the silence of organized religion, Christianity, Islam, Buddhism, and other faiths. There is no doubt that the rescue work of Church officials who in the spirit of Christian charity opened their cloisters and monasteries to the harried Jews was an important factor in the survival of individual Jews. The courageous denunciation of Nazi barbarities by church dignitaries of western Europe and especially the statement of Pope Pius XI that "in spirit we are Semites" had a considerable impact on many clergymen. The daring pronouncements against Nazi terror by Pastors Niemöller in Germany and Boegner in France rank high as inspiring acts of courage. By the same token the defiance of cardinals and bishops in France, Belgium, Galicia, and Netherlands are examples of true heroism—some paid with their lives for their compassion. There is no doubt that many of the survivors owe their lives to the humanitarian acts of both the clerics and compassionate laymen. But these righteous acts were isolated instances: they were the exception to the rule.

The fact is that no official representation was ever made by the heads of the Christian Churches (nor by the spokesmen of Islam and Buddhism) which could have expressed in the strongest possible terms the protest of all true believers. While the death factories operated at full blast, the papacy itself was silent. The silence of the Pope has been a subject of debate for 15 years. The playwright Rolf Hochhuth expressed the view in his play *The Deputy* that the Pope's failure to speak out against Nazi brutalities should be considered as telling evidence of his indifference to the plight of the Jews and thus a serious moral lapse. In "Sidelines on History," the appendix to his play, Hochhuth writes: ". . . It remains incomprehensible that His Holiness did not bestir himself to protest against Hitler, when it was clear that Germany had lost the war, while at the same time Auschwitz was just beginning its highest daily quota of killings." Other writers are not as ready to blacken the character of the Pope. Léon Poliakov, one of the outstanding researchers of the Holocaust, finds an explanation for the silence of the Pope. He writes:

> The immense church interests which were the Pope's responsibility, the extensive means for blackmail which the Nazis enjoyed on a scale commensurate with the Universal Church, probably account for his failure to issue that solemn and public declaration which the persecuted looked forward to so ardently.

Guenther Lewy, on the other hand, explains the inaction of the Pope thus: "He did not view the plight of the Jews with a real sense of urgency and moral courage"; while Father Edward H. Flannery refutes the accusations against the Pope by saying that, "at the insistence of the Vatican, protests against the deportations *were* made to several governments with Catholic majorities, such as Slovakia, Poland, Italy and Hungary." But no matter what the reasons for the Vatican's silence, and no matter whether Hochhuth's conclusions are right or wrong—all agree that the Pope *was* silent. For the same writers who try to justify his silence are, nonetheless, disturbed about it. Poliakov states: "It is painful to have to say that during the war, while the death factories ran full blast, the Papacy kept silent." Flannery notes: "Pius XII made only indirect allusions to the anti-Semitic campaign in his public pronouncements but encouraged the use of his nunciatures and chanceries throughout Europe to protect and save Jews."

We thus see that no attempt was made to mobilize the resources of the world religious institutions for the defense of Nazi victims. The religious leaders were no doubt concerned but apparently did not want to antagonize the Nazis lest they take vengeance on Church functionaries and properties. The Catholic Church did not even deem it advisable to use its power to threaten with excommunication those Catholics who participated in the Nazi treatment of Jews and other "undesirables." In the midst of the enormity of the Nazi atrocities the "true believers" conducted their affairs by the discreet rule of "business as usual."

The Silence of the Intellectual Community

As for the intellectual community, save for a number of sporadic denunciations by some writers, scientists, and academicians, the majority did not raise their voices in protest against Nazi genocide. The academic communities did not react en masse in a collective *J'accuse*. The pen clubs of the world did not sow the seed of revolt in the 1930s when outside of Germany it was still possible to arouse the people against Nazi theory and practice. They did not issue proclamations calling upon millions of readers to stand up and be heard. There were few anti-Nazi rallies conducted by the intellectuals on the campuses, in public forums, and there was little utilization of the mass media for the purpose of informing the public of the Hitlerite menace. The reactions of the liberals and progressives in the labor movement and in socio-cultural organizations were those of sympathy for and solidarity with the suffering Jews, but these feelings were not translated in terms of active and positive actions on their behalf. Had the multitudes of free men in the free world reacted courageously and vigorously, many of the Nazi acts of terror might have been averted.

Did Jewry Do Everything Possible?

There is also the very disturbing fact of the lack of mass action by the Jewish communities in the countries not overrun by the Nazis, especially in America. It has been pointed out by students of the Holocaust period that the masses of the Jewish people could not believe the news which reached them from the ghettos of Europe and the death camps and that the true facts, when they became known, had a paralyzing effect upon most of them. Furthermore, the loyalty of Jews as citizens of the free countries made them sensitive to the plea not to hamper the war effort by any "exaggerated" demands. Thus, rescue activities were confined to the philanthropic agencies and to the Palestinian Jews through the Jewish Agency. In America, the anti-Nazi boycott conducted by the Joint Boycott Council, which resulted in a decline of Germany's place in the world economy, and the anti-Nazi campaign carried out by the various organizations were efforts to unmask the true face of the Nazis and to combat mounting anti-Jewish feeling on the American continent. But the *masses* of Jews in the U.S. and in other free lands did not make *extraordinary* efforts to impress on their governments that official inaction doomed their brethren to certain death. Those American Jews who were ready to take overall collective actions of protest and rescue found themselves in a very awkward position because the State Department argued that any independent rescue action would hamper the Allied war effort. The facts are that during the period 1933–45 there were no "sit-ins" nor mass demonstrations in the dense Jewish population centers. There were no marches of Jewish masses to Washington, Ottawa, London, Johannesburg, Buenos Aires, and Rio de Janeiro. No public fast days were instituted to express solidarity with the victims. Most of the protests that took place were a byproduct of the feverish activities of a number of restless Jewish lay leaders and professional workers. The average Jew, however, although intensely hurt, did not do the impossible. This pitiful inertia of world Jewry was prophetically foreshadowed in a verse by Bialik, written in the days of Herzl's call to action (by joining the Zionist movement): *"we-lo na we-low za we-lo harad ha-am"* (and the people did not stir and were not agitated). The majority of the Jewish people during the period of the great catastrophe did not tremble sufficiently to inject a chill into the hearts of their Christian neighbors. There are now young Jews and Jewesses who fight for civil rights for the Negro, a cause that is cherished by every person of conscience as well as by the intelligent Jew who is committed to the Jewish concept of liberty. But in the years of the Holocaust there were no demonstrations by Jewish youth in the cause of their own kin trapped in the Nazi web of destruction. They did not parade; they did not go on hunger strikes. Young Jews were not ready to destroy their citizenship papers and denounce the Roosevelt administration, especially the State Department, for its apathy to the Jewish agony. Recipients of honors did not return their medals in protest. Leaders of Jewish religious schools did not assemble their pupils in the public squares to protest the persecution of their coreligionists, especially the fate of the children of their own age who were so cruelly done away with. Jews did not pluck up the courage to follow the deed of their ancestor Mordecai by assembling in the streets and "shouting bitterly" because of the threat of the Haman of their day. None proclaimed their readiness to follow the example of their Palestinian brethren who dared to parachute into Nazi-occupied territory for specific rescue missions.

Nelly Sachs, the recipient of the Nobel Award in Literature in 1966 in whose poetry we find a very intense reaction to the Tragedy, echoes its realities in one of her poems. The last stanza of this poem from *The Chorus of the Orphans* reads as follows:

> *We Orphans we lament to the world:*
> *World, why have you taken our soft moth-*
> *ers from us.*
> *And the fathers who say: My child you are*
> *like me!*
> *We Orphans are like no one in this world*
> *any more.*
> *Oh world*
> *We accuse you!*

One small country put moral principle above all other considerations. This selection is by Abraham Foxman, from *The Jewish Catastrophe in Europe.*

49.   The Righteous Danes
Abraham Foxman

On the outskirts of Jerusalem stands a large building known as Yad Yashem. It is a national documentation center of the atrocities perpetrated against the Jews during World War II. It is the world's foremost research and recording center of the Holocaust. Near the museum there is a grove where trees have been planted to honor those Christians who at the risk, and sometimes the cost, of their lives helped to rescue Jews.

These are the Righteous, whose actions were those of one who says: *"I am* my brother's keeper."

King Christian X of Denmark

The German army invaded Denmark in 1940. For two years the Germans did not take stringent actions against the Jews because of the Danes' persistent resistance against Nazi anti-Jewish measures. It is reported that King Christian X, in a conversation with a German official who used the phrase "Jewish problem," replied, "There is no Jewish problem in this country. There is only my people." It is also told that when the German officials reproached King Christian for his "negligence in resolving the Jewish problem," he answered, "Gentlemen, since we have never considered ourselves inferior to the Jews, we have no such problem here." On another occasion, King Christian announced, "If the Germans want to introduce the yellow star in Denmark, I and my whole family will wear it as a sign of the highest distinction." When in August 1943 a Nazi order was issued to deport all Jews, the Danish population mobilized all its resources to rescue the Jews. They succeeded in "smuggling" some 7,000 Jews to neutral, unoccupied Sweden. No other occupied country has achieved the distinction of rescuing the major part of its Jewish population.

Congressman Arthur W. Mitchell (1934–42) of Chicago was the first Negro Democrat elected to Congress. Born to former slaves, Mitchell once served as office boy for Booker T. Washington. When he was forced to leave a Pullman car because of his race, Congressman Mitchell took his case to the Supreme Court and won.

Congressman Mitchell expressed his concern over the Nazi persecution of Jewish peo-

ple in this letter to President Franklin D.
Roosevelt of October 12, 1938.

50.   A Negro Congressman Speaks
    for Minority Rights
                    Arthur W. Mitchell

As a representative of a minority group in America, an underprivileged group which has been subjected
to prejudice and mistreatment from time to time, we
are interested in the attitude of majority groups
throughout the world toward minority groups. At the
present time we are greatly disturbed because of the
intolerance of certain major groups toward the Jewish
people residing in European countries and wish to have
our voice heard in the interest of justice and fair
play for all racial groups. We believe that the same
spirit of intolerance which is working so tremendously
against the safety and sacred rights of the Jewish people, if permitted to go unchallenged, will manifest itself sooner or later against all minority groups, perhaps
in all parts of the world. [We] request you, the highest
representative of our Government, to use every reasonable and peaceable means at your command in securing protection for the Jewish people in this hour of sad
calamity.

This account of a murder that took place in
1964, in a quiet residential neighborhood of
New York City, appears to have no bearing on
the Holocaust. But as you read it, compare the
behavior of the "38 witnesses" to that of millions of ordinary citizens in Germany in the
1930s. They, too, were witnesses.

The selection is from *The New York Times,*
March 27, 1964.

51. Thirty-Eight Witnesses
Martin Gansberg

For more than half an hour 38 respectable, law-abiding citizens in Queens watched a killer stalk and stab a woman in three separate attacks in Kew Gardens.

Twice the sound of their voices and the sudden glow of their bedroom lights interrupted him and frightened him off. Each time he returned, sought her out and stabbed her again. Not one person telephoned the police during the assault; one witness called after the woman was dead.

That was two weeks ago today. But Assistant Chief Inspector Frederick M. Lussen, in charge of the borough's detective force and a veteran of 25 years of homicide investigations, is still shocked.

He can give a matter-of-fact recitation of many murders. But the Kew Gardens slaying baffles him—not because it is a murder, but because the "good people" failed to call the police.

"As we have reconstructed the crime," he said, "the assailant had three chances to kill this woman during the 35-minute period. He returned twice to complete the job. If we had been called when he first attacked, the woman might not be dead now."

This is what the police say happened beginning at 3:20 A.M. in the staid, middle-class, tree-lined Austin Street area:

Twenty-eight-year-old Catherine Genovese, who was called Kitty by almost everyone in the neighborhood, was returning home from her job as a manager of a bar in Hollis. She parked her red Fiat in a lot adjacent to the Kew Gardens, Long Island, Railroad Station, facing Mowbray Place. Like many residents of the neighborhood, she had parked there day after day since her arrival from Connecticut a year ago, although the railroad frowns on the practice.

She turned off the lights of her car, locked the door and started to walk the 100 feet to the entrance of her apartment at 82-70 Austin Street, which is in a Tudor building, with stores on the first floor and apartments on the second.

The entrance to the apartment is in the rear of the building because the front is rented to retail stores. At night the quiet neighborhood is shrouded in the slumbering darkness that marks most residential areas.

Miss Genovese noticed a man at the far end of the lot, near a seven-story apartment house at 82-40 Austin Street. She halted, then, nervously, she headed up Austin Street toward Lefferts Boulevard, where there is a call box to the 102nd Police Precinct in nearby Richmond Hill.

She got as far as a street light in front of a bookstore before the man grabbed her. She screamed. Lights went on in the 10-story apartment house at 82-67 Austin Street, which faces the bookstore. Windows slid open and voices punctured the early morning stillness.

Miss Genovese screamed: "Oh, my God, he stabbed me! Please help me! Please help me!"

From one of the upper windows in the apartment house, a man called down: "Let that girl alone!"

The assailant looked at him, shrugged and walked down Austin Street toward a white sedan parked a short distance away. Miss Genovese struggled to her feet.

Lights went out. The killer returned to Miss Genovese, now trying to make her way around the side of the building by the parking lot to get to her apartment. The assailant stabbed her again.

"I'm dying!" she shrieked. "I'm dying!"

Windows were opened again, and lights went on in many apartments. The assailant got into his car and drove away. Miss Genovese staggered to her feet. A city bus, Q-10, the Lefferts Boulevard line to Kennedy International Airport, passed. It was 3:35 A.M.

The assailant returned. By then, Miss Genovese had crawled to the back of the building, where the freshly painted brown doors to the apartment house held out hope of safety. The killer tried the first door; she wasn't there. At the second door, 82-62 Austin Street, he saw her slumped on the floor at the foot of the stairs. He stabbed her a third time—fatally.

It was 3:50 by the time the police received their first call from a man who was a neighbor of Miss Genovese. In two minutes they were at the scene. The neighbor, a 70-year-old woman, and another woman were the only persons on the street. Nobody else came forward.

The man explained that he had called the police after much deliberation. He had phoned a friend in Nassau County for advice and then he had crossed the roof of the building to the apartment of the elderly woman to get her to make the call.

"I didn't want to get involved," he sheepishly told the police. . . .

TWENTIETH CENTURY MAN

The evidence has mounted before us—
cruelty, cowardice, callous indifference, crazed
thirst for blood, counterpoised against courage,
kindness, willingness to sacrifice self for the
good of others. Is man beast or angel?

The next selection, taken from the book
Human Aggression by Anthony Storr, argues
that aggression is a fundamental and necessary
part of human nature, but one which can be
either a positive or a negative force.

52. Man As Aggressor

Anthony Storr

That man is an aggressive creature will hardly be
disputed. With the exception of certain rodents, no
other vertebrate habitually destroys members of his
own species. No other animal takes positive pleasure in
the exercise of cruelty upon another of his own kind.
We generally describe the most repulsive examples of
man's cruelty as brutal or bestial, implying by these
adjectives that such behavior is characteristic of less
highly developed animals than ourselves. In truth, however, the extremes of "brutal" behavior are confined to
man; and there is no parallel in nature to our savage
treatment of each other. The somber fact is that we
are the cruellest and most ruthless species that has ever
walked the earth; and that, although we may recoil in

horror when we read in newspaper or history book of the atrocities committed by man upon man, we know in our hearts that each one of us harbors within himself those same savage impulses which lead to murder, to torture and to war.

To write about human aggression is a difficult task because the term is used in so many different senses. Aggression is one of those words which everyone knows, but which is nevertheless hard to define. As psychologists and psychiatrists use it, it covers a very wide range of human behavior. The red-faced infant squalling for the bottle is being aggressive; and so is the judge who awards a 30-year sentence for robbery. The guard in a concentration camp who tortures his helpless victim is obviously acting aggressively. Less manifestly, but no less certainly, so is the neglected wife who threatens or attempts suicide in order to regain her husband's affection. When a word becomes so diffusely applied that it is used both of the competitive striving of a footballer and also of the bloody violence of a murderer, it ought either to be dropped or else more closely defined. Aggression is a portmanteau term which is fairly bursting at its seams. Yet, until we can more clearly designate and comprehend the various aspects of human behavior which are subsumed under this head, we cannot discard the concept.

One difficulty is that there is no clear dividing line between those forms of aggression which we all deplore and those which we must not disown if we are to survive. When a child rebels against authority it is being aggressive: but it is also manifesting a drive toward independence which is a necessary and valuable part of growing up. The desire for power has, in extreme form, disastrous aspects which we all acknowledge: but the drive to conquer difficulties, or to gain mastery over the external world underlies the greatest of human achievements. Some writers define aggression as "that response which follows frustration," or as "an act whose goal-response is injury to an organism (or organism surrogate)." In the author's view these definitions impose limits upon the concept of aggression which are not in accord with the underlying facts of human nature which the word is attempting to express. It is worth noticing, for instance, that the words we use to describe intellectual effort are aggressive words. We *attack* problems, or *get our teeth into* them. We *master* a subject when we have *struggled with* and *overcome* its difficulties. We *sharpen* our wits, hoping that our mind will develop *a keen edge* in order that we may better *dissect* a problem into its component parts. Although intellectual tasks are often frustrating, to argue that all intellectual effort is the result of frustration is to impose too negative a coloring upon the positive impulse to comprehend and master the external world.

The aggressive part of human nature is not only a necessary safeguard against predatory attack. It is also the basis of intellectual achievement, of the attainment of independence, and even of that proper pride which enables a man to hold his head high among his fellows.

The following selections, by two writers who experienced the Holocaust, reflect an amazing human capacity to be optimistic, and to believe in human goodness, in the face of considerable evidence to the contrary. The first is from Anne Frank's *The Diary of a Young Girl*, the second from *Man's Search for Meaning* by Viktor Frankl.

53. People Are Really Good at Heart
Anne Frank

"For in its innermost depths youth is lonelier than old age." I read this saying in some book and I've always remembered it, and found it to be true. Is it true then that grownups have a more difficult time here than we do? No. I know it isn't. Older people have formed their opinions about everything, and don't waver before they act. It's twice as hard for us young ones to hold our ground, and maintain our opinions, in a time when all ideals are being shattered and destroyed, when people are showing their worst side, and do not know whether to believe in truth and right and God.

Anyone who claims that the older ones have a more difficult time here certainly doesn't realize to what extent our problems weigh down on us, problems for which we are probably much too young, but which thrust themselves upon us continually, until, after a long time, we think we've found a solution, but the solution doesn't seem able to resist the facts which reduce it to nothing again. That's the difficulty in these times: ideals, dreams, and cherished hopes rise within us, only to meet the horrible truth and be shattered.

It's really a wonder that I haven't dropped all my ideals, because they seem so absurd and impossible to carry out. Yet I keep them, because in spite of everything I still believe that people are really good at heart. I simply can't build up my hopes on a foundation consisting of confusion, misery, and death. I see the world gradually being turned into a wilderness, I hear the ever approaching thunder, which will destroy us too, I can feel the sufferings of millions and yet, if I look up into the heavens, I think that it will all come right, that this cruelty too will end, and that peace and tranquillity will return again.

---

54. The Decent and the Indecent
Victor Frankl

It is apparent that the mere knowledge that a man was either a camp guard or a prisoner tells us almost nothing. Human kindness can be found in all groups, even those which as a whole it would be easy to condemn. The boundaries between groups overlapped and we must not try to simplify matters by saying that these men were angels and those were devils. Certainly, it was a considerable achievement for a guard or foreman to be kind to the prisoners in spite of all the camp's influences, and, on the other hand, the baseness of a prisoner who treated his own companions badly was exceptionally contemptible. Obviously the prisoners found the lack of character in such men especially upsetting, while they were profoundly moved by the smallest kindness received from any of the guards. I remember how one day a foreman secretly gave me a piece of bread which I knew he must have saved from his breakfast ration. It was far more than a small piece of bread which moved me to tears at that time. It was the human "something" which this man also gave to me—the word and look which accompanied the gift.

From all this we may learn that there are two races of men in this world, but only these two—the "race" of the decent man and the "race" of the indecent man. Both are found everywhere; they penetrate into all groups of society. No group consists entirely of decent or indecent people. In this sense, no group is of "pure race"—and therefore one occasionally found a decent fellow among the camp guards.

BEHAVIOR UNDER STRESS

Optimism, faith, a tenacious holding on to life. These persisted in some people even as their world lay shattered about them. Behind the barbed wire, men, women, and children actually composed and sang songs of hope; they wrote poetry and painted pictures to express their deepest yearnings.

55. Music Out of Pain

Peat Bog Soldiers

German Concentration Camp Song

[Political prisoners, who composed this song while marching to and from their work in the peat bog, sang it with such enthusiasm, particularly in the last chorus, with its veiled meaning, that it was finally forbidden.]

1. Far and wide as the eye can wander
   Heath and bog are everywhere,
   Not a bird sings out to cheer us
   Oaks are standing gaunt and bare.

177

CHORUS:

We are the peat bog soldiers,
Marching with our spades—to the bog.

2. Up and down the guards are pacing,
   No one, no one can go through
   Flight would mean a sure death facing,
   Guns and barbed wire greet our view.

CHORUS:

We are ...

3. But for us there is no complaining
   Winter will in time be past
   One day we shall cry rejoicing,
   Homeland, dear, you're mine at last!

CHORUS:

Then will the peat bog soldiers
March no more with their spades—to the
   bog.

Ani Ma'amin

[This song was sung by Jews who were about to
be cremated by the Nazis.]

I believe with complete faith in the coming of
the Messiah. And though he tarry, still shall I believe
and await his coming.

Jewish Partisan Song

[Throughout Europe, groups of partisans, Jews
and non-Jews, formed to fight a guerrilla war and

carry out acts of sabotage against the Nazis and their collaborators. Their natural bases were the forests and swamps and mountain caves.]

Never say that there is only death for you
Though leaden skies may be concealing days
     of blue—
Because the hour we have hungered for is near;
Beneath our tread the earth shall tremble:
     We are here!

From land of palm-tree to the far-off land of
     snow
We shall be coming with our torment and our
     woe,
And everywhere our blood has sunk into the
     earth
Shall our bravery, our vigor blossom forth!

We'll have the morning sun to set our day
     aglow,
And all our yesterdays shall vanish with the foe,
And if the time is long before the sun appears,
Then let this song go like a signal through the
     years.

This song was written with our blood and not
     with lead;
It's not song that birds sing overhead,
It was a people, among toppling barricades,
That sang this song of ours with pistols and
     grenades.

So never say that there is only death for you.
Leaden skies may be concealing days of blue—
Yet the hour we have hungered for is near;
Beneath our tread the earth shall tremble:
     We are here!

Some 15,000 children under the age of 15 passed through this camp between the years 1942 and 1944. About 150 of them survived. In all, more than 1,000,000 Jewish children were killed by the Nazis. In Terezín, children were housed in separate barracks, and at the request of Jewish leaders, a kind of school was actually organized for them. These and other poems, and numerous drawings, were created in that makeshift school.

The poems are reprinted from the book *I Never Saw Another Butterfly.*

56. Children's Writings

We Got Used to . . .

. . . We got used to standing in line at 7 o'clock in the morning, at 12 noon and again at seven o'clock in the evening. We stood in a long queue with a plate in our hand, into which they ladled a little warmed-up water with a salty or a coffee flavor. Or else they gave us a few potatoes. We got used to sleeping without a bed, to saluting every uniform, not to walk on the sidewalks and then again to walk on the sidewalks. We got used to undeserved slaps, blows and executions. We got accustomed to seeing people die in their own excrement, to seeing piled-up coffins full of corpses, to seeing the sick amidst dirt and filth and to seeing the helpless doctors. We got used to it that from time to time, one thousand unhappy souls would come here and that, from time to time, another thousand unhappy souls would go away. . . .

From the prose of 15 year old Petr Fischl (born September 9, 1929), who perished in Auschwitz in 1944.

I'd Like to Go Alone

I'd like to go away alone
Where there are other, nicer people,
Somewhere into the far unknown,
There, where no one kills another.

Maybe more of us,
A thousand strong,
Will reach this goal
Before too long.

Alena Synková

It All Depends on How You Look at It

I.

Terezín is full of beauty.
It's in your eyes now clear
And through the street the tramp
Of many marching feet I hear.

In the ghetto at Terezín,
It looks that way to me,
Is a square kilometer of earth
Cut off from the world that's free.

II.

Death, after all, claims everyone,
You find it everywhere.
It catches up with even those
Who wear their noses in the air.

The whole, wide world is ruled
With a certain justice, so
That helps perhaps to sweeten
The poor man's pain and woe.

Miroslav Košek

Homesick

I've lived in the ghetto here more than a year,
In Terezín, in the black town now,
And when I remember my old home so dear,
I can love it more than I did, somehow.

Ah, home, home,
Why did they tear me away?
Here the weak die easy as a feather
And when they die, they die forever.

I'd like to go back home again,
It makes me think of sweet spring flowers.
Before, when I used to live at home,
It never seemed so dear and fair.

I remember now those golden days . . .
But maybe I'll be going there soon again.

People walk along the street,
You see at once on each you meet
That there's a ghetto here,
A place of evil and of fear.
There's little to eat and much to want,
Where bit by bit, it's horror to live.
But no one must give up!
The world turns and times change.

Yet we all hope the time will come
When we'll go home again.
Now I know how dear it is
And often I remember it.

Anonymous 9. 3. 1943

The Butterfly

The last, the very last,
So richly, brightly, dazzlingly yellow.
   Perhaps if the sun's tears would sing
   against a white stone . . .

Such, such a yellow
Is carried lightly 'way up high.
It went away I'm sure because it wished to
   kiss the world goodbye.

For seven weeks I've lived in here,
Penned up inside this ghetto
But I have found my people here.
The dandelions call to me
And the white chestnut candles in the court.
Only I never saw another butterfly.

That butterfly was the last one.
Butterflies don't live in here,
   In the ghetto.

Pavel Friedmann 4. 6. 1942

The Garden

   A little garden,
   Fragrant and full of roses.
   The path is narrow
   And a little boy walks along it.

   A little boy, a sweet boy,
   Like that growing blossom.
   When the blossom comes to bloom,
   The little boy will be no more.

Franta Bass

Why didn't more victims fight back? Was revolt possible? Would any act of retaliation have been preferable to passive acceptance of death? These questions have been raised again and again by students of the Holocaust. The next four selections may not give you definitive answers to these questions, but they will provide you with additional insights into the whole problem of resistance.

Scholars and researchers have discovered that there was much more active resistance by Jews than was previously thought. Perhaps the reason so little was known about this subject is that most resistance efforts were fruitless. Nevertheless, they did occur. When we speak of "fighting back," remember that we are talking of civilian populations, unarmed, weakened and demoralized, matching their strength against legions of highly trained soldiers, guns, and tanks. Two other factors militated against the use of force: one, the lack of dependable support from non-Jews outside the ghettos, and two, fears on the part of many, particularly older people, that any action against the Nazis would bring retaliation and make matters worse. The conflict seemed to boil down to these two views: to die "with honor," as most resistance leaders urged, or to try and find ways to survive, hoping for Nazi lenience.

The first reading, from *Encyclopedia Judaica,* presents a broad view of the subject, including comparisons with other prisoner situations.

57. The Behavior of the Victims
Encyclopedia Judaica

After the life in the ghettos and camps, after having lost the power of resistance under the constant Nazi terror, and often having also lost entire or part of their families, nothing but blind obedience could have been expected of these former persons when they were shipped to gas chambers which were disguised as showers. All thoughtful observers agree that in the death camps the normality of death "caused death to lose its terror." The calm that reigned among death candidates impressed various witnesses, some of them seeing it as a characteristic of dignified death in view of the impossibility to live a dignified life. The special commandos in the death camps were forced to perform the macabre job of sometimes accompanying (in Auschwitz) the victims to the gas chambers and, after their death, disposing of the corpses, extracting gold teeth, cutting hair, etc. In a later period, people of this category (when in Auschwitz they were threatened with physical destruction) or of the working groups in other camps took active parts in uprisings which occurred in Treblinka (August 2, 1943), Sobibor (October 14, 1943), and Chelmno (January 1945) at the cost of many Jewish lives as against the loss of only relatively few Nazi lives.

In the daily dilemma of the conflict between the instinctive will to remain alive at all cost and the faint hope of maintaining at least a certain amount of "God's image," the depth of human degradation for the condemned Jews was reached in the death camps. A look at comparable situations may be in order. In terms of numbers and ultimate fate, the Soviet prisoners of war came closest to the Jews, with two significant differences: they were young and mostly single and thus— among other things—spared the fate of having to witness the agony of their loved ones; and they were military men trained in the use of arms and indoctrinated with Soviet and Russian patriotism. Like the Jews, who were not protected by any international convention, these prisoners were also unprotected, since their government considered all of them as deserters and did not invoke the Geneva Convention on Prisoners of War. The remarks of a sympathetic observer, who spent some four months in three prisoners' camps in Soviet-occupied areas with a capacity of 90,000 prisoners, have a familiar ring: "It was intolerable to realize that before the eyes of the whole civilized world millions of innocent people died a slow death."

Here are a few Dantesque scenes of their behavior:

> The exhausted comrades were considered by the less exhausted ones as living corpses, and some of the stronger prisoners watched the dying and upon their death stripped them naked, sometimes even before they gasped their last breath. Despite cruel punishment meted out to marauders by their own comrades, these crimes continued, since in the climate of total demoralization punishment did not work. Groups of marauders—each with their own sphere of influence—acted collectively and with exclusive claim to the "property" of their victims. Another phenomenon in these camps was cannibalism. Corpses were found in the morning with hearts, livers, and large pieces from their insides cut out. The cannibals, if caught, were delivered to the Germans for death by shooting. And still it went on.

Under the circumstances, Jewish masses could not and did not—as a rule—revolt. No significant acts of sabotage or other forms of resistance have been recorded for their part by prisoners of war (both those internationally protected by the Geneva Convention and remaining mostly in camps in their home countries

and—a fortiori—unprotected Soviet prisoners of war)
or the millions (on September 30, 1944—some seven
and a half million) of European workers situated in
the heart of Germany, many of them enjoying wide
freedom of movement and other privileges or by non-
Jewish prisoners of concentration camps (prior to
1945).

A problem that has been hotly debated between
survivors and outsiders has been: who is competent
to describe and evaluate authoritatively the behavior of
the victims and their leaders. Many survivors held
the view that "no one who has not had any personal
experience of a German concentration camp can possibly have the remotest conception of concentration
camp life." "Little does the outsider know of the hard
fight for existence which raged among prisoners." Admittedly, they have the advantage of the immediate
personal experience of a phenomenon not easily imag-
inable. But acceptance of this claim at its face value
would mean that with the last survivor gone, research
and evaluation of such behavior would also come to an
end. Nor could the danger be ignored of generalization
by survivors who sometimes on the basis of brief and
local experience in a camp or in a ghetto, arrive at
conclusions of broader applications. On the other hand,
it is not beyond the capacities of a conscientious witness or student to acquire knowledge and understanding, and to arm himself with *Einfuehlungsvermoegen*
which is the proper meaning of the talmudic saying,
"Judge not thy neighbor until thou art come into his
place," as formulated in modern terms by Victor
Frankl: "No man should judge unless he asks himself
in absolute honesty whether in a similar situation he
might not have done the same."

Any attempt to apply to the victims of the Holocaust or of comparable situations standards of behavior
of a civilized society must fail. "Standards of normal
society did not obtain in the ghettos and concentration
camps. Theft, egotism, lack of consideration for

others, disregarding all laws, all this was prohibited in preconcentration camp days; inside the concentration camp, however, it was normal." In these conditions, "there was neither the time nor the desire to consider moral issues. Every man was controlled by one thought only: how to keep himself alive." The admitted purpose of the Nazis in regard to the Jewish victim—as long as he was alive—was to reduce the homo sapiens to the category of a primitive creature with steadily decreasing needs which were finally reduced to craving for food ("two hundred grams of bread ruled over life"—Solzhenitsyn; "general preoccupation with food" —Frankl; "I am hungry, I am cold; when I grow up I want to be a German, and then I shall no longer be hungry, and no longer be cold"—diary of a child in the Warsaw ghetto).

––––––––––

In a number of cities, Jews were ordered to move into walled-off neighborhoods so that they would be isolated and imprisoned in one area. They lived in vastly overcrowded, unsanitary conditions, never knowing what their fate would be. Many ghetto inhabitants were subsequently transferred to extermination camps.

Despite incredible odds, resistance groups did form in various ghettos, managing to smuggle in small quantities of arms, or to make their own crude weapons. Only in one ghetto, however, that of Warsaw, did the Jewish Combat Organization, as it was called, succeed in holding off the Nazis for any time. There, too, success was only for an instant; the Nazis set the ghetto ablaze. Some 75 survivors crawled through the sewers of Warsaw to safety.

In this selection, which is a composite of excerpts from diaries and memoirs, we see again that some people resisted giving way to

despair, and carried on active, useful lives.
Nothing could rob them of their basic humanity.

58. The Warsaw Ghetto

At the beginning of September, 1940, the Central Entertainment Committee was established, and I was designated as the head of this body. The Central Entertainment Committee sought to raise the level of the performances and to lend its protective hand to all professional Jewish artists, such as actors, musicians, painters, dancers and to all who were professionally employed in this field. Special care was also devoted to the fostering of young talent. If anybody revealed extraordinary gifts at an early age, the Central Entertainment Committee agreed to public performances, as was the case with the eighteen-year-old Marysia Ajzensztadt, who later acquired such enormous popularity in the ghetto.

Then there was also the phenomenally gifted eight-year-old composer and pianist Yossimah Feldschuh.

In the short period from September, 1940 to September, 1941 (inclusive) we arranged 1,814 artistic spectacles, among them light symphony concerts. . . .

Besides the great symphony orchestra, which gave symphonic matinees once a week, (on Saturday or Sunday), there were also a few chamber music ensembles. . . .

There were also several choirs in the ghetto.

BENEK, ABRAM. 50 years old, 3 Krochmalna Street, apt. 27.

In re placement of the children in a children's home.

The applicant, a hatmaker by profession, became a widower at the start of the war. Lives in utter misery. He just sold his last piece of bedding and he is tearing out planks from the floor for fuel.

The study of starvation was started in February, 1942. At that time hunger was the key to everyday life within the walls of the Warsaw Ghetto. Some of its manifestations were: crowds of beggars you often encountered in the streets, corpses covered with paper, statistics of mortality in the refugee centers and orphan homes and specific symptoms of starvation requiring hospitalization, with their ramifications: TB and typhoid fever.

A group of my fellow physicians, witnessing the manifestations of community life in the ghetto, grew increasingly aware that this tragic outcome of our gloomy epoch must be transformed into a scientific record. Ignoring all the obstacles, these physicans plunged into their work with great enthusiasm and devotion. External conditions were by no means favorable for their endeavor. . . .

March . . . From the highest ranks of the Roman-Catholic hierarchy suddenly came the proposal to save the last three rabbis who still remained in the Warsaw Ghetto. The three rabbis now had to decide what to do, whether to accept or to reject. They had to make the decision quickly, and no time was to be lost, since the Nazis constantly kept asking the members of the Community Council whether there were still some rabbis in the ghetto.

So the last three Warsaw rabbis were sitting in a room and discussing the Roman Catholic offer. "Discussing" . . . in reality they were sitting silent, and did not utter a word.

Suddenly the silence was interrupted, and it was Rabbi Szapiro who broke it, uttering the following words:

"I am the youngest among you, and therefore my words are not binding on you. We already know that we cannot help them any longer, but by staying with them and by not abandoning them, we encourage them and strengthen their hopes, and this is the only encouragement we are able to give the last Jews. I simply do not have the strength to abandon these wretched people."

The end is well known. Rabbi Zemba and Rabbi Stockhamer went the way of annihilation. Only Rabbi David Szapiro was not burned. And he wears now the ghostly and tragic crown of the "last Warsaw rabbi," the last rabbi of a city of rabbis.

(*Marian Zyd, in the article, "With the last Warsaw Rabbi," in Forwards, of March 1, 1942. Quoted from Niger, pp. 161-162*)

Wednesday, August 12, 1942   Today Korczak's orphanage is to be "evacuated." . . . Korczak himself may remain, physicians are needed. They are not marked for deportation.

But Korczak refuses to stay behind. He will not abandon "his" children, he will go with them.

And so a long line is formed in the front of the orphanage on Sliska Street. A long procession, children, small, tiny, rather precocious, emaciated, weak, shriveled and shrunk. They carry shabby packages, some have schoolbooks, notebooks under their arms. No one is crying.

Slowly they go down the steps, line up in rows, in perfect order and discipline, as usual. Their little eyes are turned towards the "doctor," they are strangely calm. The "doctor" is going with them. They are not alone, they are not abandoned.

Dr. Korczak busies himself with the children with a sober earnestness. He buttons the coat of one child, ties up a package of another, or straightens the cap of a third. Then he wipes off a tear which is rolling down the thin little face of a child . . .

Then the procession starts out. The children are marching quietly in orderly rows, calm and earnest, and at the head of them is Janusz Korczak. . . .

(*Seidman, pp. 66-67*)

Even in the concentration camps, where
conditions were least amenable to it, sporadic
attempts at revolt occurred. One such episode
is recounted here by Abraham Foxman, in an
excerpt from the book *The Jewish Catastrophe
in Europe.*

59. Resistance in the Concentration Camps

Abraham Foxman

To survive in a concentration camp for one day
could be considered a form of resistance. Even had the
Nazis not introduced direct methods of extermination,
it would not have taken long for the inmates to die of
starvation, exhaustion or disease. But the Jews of the
camps kept alive a spark of hope for ultimate survival.
What other goal could there be for those doomed to
mass extermination? The hope of survival wrought
miracles, giving superhuman strength and endurance
to the Jewish prisoners. It sustained them while they
gritted their teeth and swallowed degradation. It nour-
ished their will to live, the predominant factor in their
ability to endure as long as they did. However, in
addition to this "passive resistance," there were many
instances of active Jewish courage and heroism.

Revolt in the Sobibor Death Camp

Under the leadership of Leon Feldhendler, a
Jewish Red Army officer, and Alexander Pechersky, a
partisan leader, a clandestine organization was established in the Sobibor death camp for the purpose of
destroying the murder factory. The "staff" of the organization consisted of five men entrusted with special assignments. Thirty fighters were designated to kill
all the guards within one hour during the planned revolt, and to gain control of the arms store. A variety of
ruses were devised to lure the German guards into cor-

ners where they could be killed surreptitiously. The men would then collect the arms and transfer them immediately to the carpentry shop. Later, the workers of this shop, together with their work-gang leaders, would appear, as usual, at the regular roll call, form ranks, and march toward the gate. Those who spoke Russian would call out to the Ukrainians not to fire but rather to escape, as the Germans had already lost the war. In the meantime, another group would rush to the arms store near the gate for additional arms to cover the fleeing inmates. Planks and stones would be thrown on the mined area to explode the mines in the ground before the gates.

The uprising, set for October 13, 1943, was for unknown reasons postponed to the next day, the 14th.

One of the survivors, Tuvia Blatt, described the events in testimony he gave to Yad Nashem in Jerusalem:

> . . . It was 4 o'clock. There was no hint as to what was about to occur. With tension that is impossible to describe I peered through the door down the road leading to the First Section, where the conspirators were to appear. The hands of the clock had passed 16:00 hours. Had there been another postponement?—"They are coming!" I heard Waytzen whisper. I looked in the direction he indicated and saw "Kali-Mali" come round the corner with a jug in his hands. His real name was Shubayev, a Soviet Jew of about 35, a traffic engineer by profession. He was accompanied by the work group leader Benya, for it was forbidden for a prisoner to cross the area without an escort. A German was standing there and I saw a youngster named Phibs invite him into the store to try on a new leather coat. The leather coat was among the clothing that was being sorted. (It was the clothing of prisoners who had already been killed.) He suspected nothing and complied . . . so it was the beginning. I left my job and went to the sorting barracks, just a minute before the German Wolf entered. In one of the compart-

ments a number of prisoners were standing and, with assumed diligence, engaged in sorting the clothes. Next to them was the bait—a smooth, shining leather coat. . . . At the order of the work leader two of them handed the coat respectfully—so to speak—to the German, and helped him put his arms into the sleeves. At that moment the picture changed. The arms caught in the sleeves could not get out. In Kali's hand an axe glinted—and the Nazi fell. In a moment the body was hidden under a heap of sand. The trap was ready for a second victim.

A moment later Phibs went out to call another German. My nervousness vanished immediately. I stood, quiet and restrained. Now the German, Beckmann, was invited into the store. He seemed to hesitate, but went over to the section where the valuables were stored. In spite of the inconvenient circumstances, they succeeded in liquidating him. After him, Staubel was killed. From the First Section came Drescher, a sanitary worker, and announced that they had killed the Deputy Commandant Neumann, the head of the camp guard named Greitschutz, and a Ukrainian named Klet.

This was how it happened. SS Officer Neumann came to the Section mounted on a horse. At that moment one of the tailors came up to him, and asked him to come in and try on a new uniform which had been made for him. (The workshops operated only for the Germans.) The tall officer tied his horse to a post and entered. As he entered he took off his belt and revolver and placed them on the table. Then he took off his tunic. The tailor saw to it that the officer would stand with his back to the Jew who was going to do the job, and the German was dead. Greitschutz, I was told, was killed in the shoemaker's shop where he had been invited to try on a pair of topboots; as he was putting them on, he was killed with a blow of an axe. At that moment Klet, the Ukrainian, came running in to call the officer to the telephone. . . .

The Ukrainian did not get out. Gotzinger was killed in like fashion.

From the tower of the camp the peal of a bell was heard. The time had come for the roll call. The Jewish work-group leaders were leading the men, singing as they went to the First Section. On the surface everything was normal. Now I saw how many people were still unaware of what was happening. Those who did know no longer thought of supper, but began to form their ranks. But the others queued up to receive their food, as on every other day. Nevertheless the queue quickly melted away. The decisive moment was approaching. Further delay could result in discovery by the Germans who had remained alive. I was in the smithy. The foreman there was an energetic fellow called Shlomo Shmayzner, from Pulawy. He was examining the rifle just brought to him by Drescher from the Ukrainian barracks. A few moments earlier, the German overseer of barracks construction had been liquidated. He had been asked to come into the barracks on the pretext that he must give instructions on how to repair the bunks that had been broken. Sasha (Pechersky) and others readied the ranks for the exit. The men of the Ukrainian guard on the towers were still ignorant of what was happening. They thought, it seems, that these were the usual preparations at this hour for the roll call.

A number of prisoners rushed to the barbed-wire fence, trying to get away. I was in the group that ran to the main gate. The gate to the First Section was already behind us. We continued running. Then suddenly . . . shots. The German cook who had remained alive was firing. He stood with his back to the casino, retreating slowly, with the intention of getting away round the corner. I was in the front row where the bullets were falling. We tried to check ourselves, but were pushed from behind. I was pushed until I found myself inside the aisle between the barbed-wire fences intended for the

Ukrainian guards. Behind us there were already two fences and a ditch full of water, and ahead there was only one wire fence and . . . mines. We stopped. Someone with a hoe in his hand tried to cut the barbed-wire fence with it. The wire was cut and we passed through. The moment I was passing through the wires, the whole fence collapsed and I under it. It is very likely that this saved my life, for while I was under the wires and the fleeing prisoners were treading on my feet I saw mines exploding. It had been said that we must put planks on the mined area to explode the mines, but the people did not do so. They could not wait, and chose the danger of sudden death, rather than to remain another minute in the place. All around was madness. There was the sound of shots, the explosion of mines, the rattle of machine-guns. As the first wave passed I tried to extricate myself from under the fence. Notwithstanding the barbed-wire I found it was quite easy. How? I got out of the coat I was wearing, leaving it on the wire, and got away. I ran through the mine line. I was free. I still had to get to the forest, which seemed to me to be so near. . . . In the field in front of me I saw bent forms, running away. I fell a number of times, thinking each time that I had been hit by a bullet. But I got up and continued running. Another 100 meters, another 50, 20 . . . then . . . I was in the forest.

From a recent study, *The War Record of Soviet Jewry,* we learn that the revolt in the Sobibor camp involved about 350 organized rebels in addition to the many inmates who assisted in the fighting. The end result of the revolt is given in the following account: "The rebels of Sobibor killed 10 SS men and wounded one; 38 Ukrainian guards were either killed or wounded in the fighting, while 40 others deserted rather than face the wrath of their Nazi masters. Almost 400 to 600 inmates broke out, but perhaps as many as half were killed or wounded in the minefield. Perchersky led his 60 men and women eastward, toward the River Bug. . . . They broke up into six groups . . . and ran into Soviet partisans shortly afterward."

Elie Wiesel, eloquent spokesman of the victims of the Holocaust, suggests reasons for the victims' behavior in this excerpt from *Legend of Our Time.* At the same time, he deplores the very question "Why so little resistance?" as if somehow it is the victims who have been placed on trial.

60. Why So Little Resistance?
Elie Wiesel

Reduced to a mere number, the man in the concentration camp at the same time lost his identity and his individual destiny. He came to realize that his presence in the camp was due solely to the fact that he was part of a forgotten and condemned collectivity. It is not written: I shall live or die, but: *someone*—today—will vanish, or will continue to suffer; and from the point of view of the collective, it makes no difference whether that someone is I or another. Only the number, only the quota counts. Thus, the one who had been spared, above all during the selections, could not repress his first spontaneous reflex of joy. A moment, a week, or an eternity later, this joy weighted with fear and anxiety will turn into guilt. *I am happy to have escaped death* becomes equivalent to admitting: *I am glad that someone else went in my place.* It was in order not to think about this that the prisoners so very quickly managed to forget their comrades or their relatives: those who had been selected. They forgot them quickly—trying to shut their eyes to the reproachful glances which still floated in the air around them.

Why did the Jews in the camps not choose a death with honor, knife in hand and hate on their lips?

It is understandable that all of us should wonder why. Putting aside the technical and psychological reasons which made any attempt at revolt impossible (the Jews knew that they had been sacrificed, forgotten, crossed off by humanity), to answer we must consider the moral aspects of the question. The Jews, conscious of the curse weighing them down, came to believe that they were neither worthy nor capable of an act of honor. To die struggling would have meant a betrayal of those who had gone to their death submissive and silent. The only way was to follow in their footsteps, die their kind of death—only then could the living make their peace with those who had already gone.

I attended the Eichmann trial, I heard the prosecutor try to get the witnesses to talk by forcing them to expose themselves and to probe the innermost recesses of their being: Why didn't you resist? Why didn't you attack your assassins when you still outnumbered them?

Pale, embarrassed, ill at ease, the survivors all responded in the same way: "You cannot understand. Anyone who was not there cannot imagine it."

Well, I was there. And I still do not understand. I do not understand that child in the Warsaw Ghetto who wrote in his diary: "I'm hungry, I'm cold; when I grow up I want to be a German, and then I won't be hungry anymore, and I won't be cold anymore."

I still do not understand why I did not throw myself on the Kapo who was beating my father before my very eyes. In Galicia, Jews dug their own graves and lined up, without any trace of panic, at the edge of the trench to await the machine-gun barrage. I do not understand their calm. And that woman, that mother, in the bunker somewhere in Poland, I do not understand her either; her companions smothered her child for fear its cries might betray their presence; that woman, that mother, having lived this scene of biblical intensity, did not go mad. I do not understand her:

why, and by what right, and in the name of what, did she not go mad?

I do not know why, but I forbid us to ask her the question. The world kept silent while the Jews were being massacred, while they were being reduced to the state of objects good for the fire; let the world at least have the decency to keep silent now as well. Its questions come a bit late; they should have been addressed to the executioner. Do they trouble us? Do they keep us from sleeping in peace? So much the better. We want to know, to understand, so we can turn the page: is that not true? So we can say to ourselves: the matter is closed and everything is back in order. Do not wait for the dead to come to our rescue. Their silence will survive them.

One explanation of Nazi behavior has been that Hitler and his followers were insane —that is, their actions could not possibly have been carried out by "normal" people. An interesting psychological study of Nazi war criminals, however, suggests that this was not the case, as summarized In this excerpt from an article by Molly Harrower in *Psychology Today* of July, 1976.

61. Were Hitler's Henchmen Mad?
Molly Harrower

It was easy to believe in 1945 that Adolf Hitler's henchmen were mad. It seemed impossible, for example, that Albert Speer, Hitler's confidant, Reich Minister for Armaments and War Production, and the man personally responsible for enslaving millions could have been anything but a maniac. The lesson Hitler and the Nazis taught us seemed simple: keep insane people out of high office and the atrocities of the Third Reich will never happen again. Unfortunately, it wasn't that simple. The Nazis who went on trial at Nuremberg were as diverse a group of people as one might find in our own government today, or for that matter, in the leadership of the PTA.

In 1945, the Nazi war criminals took the Rorschach ink-blot test while they awaited trial. The Rorschach is a series of 10 cards with ink blots, some black and white, some with blobs of red, blue or yellow. The person being tested looks at each card and describes what the ink blot looks like to him. The ink blots are not intended to look like anything, so there is no right or wrong answer as there is, say, in an IQ test. The idea behind the Rorschach technique is that when a person describes what he sees, he reveals aspects of his personality, particularly his unconscious needs and desires.

In 1947, 10 Rorschach experts, including myself, received copies of the Nazi Rorschach answers and were asked to comment on them. Although all of us agreed to respond, not one of us followed through. I was vice chairman of the committee that initiated this project, so my own failure to participate was particularly puzzling to me. Over the years, I have come to believe that our reason for not commenting on the test results was that they did not show what we expected to see, and what the pressure of public opinion demanded that we see—that these men were demented creatures, as different from normal people as a scorpion is different from a puppy. What we saw was a wide range of personalities, from severely disturbed neurotics to the superbly well-adjusted. But only Douglas Kelley, the Nuremberg psychiatrist who interviewed the Nazis, said aloud in 1946 "that such personalities are not unique or insane [and] could be duplicated in any country of the world today." . . .

These results do not excuse the acts of the Nazis. Instead, they demonstrate that well-adjusted people may get caught up in a tangle of social forces that makes them goose-step their way toward such abominations as the calculated execution of 6 million Jews and the systematic elimination of the elderly and other unproductive people. It may be comforting to believe that the horrors of World War II were the work of a dozen or so insane men, but it is a dangerous belief, one that may give us a false sense of security.

It *can* happen here.

V

AFTERMATH

"After the war the weary world will return **to its** daily turmoil and struggle. Such is the law of life. Bread and circuses. Birkenau may drop out of the human vocabulary, and the terrible lesson of Auschwitz may fall on deaf ears. The human mind cannot conceive of extinction, but in this last terrible and miraculous moment I see life in all its four dimensions. I believe that the small still voice of Israel will remain and continue to proclaim the law of truth and justice."

—IRENE SCHWARTZ
The Root and the Bough

This excerpt from Richard Mayne's book
The Recovery of Europe reveals the staggering
impact of the war on the people of Europe:
60 million persons were uprooted from their
homes. Numbers, of course, tell only part of the
story; the real effects of the war, on individuals
and on nations, can still be perceived in the
world today.

62. The Uprooted

Richard Mayne

Between 1939 and the end of 1945, at least 60
million Europeans—not counting servicemen and prisoners of war—had been uprooted from their homes.
Twenty-seven million of them had left their own countries, or been driven out by force. Four and a half
million had been deported by the Nazis for forced labor; many thousands more had been sent to Siberia by
the Russians. When the war ended, two and a half
million Poles and Czechs were transferred to the Soviet Union, and more than 12 million Germans fled or
were expelled from Eastern Europe. At one period
in 1945, 40,000 refugees a week were streaming into
northwest Germany. All told, the shifts of population
involved 55 ethnic groups from 27 countries. Some
had been displaced more than once: one group—
420,000 Karelians from between the Gulf of Finland

and the White Sea—was shuttled to and fro no less
than three times.

The homeless became known as DP's,
"displaced persons," and they were cared for
in special camps set up by the United Nations
and the Allied armies. By mid-1946, some
230,000 Jews were in DP camps. Some were
survivors of concentration camps, others had
been in hiding or with partisan groups, and
still others had successfully posed as Aryans
during the war. Most Jews could not, and would
not, return to their former homes.

This next selection, excerpted from a collective journal written by a group of survivors
and published originally in *Commentary* Magazine of July and August, 1946, describes the
end of the war and the group's decision to
settle in Palestine, in a kibbutz, a collective
settlement. At that time, Palestine was not open
to free immigration, and it was a dangerous undertaking to travel there. Ultimately, however,
nearly two-thirds of the Jewish DP's settled in
the new State of Israel, created in 1948. About
25 percent emigrated to the U.S., Canada,
and other countries, and a small number remained in Europe.

63. Kibbutz Buchenwald

Commentary

Those were dreary, endlessly monotonous days,
the last days in Buchenwald. Gray heavy hours went
by. We lived in the barracks, slept on dirty narrow
benches, and crept around the camp; in passing each
other, we exchanged whispers about our fate. Would
it soon be changed? We exchanged whispers in passing,

whispers in all the languages of the world. For there were people from all lands, from all nations; there were French, Belgians, Dutch, Hungarians, Russians, Poles, Italians. And also, of course, Jews.

But during this last period there was no distinction of race in the concentration camp; all, even the Jews, were treated on the same level. All were hungry, all were oppressed, beaten, degraded. Therefore, there were no separate problems for people belonging to one nationality or another. The long gray hopeless days dragged on. Wraiths of human beings dragged themselves around the camp or sat against their barracks walls, staring with vacant eyes, and thinking of nothing. They were broken and apathetic.

But there was another world in the camp. This was the secret world of the underground. Here, too, there were people of all nations and all languages, including, of course, Jews. And there, too, there was no distinction of race or nationality. Their united interests held them together: the war against the Nazis, against evil and oppression, the will to live and free themselves. And they worked together, all, including the Jews, not as representatives of their nations, but as people.

Then came April 11, 1945. Liberation. An American commander took over the camp. Immediately, an international camp committee was set up. People now grouped themselves according to nationality, and there was a representative of each group on this committee. There were a few Jews on this committee, it is true, but not as Jews; they represented the countries of their birth. The entire committee was drawn from the former underground organization, and its Jewish members were men who had been leaders in the struggle for freedom.

Now, gradually, after the liberation, the inmates of Buchenwald began to live again. Once apathetic and hopeless, they now nearly went mad with joy. Freedom! Freedom! We lived to see it!

Their faces were ablaze. They began to talk about going home. To their own countries, to father, mother, wife, and child.

And the Jews? Well—the Jews . . .

The Jews suddenly faced themselves. Where now?
Where to? They saw that they were different from all
the other inmates of the camp. For them things were
not so simple. To go back to Poland? To Hungary? To
streets empty of Jews, towns empty of Jews, a world
without Jews. To wander in those lands, lonely, homeless, always with the tragedy before one's eyes . . . and
to meet, again, a former Gentile neighbor who would
open his eyes wide and smile, remarking with double
meaning, "What! Yankel! You're still alive!"

Perhaps for the thousandth time the Jewish committee in Buchenwald was holding a meeting on the
question: Where to? A Polish Jew, a German, a
Czech, a Hungarian—each faced the same burning
problem. . . . The world, we had thought, would welcome our few survivors with open arms!

July 27th—A boy, Moshe, came to us today from
Poland. He had been in Buchenwald until the liberation,
and then had returned to Poland with a group of
Buchenwald Jews. Poland, he told us, was ridden
with anti-Semitism. He told of the loneliness and the
fear of the handful of Jews remaining there. The majority of the Polish people, Moshe declared, have only
one idea: to eliminate the Jews. In small towns, there
are no Jews to be found; they have fled in terror to the
cities. Moshe had once lived in the village of Koszenitz, and he had returned to Poland hoping to go
home, but when he spoke to the Jews in Lodz, he realized that he would be risking his life in going alone to a
small town like Koszenitz, and so he fled Poland. He
wandered on the roads for several days, stole across
borders, and managed somehow to get back to the region of Buchenwald. [One year later, on July 4, 1946,
in the town of Kielce, Poland, a pogrom erupted. For-
ty-one Jews who had returned to their hometown were
murdered. Like an epidemic, pogroms broke out all
over Poland.]

Quickly enough, we saw that the world had other things on its mind than Jewish suffering. So where to?

Comrade Posnansky put forth an idea: into our own kibbutz. To build a group of Buchenwald's youth, and find a farm where we could prepare for Palestine. A wonderful idea. There would be no lack of candidates for the kibbutz, for energy was reawakening in the survivors and seeking an outlet.

From that idea sprang Kibbutz Buchenwald. . . .

September 3rd—We sailed from the French port of Toulon at 7:30 P.M. and a great crowd was assembled on the shore.

The *Matroah* is a military transport, normally carrying about 200 men; aboard her now are a thousand refugees, so the crowding can be imagined. The refugees are from four centers: Switzerland, Belgium, France, and Buchenwald.

There are old men and women with little children who were given refuge in Switzerland, and thus escaped the Hitler regime; there are prisoners who were saved by a succession of miracles; there are *halutzim* [pioneers] with work-roughened hands, and there are even women with painted mouths and lacquered fingernails.

September 8th—Sabbath, and the first day of Rosh Hashanah, and the day we first saw our homeland! We ate a hasty lunch, took our baggage in hand, and went on deck, impatiently awaiting the sight of Eretz Yisrael. Then we saw the distant shore. Many people had tears in their eyes. As the shore became clearer and English vessels passed near by, greeting us, loud cries of joy broke out. At 2:30 P.M. we came to Haifa port, singing "Hatikvah."

The next three readings deal with the fate of the Nazis at war's end, and with international efforts to prevent future catastrophes like the Holocaust.

The first selection, from *New Catholic Encyclopedia*, explains how the term "genocide" came into being, and discusses the Convention on Genocide adopted by the United Nations in 1948.

64.   On the Genocide Convention
New Catholic Encyclopedia

When the victorious Allies brought the German leaders to trial after the war, international lawyers found it difficult to find a legal concept adequate for the crimes against minority groups. It was at this time that Professor Raphael Lemkin coined the hybrid word "genocide." It combines the Greek *genos* (race, nation, or tribe) with the Latin suffix *cide* (killing). The word was adopted in the Nuremberg trial, notably by the British prosecutor, Sir Hartley Shawcross, but this crime was included under the broader category of "crimes against humanity."

The Nazi leaders were convicted of crimes against humanity, but only with respect to acts committed during the war. Thus acts of genocide against their own people or peoples taken over before the war were not punished. This gap in international law has been filled by the development of the concept of genocide as a crime under both conventional and customary international law. On December 11, 1946, the UN General Assembly unanimously adopted a resolution affirming that "genocide is a crime under international law" and advising that international and unilateral measures be taken to suppress it. On December 9, 1948, the General Assembly adopted a Convention on Genocide. The Convention received sufficient adhesions to enter into force on January 12, 1951, but the U.S. has not ratified it partly because of a fear that foreign powers might seek to intervene in American racial difficulties.

The Convention defines genocide as any of the following acts: "(a) Killing members of the group; (b)

Causing serious bodily or mental harm to members of the group; (c) Deliberately inflicting on the group conditions of life calculated to bring about its physical destruction in whole or in part; (d) Imposing measures intended to prevent births within the group; (e) Forcibly transferring children of the group to another group" (Article 2). The parties to the Convention "undertake to enact, in accordance with their respective Constitutions, the necessary legislation to give effect to the Convention and . . . to provide effective penalties" (Article 5). Following the Nuremberg precedent, genocide is treated as a crime for which individuals may be tried "by a competent tribunal of the state in the territory of which the act was committed, or by such international penal tribunal as may have jurisdiction with respect to those contracting parties which shall have accepted its jurisdiction" (Article 6).

No international penal tribunals have yet been established and the repression of genocide remains primarily a matter of unilateral action supported by world public opinion. To the extent that the UN develops a capacity to intervene on behalf of victims of policies of genocide, the Convention could be implemented on a truly international basis. Article 8 provides that "Any contracting Party may call upon the competent organs of the United Nations to take such action under the Charter of the United Nations as they consider appropriate for the prevention and suppression of acts of genocide or any of the other acts enumerated in Article III." The acts covered by Article 3 are: "genocide, conspiracy to commit genocide, direct and public incitement to commit genocide, complicity in genocide."

In 1945 and 1946, an International Military Tribunal met in Nuremberg, Germany, to try former Nazi leaders. The judges were representatives of the United States, Great Britain, France, and the Soviet Union. The following selections, from the book *The Nuremberg Trials* by Leo Kahn, first define the crimes over which the court had jurisdiction, then present a discussion of the arguments used by the Defense. Although the evidence against the defendants was overwhelming, the Defense fought hard, and used very interesting arguments, to try and win reduced sentences for the accused. This section concludes with a chart showing the sentences imposed by the International Military Tribunal on those tried.

The Nuremberg Trials passed judgment on many of the Nazis' top leaders, but others had escaped capture. Many fled to foreign countries where they took assumed names, and others remained in hiding in Germany. In the years since the end of World War II, and using the precedents established at Nuremberg, hundreds of ex-Nazis have been caught and tried in various countries. In 1962, Israeli undercover agents in Argentina captured Adolf Eichmann, a high-ranking officer who had been in charge of transporting prisoners to the camps. Eichmann was tried in Jerusalem, in a trial that drew worldwide attention, and was subsequently executed.

At the present time, more than 80 persons living in the United States are under investigation as alleged Nazi war criminals.

65. The Nuremberg Trials

Leo Kahn

The following acts, or any of them, are crimes coming within the jurisdiction of the Tribunal for which there shall be individual responsibility:

(a) **CRIMES AGAINST PEACE:** namely, planning, preparation, initiation or waging of a war of aggression, or a war in violation of international treaties, agreements or assurances, or participation in a common plan or conspiracy for the accomplishment of any of the foregoing;

(b) **WAR CRIMES:** namely, violations of the laws or customs of war. Such violations shall include, but not be limited to, murder, ill-treatment or deportation to slave labor or for any other purpose of civilian population of or in occupied territory, murder or ill-treatment of prisoners of war or persons on the seas, killing of hostages, plunder of public or private property, wanton destruction of cities, towns or villages, or devastation not justified by military necessity;

(c) **CRIMES AGAINST HUMANITY:** namely, murder, extermination, enslavement, deportation, and other inhumane acts committed against any civilian population, before or during the war; or persecutions on political, racial or religious grounds in execution of or in connection with any crime within the jurisdiction of the Tribunal, whether or not in violation of the domestic law of the country where perpetrated.

Leaders, organizers, instigators and accomplices participating in the formulation or execution of a common plan or conspiracy to commit any of the foregoing crimes are responsible for all acts performed by any persons in execution of such plan.

It took the prosecution teams almost four months to present their case, but when it was completed the defendants and their lawyers realized that they had to contend with a body of evidence much more extensive and concrete than they had thought possible when the trial started. A denial of the facts named in the indictment would clearly be futile, and so would any attempt to belittle their gravity. There was only limited scope for defensive strategy, but within those limits the Defense fought a tenacious struggle.

In the early stages of the trial, on 19th November 1945, all defense counsel adopted a joint motion challenging the validity of the International Military Tribunal charter inasmuch as it made individuals accountable for "crimes against peace": this, they argued, offended against the ancient principle that an act should not be treated as a crime, and nobody should be punished for it, unless it had been declared criminal by a law already in existence when the act was done—*nullum crimen sine lege, nulla poena sine lege* in its conventional Latin formulation. The problem, it will be remembered, had been a subject of discussion at the London Conference. It is a very difficult one, one which cannot be dealt with adequately in a few sentences. The tribunal rejected the Defense motion, not without some elaborate reasoning, but among lawyers the tribunal's ruling has caused more criticism than approval.

The Defense tried to make the most of an argument also best known in the form of a Latin tag: *tu quoque* ("you're another"), claiming that among the crimes charged there were at least some that had also been committed on the Allied side. Strictly speaking, the alleged or even proved similar guilt of somebody else can never be admissible as a valid legal defense, but its normal and psychological effect can be considerable; a fact which may well have saved the lives of Admirals Doenitz and Raeder. Both had been charged with "waging unrestricted submarine warfare," and both were acquitted of this particular charge on the ground that Great Britain and the United States had admittedly done the same. It is true that Doenitz's counsel very skilfully drew a fine distinction between the legal point he was making in this context and the ordinary *tu quoque* argument, but it is doubtful whether the judges would have accepted his rather subtle legal reasoning if they had not welcomed this way of avoiding the reproach of "one law for the victor, another for the vanquished."

A more fundamental issue was the defense of

"superior orders," for in most instances the defendants could rightly claim that they had issued their orders and decrees in obedience to the directives of Hitler as the Head of the Government and Supreme Commander of the Armed Forces. Under Article 8 of the IMT Charter this argument was available only as a plea in mitigation of punishment, and it cannot be said that the charter introduced a new principle in this respect. The position was as the tribunal defined it in the judgment: "The provisions of this article are in conformity with the law of all nations. That a soldier was ordered to kill or torture in violation of the international law of war has never been recognized as a defense to such acts of brutality. . . . The true test, which is found in varying degrees in the criminal law of most nations, is not the existence of the order, but whether moral choice was in fact possible."

This legal rule is unpopular with most military Establishments, but it really represents sound common sense. A man subject to military, or indeed any other similarly strict discipline does not thereby become an automaton without responsibility for criminal actions. On the other hand, he is neither supposed to query the legality of an order where its illegality is not blatantly illegal, nor is he required to be a hero. What he may or may not do depends on circumstances. He is entitled to take into account the risks of disobedience, but he must weigh them against the gravity of the crime he is ordered to commit. There must be a reasonable balance between the need for discipline and the duty to avoid crime. The higher the rank, the wider the scope for a "moral choice" is likely to be, and in the trial of the major war criminals there was actually not much scope for the defense of "superior orders"; but this was not so clearly recognized at the time.

Goering's attempt to create a united front among the defendants was frustrated as the evidence of the prosecution in all its strength became gradually known. Nobody wanted to be identified with the horrors of concentration camps, mass murder, and slave labor.

Goering himself made a last determined effort to defend the Nazi regime and his own reputation during the nine days he was on the witness stand (from 13th to 22nd March 1946). Since the prosecution had made accusations of a general, political kind, the judges thought it right that at least one of the accused should be allowed to reply in kind. They regarded Goering as the most suitable spokesman for the rest, and Goering was thus able to make lengthy speeches instead of giving brief replies to the question of counsel. Employing the tactics and manner which we have tried to describe he gained a triumph of prestige at first. He also did well, on the whole, under cross-examination by Jackson, who had been so sure of the righteousness of his cause that he made the fatal mistake of losing his temper when he met Goering's clever and arrogantly defiant resistance. But the cross-examination by Maxwell-Fyfe, which followed, was cool, patient, and matter-of-fact, and under this thoroughly professional questioning Goering's defense soon began to crumble. In the end he too, like the rest, was reduced to denying that he had been aware of facts which, in the light of the evidence, he must have known, and to assigning the ultimate responsibility for the worst crimes to the dead Führer, who "let Bormann and Himmler have their way." About Goering's guilt there remained no doubt, but at least he had relieved the growing tedium of the proceedings by his spirited duel with the prosecution, so that many people were not sorry when he managed to commit suicide before he could be delivered to the hangman.

The evidential material contained abundant proof, not only that the gravest possible crimes had been perpetrated in the systematic, centrally controlled manner alleged, but also that all the accused were, at least in a general way, implicated in this criminal system: so that at first the Prosecution, relying on an extensive interpretation of "conspiracy," felt certain that the trial could have no other outcome than conviction and sentence of death in the case of each defendant. But the Bench soon made it clear that they would not regard a general involvement, whatever its moral or political significance, as sufficient for a criminal conviction; the Prosecution must show in every individual case that an accused was specifically and concretely implicated in the crime charged. A hard task, for it must be remembered that except in a few instances these defendants had neither initiated the crimes nor personally taken part in their physical execution: they were accused of having knowingly and willingly provided the necessary link between Hitler's intentions and their final realization. Knowledge and willingness, however, are states of mind, the existence of which is exceedingly difficult to prove "beyond reasonable doubt." A Nuremberg defendant would sometimes deny knowledge of an event even when shown his own signature on a document referring to that event; he had been too busy, he would claim, to read everything he was given to sign. Or he would plead in mitigation that behind the scenes he had remonstrated against a criminal order by Hitler, or tried to soften its impact, although in public he had made a show of eager obedience. Explanations of this kind were hardly ever convincing, and often patently absurd, yet just occasionally they had some substance; at any rate, they had to be listened to and meticulously examined, and this the tribunal did during a further seven weary months.

The table presents the judgment of the tribunal and the sentences passed. . . . With 19 convictions against only three acquittals the Prosecution could be well content. On the other hand, the fact that in a trial of this nature 10 out of 22 defendants escaped with their lives seems to demonstrate how carefully the legal point in their favor and all extenuating circumstances were taken into account.

Without attempting the impossible task of reviewing the whole of the evidence in detail the judgment could give no more than a mere indication of the reasoning behind particular findings; an unsatisfactory, if inevitable, feature of the trial. The death sentences were pronounced in those 12 cases where most people would expect it. Goering was obviously guilty on all

counts, with practically nothing to be said in mitigation. "Goering was often, indeed almost always, the
moving force, second only to his leader," said the
judgment. Ribbentrop, not content with his part in
bringing about the war, had also given zealous support
to the wartime policies of oppression and genocide.
Nobody has queried the unqualified guilt of Kaltenbrunner, second man in the SS "state within a state," or
Bormann, in the last few years of the Third Reich
probably the most powerful of Hitler's lieutenants, or
Rosenberg, Frank and Seyss-Inquart, Hitler's satraps
in occupied territories. Frick had supplied the administrative tools for the incorporation and "Germanization" of conquered countries, and had also had administrative responsibility for the murder of several
hundred thousand "useless eaters" under the so-called
"euthanasia" program. Although Streicher's influence
had been at its peak in Germany before the war, he
had done enough to encourage genocide during the war
to justify his conviction on Count Four. Sauckel had
been in charge of a program which "involved deportation for slave labor of more than 5 million human
beings." In respect of Keitel and Jodl it has sometimes
been claimed that as professional soldiers they did not
belong in the same category, even though they had
gone too far in their obedience to superior orders.
But would they really have deserved a more lenient
sentence? Even from the few pieces of evidence which
we have cited it is apparent that the Wehrmacht was
deeply implicated in the crimes of aggression and terrorism. Among the German officers and other ranks in
the field there had indeed been many who had felt
disgraced by the barbarities which they had been ordered to assist or tolerate, and some had been brave
enough to protest. But such sense of honor and moral
courage had been sadly lacking at the top—where they
should have been strongest.

   Von Papen and Schacht had rendered great services
to Nazism during the last phase of the Weimar Republic and the period known as the "consolidation of
power," and even then they must have been aware of

Hitler's general intentions. But the tribunal acquitted them, though not without some scathing remarks on the moral guilt of these two cunning and shifty gentlemen, on the ground that they had no longer been in positions of influence during the crucial time from 1937 onward. The Russian judge delivered a dissenting opinion in all three cases.

Lastly, a few comments on the prison sentences. Those of von Neurath (15 years) and Funk (life) have been criticized as comparatively harsh. Neurath's case was not so very different from that of Schacht and Papen, except that he was less adroit. Funk was not held to be one of the leading figures in the planning of aggressive war, though found guilty of taking part in the economic preparations, and the worst point against him in the context of atrocities was that as Reichsbank president he had accepted deposits of valuables which the SS had taken from their murdered victims. It should be noted that von Schirach was not convicted on account of his pernicious activities as leader of the Hitler Youth, but in connection with the deportation of Jews from Vienna. Speer had supported and used the slave labor program, but his responsibility was clearly not so heavy as Sauckel's. The two admirals, Doenitz and Raeder, were found guilty of having been "active in waging aggressive war" (Raeder also of taking part in the planning), and both had issued some of Hitler's criminal orders without protest, but they had been much less involved in war crimes than the army leaders, and they had not even been indicted for "crimes against humanity."

In our short exposition we have not been able to deal with the prosecution of the seven organizations or groups, of which four were declared criminal by the tribunal. Legally these prosecutions were something of an oddity, which practical effect only in the subsequent trials of war criminals. In future, membership in one of the criminal organizations could be an additional count in an indictment for other offenses, though it was not to be regarded as a separate offense. The evidence submitted on both sides has been an important historical source, but in all other respects the value of the proceedings against organizations is questionable.

---

66. The Sentences Imposed by the International Military Tribunal

Hermann Goering—death
Rudolph Hess—life imprisonment
Hans Frank—death
Wilhelm Frick—death
Julius Streicher—death
Walter Funk—life imprisonment
Fritz Sauckel—death
Alfred Jodl—death
Martin Bormann—death (in absentia)
Franz von Papen—acquittal
Joachim von Ribbentrop—death
Wilhelm Keitel—death
Ernst Kaltenbrunner—death
Alfred Rosenberg—death
Hjalmar Schacht—acquittal
Karl Doenitz—10 years imprisonment
Erich Raeder—life imprisonment
Baldur von Schirach—20 years imprisonment
Artur Seyss-Inquart—death
Albert Speer—20 years imprisonment
Constantin von Neurath—15 years imprisonment
Hans Fritzsche—acquittal

For survivors of the Holocaust, and for Jews elsewhere in the world, there were two matters of urgent priority: to provide a home for the displaced persons, and to make sure that Jews would never again be defenseless victims. The vehicle for accomplishing both these goals was to be an independent Jewish state, the State of Israel, situated in the ancient Jewish homeland. The dream of such a "national home" was not new by any means, and in fact the Jews had already built up a thriving community in Palestine. Nevertheless, it took the tragedy of the Holocaust, and the subsequent outpouring of sympathy on the part of people everywhere, to bring about the actual establishment of a recognized sovereign and independent state. This was in 1948.

The next reading is the complete text of Israel's "Proclamation of Independence," which sets forth the Jewish people's claims to an independent national existence, on its own soil.

---

67. State of Israel Proclamation of Independence

The Land of Israel was the birthplace of the Jewish people. Here their spiritual, religious and national identity was formed. Here they achieved independence and created a culture of national and universal significance. Here they wrote and gave the Bible to the world.

Exiled from the Land of Israel the Jewish people remained faithful to it in all the countries of their dispersion, never ceasing to pray and hope for their return and the restoration of their national freedom.

Impelled by this historic association, Jews strove throughout the centuries to go back to the land of their fathers and regain their statehood. In recent decades they returned in their masses. They reclaimed the wilderness, revived their language, built cities and villages, and established a vigorous and ever-growing community, with its own economic and cultural life. They sought peace, yet were prepared to defend themselves. They brought the blessings of progress to all inhabitants of the country and looked forward to sovereign independence.

In the year 1897 the First Zionist Congress, inspired by Theodor Herzl's vision of the Jewish State, proclaimed the right of the Jewish people to national revival in their own country.

This right was acknowledged by the Balfour Declaration of November 2, 1917, and reaffirmed by the Mandate of the League of Nations, which gave explicit international recognition to the historic connection of the Jewish people with Palestine and their right to reconstitute their National Home.

The recent Holocaust, which engulfed millions of Jews in Europe, proved anew the need to solve the problem of the homelessness and lack of independence of the Jewish people by means of the reestablishment of the Jewish State, which would open the gates to all Jews and endow the Jewish people with equality of status among the family of nations.

The survivors of the disastrous slaughter in Europe, and also Jews from other lands, have not desisted from their efforts to reach Eretz-Yisrael, in face of difficulties, obstacles and perils; and have not ceased to urge their right to a life of dignity, freedom and honest toil in their ancestral land.

In the Second World War the Jewish people in Palestine made their full contribution to the struggle of the freedom-loving nations against the Nazi evil. The sacrifices of their soldiers and their war effort gained them the right to rank with the nations which founded the United Nations.

On November 29, 1947, the General Assembly of the United Nations adopted a Resolution requiring the establishment of a Jewish State in Palestine. The General Assembly called upon the inhabitants of the country to take all the necessary steps on their part to put the plan into effect. This recognition by the United Nations of the right of the Jewish people to establish their independent State is unassailable.

It is the natural right of the Jewish people to lead,

as do all other nations, an independent existence in its
sovereign State.

ACCORDINGLY WE, the members of the National
Council, representing the Jewish people in Palestine
and the World Zionist Movement, are met together in
solemn assembly today, the day of termination of the
British Mandate for Palestine; and by virtue of the
natural and historic right of the Jewish people and of
the Resolution of the General Assembly of the United
Nations.

WE HEREBY PROCLAIM the establishment of the
Jewish State in Palestine, to be called Medinath Yisrael
(The State of Israel).

WE HEREBY DECLARE that, as from the termination
of the Mandate at midnight, the 14th–15th May, 1948,
and pending the setting up of the duly elected bodies
of the State in accordance with a Constitution, to be
drawn up by the Constituent Assembly not later than
the 1st October, 1948, the National Council shall act
as the Provisional State Council, and that the National
Administration shall constitute the Provisional Government of the Jewish State, which shall be known as
Israel.

THE STATE OF ISRAEL will be open to the immigration of Jews from all countries of their dispersion; will
promote the development of the country for the benefit
of all its inhabitants; will be based on the principles of
liberty, justice and peace as conceived by the Prophets
of Israel; will uphold the full social and political equality of all its citizens, without distinction of religion,
race, or sex; will guarantee freedom of religion, conscience, education and culture; will safeguard the Holy
Places of all religions; and will loyally uphold the principles of the United Nations Charter.

THE STATE OF ISRAEL will be ready to cooperate
with the organs and representatives of the United Nations
in the implementation of the Resolution of the Assembly of November 29, 1947, and will take steps to bring
about the Economic Union over the whole of Palestine.

We appeal to the United Nations to assist the

Jewish people in the building of its State and to admit Israel into the family of nations.

In the midst of wanton aggression, we yet call upon the Arab inhabitants of the State of Israel to pre-serve the ways of peace and play their part in the development of the State, on the basis of full and equal citizenship and due representation in all its bodies and institutions—provisional and permanent.

We extend our hand in peace and neighborliness to all the neighboring states and their peoples, and in-vite them to cooperate with the independent Jewish na-tion for the common good of all. The State of Israel is prepared to make its contribution to the progress of the Middle East as a whole.

Our call goes out to the Jewish people all over the world to rally to our side in the task of immigration and development, and to stand by us in the great strug-gle for the fulfilment of the dream of generations for the redemption of Israel.

With trust in the Rock of Israel, we set our hand to this Declaration, at this Session of the Provisional State Council, on the soil of the Homeland, in the city of Tel-Aviv, on this Sabbath eve, the fifth of Iyar, 5708, the fourteenth of May, 1948.

At the end of the war, many Germans and Poles undoubtedly wished to see razed to the ground all vestiges of the infamous camps and crematoria. A number of camps were de-stroyed. At the insistence of the Allies, how-ever, some camps were preserved, and des-ignated as memorials or as places of historic interest. Many people felt, and still feel, that the people of Germany and Poland, where the camps were situated, should not be allowed to forget what took place in them. These memorials are also intended to teach the rest of the world the importance of remembering—however painful—in the hope that we will be alert to the danger of similar occurrences in our own time.

The next two selections describe the fate of two of the camps—Dachau in Germany, and Auschwitz in Poland. The first is excerpted from the publication *In Everlasting Remembrance,* published by the American Jewish Congress; the second is by William Helmreich, from an article in the book *Living After the Holocaust.*

68.   Dachau: Munich Suburb

It was in Munich that Adolf Hitler made his first bid for power in the abortive beerhall putsch of 1923. It was in Munich that the Nazi Party's monster rallies were held—the boots in goose-step and the shouts of "Sieg Heil." When war came the city was all but destroyed by American B-17's. When war ended, the bombers were replaced by bulldozers and a new city arose, thanks in no small measure to American aid. But some reminders of the old Munich remain. The *Oktoberfest*—the month-long beer festival—still takes place every year. And the village of Dachau still stands, just 10 miles outside the city.

Dachau occupies a special niche in the hierarchy of Nazi concentration camps. It was here that the "medical" experiments were undertaken by German "doctors," among them a research project requested by the German Air Force to study the effects of immersing human beings in freezing water.

Today at Dachau the materials are gone and the concentration camp itself has vanished. In its place are two memorials. One is a set of stone blocks, placed one upon the other, with a Menorah carved on the uppermost stone. Engraved in German, Hebrew, and English is the inscription, "Remember the Victims."

The second memorial to the victims of Dachau is a Carmelite convent known as the Convent of Atonement. Here live 21 nuns who have taken a vow never to leave. The prioress of the convent was a member of the group led by a Jesuit priest, Alfred Delp, one of those executed by the Nazis for his part in the attempt to assassinate Hitler on July 20, 1944.

To enter the outer courtyard of the convent, one walks beneath an old watch tower, within the wall of the camp. The convent itself is new; each nun has her own cell.

Why did the Carmelites put a convent there? They gave this answer: The ground Dachau stood on can never be allowed to return to "normal" use. The convent is there to remind the visitor that when he leaves bright and busy Munich and arrives at Dachau, he is in another world.

69. A Visit to Auschwitz
William Helmreich

In the summer of 1972 I had the opportunity to travel through Poland. There I visited Auschwitz. As I got off the steps of the train I noticed that the supporting poles of the station were painted in alternating red and white stripes like pieces of peppermint candy. The litter baskets were shaped in the form of penguins with their mouths open. The atmosphere was a festive one as people waited for the buses to the camp. (As a matter of fact, one person on the train, a youth of about 20, informed me that the Auschwitz museum was a beautiful and fascinating place to visit.)

Upon arriving at the camp I was surprised to see that much of it had been preserved. The "Arbeit Macht Frei" sign was still there, as were the barracks (that had once housed the inmates) and several crematoria. Barbed wire surrounded the camp. Inside one of the buildings were exhibits behind glass walls showing human hair, articles of clothing, and various other items that had been in the camp storehouses when Auschwitz was liberated. Yet with the exception of one or two small exhibits (i.e., several prayer shawls suspended on what looked like clothes lines) there was little indication that Jews had been there, much less that they had died there in great numbers. . . .

I did not, however, find this nearly as disturbing as the general way in which the Holocaust was treated, an attitude of casualness and callousness that was impossible to miss. A hotel and two restaurants have been built on the premises of the camp. A souvenir stand sold pennants depicting the prison uniform on one side and a drawing of a guard looking out over a barbed wire enclosure on the other. Picture postcards and lapel pins were also available. Little children ran through the halls of a building laughing, shouting, and playing ball where ghastly medical experiments had once been performed. Inside another building were some teenage youths leaning out of a window and listening to popular music on a radio. In general people appeared to regard their visit to the camp as a family outing and a pleasurable experience. As I walked past one of the crematoria I stopped short. A woman of about 60 with a *babushka* on her head had clambered into the crematorium. She smiled broadly as a child of about 12 took her picture. At this point, I left the camp as quickly as possible.

IV

VI

COULD IT HAPPEN AGAIN?

"Political analysts talk of nuclear holocaust. Racism, fascism, totalitarian dictatorship, complicity, passivity: words heavy with past significance which explains their impact on your comrades. By criticizing regimes, they indite yesterday's corruption. That is why it is important to put society on trial, this society which was and still is ours. By scorning its defenders, you place yourself on the side of the victims."

—ELIE WIESEL
"To A Young Jew of Today"

PARALLELS IN LITERATURE AND LIFE

In this final section, we ask the reader to consider whether events similar to the Holocaust have occurred or could ever occur again. Specifically, could another innocent people be singled out for mass destruction while the rest of the world closes its eyes to what it would rather not see? Could another crazed fanatic seek—and achieve—total domination over millions of compliant subjects?

While there has been nothing in history to equal the dimensions of the Holocaust, movements like Nazism and attempts to wipe out entire groups of people have taken place— may even be taking place now.

In 1932, just as Hitler was beginning his rise to power, Aldous Huxley wrote a book of science fiction that turned out to be amazingly prophetic. As you read this excerpt from *Brave New World*, try to find parallels between the controlled society that Huxley created from his imagination, and the real policies and programs of the Third Reich.

70. Utopia: The Controlled Society
Aldous Huxley

The room into which the three were ushered was the Controller's study.

"His fordship will be down in a moment." The Gamma butler left them to themselves.

Helmholtz laughed aloud.

"It's more like a caffeine-solution party than a trial," he said, and let himself fall into the most luxurious of the pneumatic arm-chairs. "Cheer up, Bernard," he added, catching sight of his friend's green unhappy face. But Bernard would not be cheered; without answering, without even looking at Helmholtz, he went and sat down on the most uncomfortable chair in the room, carefully chosen in the obscure hope of somehow deprecating the wrath of the higher powers.

The Savage meanwhile wandered restlessly round the room, peering with a vague superficial inquisitiveness at the books in the shelves, at the sound-track rolls and reading machine bobbins in their numbered pigeon-holes. On the table under the window lay a massive volume bound in limp black leather-surrogate, and stamped with large golden T's. He picked it up and opened it. MY LIFE AND WORK, BY OUR FORD. The book had been published at Detroit by the Society for the Propagation of Fordian Knowledge. Idly he turned the pages, read a sentence here, a paragraph there, and had just come to the conclusion that the book didn't interest him, when the door opened, and the Resident World Controller for Western Europe walked briskly into the room.

Mustapha Mond shook hands with all three of them; but it was to the Savage that he addressed himself. "So you don't much like civilization, Mr. Savage," he said.

The Savage looked at him. He had been prepared to lie, to bluster, to remain sullenly unresponsive; but, reassured by the good-humoured intelligence of the Controller's face, he decided to tell the truth, straightforwardly. "No." He shook his head.

Bernard started and looked horrified. What would the Controller think? To be labelled as the friend of a man who said that he didn't like civilization—said it openly and, of all people, to the Controller—it was terrible. "But, John," he began. A look from Mustapha Mond reduced him to an abject silence.

"Of course," the Savage went on to admit, "there are some very nice things. All that music in the air, for instance . . ."

"Sometimes a thousand twangling instruments will hum about my ears and sometimes voices."

The Savage's face lit up with a sudden pleasure. "Have you read it too?" he asked. "I thought nobody knew about that book here, in England."

"Almost nobody. I'm one of the very few. It's prohibited, you see. But as I make the laws here, I can also break them. With impunity, Mr. Marx," he added, turning to Bernard. "Which I'm afraid you *can't* do."

Bernard sank into a yet more hopeless misery.

"But why is it prohibited?" asked the Savage. In the excitement of meeting a man who had read Shakespeare he had momentarily forgotten everything else.

The Controller shrugged his shoulders. "Because it's old; that's the chief reason. We haven't any use for old things here."

"Even when they're beautiful?"

"Particularly when they're beautiful. Beauty's attractive, and we don't want people to be attracted by old things. We want them to like the new ones."

"But the new ones are so stupid and horrible. Those plays, where there's nothing but helicopters flying about and you *feel* the people kissing." He made a grimace. "Goats and monkeys!" Only in Othello's word could he find an adequate vehicle for his contempt and hatred.

"Nice tame animals, anyhow," the Controller murmured parenthetically.

"Why don't you let them see *Othello* instead?"

"I've told you; it's old. Besides, they couldn't understand it."

Yes, that was true. He remembered how Helmholtz had laughed at *Romeo and Juliet*. "Well then," he said, after a pause, "something new that's like *Othello*, and that they could understand."

"That's what we've all been wanting to write," said Helmholtz, breaking a long silence.

"And it's what you never will write," said the Controller. "Because, if it were really like *Othello* nobody could understand it, however new it might be. And if it were new, it couldn't possibly be like *Othello*."

"Why not?"

"Yes, why not?" Helmholtz repeated. He too was forgetting the unpleasant realities of the situation. Green with anxiety and apprehension, only Bernard remembered them; the others ignored him. "Why not?"

"Because our world is not the same as Othello's world. You can't make flivvers without steel—and you can't make tragedies without social instability. The world's stable now. People are happy; they get what they want, and they never want what they can't get. They're well off; they're safe; they're never ill; they're not afraid of death; they're blissfully ignorant of passion and old age; they're plagued with no mothers or fathers; they've got no wives, or children, or lovers to feel strongly about; they're so conditioned that they practically can't help behaving as they ought to behave. And if anything should go wrong, there's *soma*. Which you go and chuck out of the window in the name of liberty, Mr. Savage. *Liberty!*" He laughed. "Expecting Deltas to know what liberty is! And now expecting them to understand *Othello!* My good boy!"

The Savage was silent for a little. "All the same," he insisted obstinately, *"Othello's* good, *Othello's* better than those feelies."

"Of course it is," the Controller agreed. "But that's the price we have to pay for stability. You've got to choose between happiness and what people used to call high art. We've sacrificed the high art. We have the feelies and the scent organ instead."

"But they don't mean anything."

"They mean themselves; they mean a lot of agreeable sensations to the audience."

"But they're . . . they're told by an idiot."

The Controller laughed. "You're not being very polite to your friend, Mr. Watson. One of our most distinguished Emotional Engineers . . ."

"But he's right," said Helmholtz gloomily. "Because it *is* idiotic. Writing when there's nothing to say . . ."

"Precisely. But that requires the most enormous ingenuity. You're making flivvers out of the absolute minimum of steel—works of art out of practically nothing but pure sensation."

The Savage shook his head. "It all seems to me quite horrible."

"Of course it does. Actual happiness always looks pretty squalid in comparison with the over-compensations for misery. And, of course, stability isn't nearly so spectacular as instability. And being contented has none of the glamour of a good fight against misfortune, none of the picturesqueness of a struggle with temptation, or a fatal overthrow by passion or doubt. Happiness is never grand."

"I suppose not," said the Savage after a silence. "But need it be quite so bad as those twins?" He passed his hand over his eyes as though he were trying to wipe away the remembered image of those long rows of identical midgets at the assembling tables, those queued-up twin-herds at the entrance to the Brentford monorail station, those human maggots swarming round Linda's bed of death, the endlessly repeated face of his assailants. He looked at his bandaged left hand and shuddered. "Horrible!"

"But how useful! I see you don't like our Bokanovsky Groups; but, I assure you, they're the foundation on which everything else is built. They're the gyroscope that stabilizes the rocket plane of state on its unswerving course." The deep voice thrillingly vibrated; the gesticulating hand implied all space and the onrush of the irresistible machine. Mustapha Mond's oratory was almost up to synthetic standards.

"I was wondering," said the Savage, "why you had them at all—seeing that you can get whatever you want out of those bottles. Why don't you make everybody an Alpha Double Plus while you're about it?"

Mustapha Mond laughed. "Because we have no wish to have our throats cut," he answered. "We believe in happiness and stability. A society of Alphas couldn't fail to be unstable and miserable. Imagine a factory staffed by Alphas—that is to say by separate and unrelated individuals of good heredity and conditioned so as to be capable (within limits) of making a free choice and assuming responsibilities. Imagine it!" he repeated.

The Savage tried to imagine it, not very successfully.

"It's an absurdity. An Alpha-decanted, Alpha-conditioned man would go mad if he had to do Epsilon Semi-Moron work—go mad, or start smashing things up. Alphas can be completely socialized—but only on condition that you make them do Alpha work. Only an Epsilon can be expected to make Epsilon sacrifices, for the good reason that for him they aren't sacrifices; they're the line of least resistance. His conditioning has laid down rails along which he's got to run. He can't help himself; he's foredoomed. Even after decanting, he's still inside a bottle—an invisible bottle of infantile and embryonic fixations. Each one of us, of course," the Controller meditatively continued, "goes through life inside a bottle. But if we happen to be Alphas, our bottles are, relatively speaking, enormous. We should suffer acutely if we were confined in a narrower space. You cannot pour upper-caste champagne-surrogate into lower-caste bottles. It's obvious theoretically. But it has also been proved in actual practice. The result of the Cyprus experiment was convincing."

"What was that?" asked the Savage.

Mustapha Mond smiled. "Well, you can call it an experiment in rebottling if you like. It began in A.F. 473. The Controllers had the island of Cyprus cleared of all its existing inhabitants and re-colonized with a specially prepared batch of twenty-two thousand Alphas. All agricultural and industrial equipment was handed over to them and they were left to manage their own affairs. The result exactly fulfilled all the theoretical predictions. The land wasn't properly worked; there were strikes in all the factories; the laws were set at naught, orders disobeyed; all the people detailed for a spell of low-grade work were perpetually intriguing for high-grade jobs, and all the people with high-grade jobs were counter-intriguing at all costs to stay where they were. Within six years they were having a first-class civil war. When nineteen out of the twenty-two thousand had been killed, the survivors unanimously petitioned the World Controllers to resume the government of the island. Which they did. And that was the end of the only society of Alphas that the world has ever seen."

The Savage sighed, profoundly.

"The optimum population," said Mustapha Mond, "is modelled on the iceberg—eight-ninths below the water line, one-ninth above."

"And they're happy below the water line?"

"Happier than above it. Happier than your friend here, for example." He pointed.

"In spite of that awful work?"

"Awful? *They* don't find it so. On the contrary, they like it. It's light, it's childishly simple. No strain on the mind or the muscles. Seven and a half hours of mild, unexhausting labour, and then the *soma* ration and games and unrestricted copulation and the feelies. What more can they ask for? True," he added, "they might ask for shorter hours. And of course we could give them shorter hours. Technically, it would be perfectly simple to reduce all lower-caste working hours to three or four a day. But would they be any the happier for that? No, they wouldn't. The experiment was tried, more than a century and a half ago. The whole of Ireland was put on to the four-hour day. What was the result? Unrest and a large increase in the consumption of *soma;* that was all. Those three and a half hours of extra leisure were so far from being a source of happiness, that people felt constrained to take a holiday from them. The Inventions Office is stuffed with plans for labour-saving processes. Thousands of them." Mustapha Mond made a lavish gesture. "And why don't we put them into execution? For the sake of the labourers; it would be sheer cruelty to afflict them with excessive leisure. It's the same with agriculture. We could synthesize every morsel of food, if we wanted to. But we don't. We prefer to keep a third of the population on the land. For their own sakes—because it takes *longer* to get food out of the land than out of a factory. Besides, we have our stability to think of. We don't want to change. Every change is a menace to stability. That's another reason why we're so chary of applying new inventions. Every discovery in pure science is potentially subversive; even science must sometimes be treated as a possible enemy. Yes, even science."

Science? The Savage frowned. He knew the word. But what it exactly signified he could not say. Shakespeare and the old men of the pueblo had never mentioned science, and from Linda he had only gathered the vaguest hints: science was something you made helicopters with, something that caused you to laugh at the Corn Dances, something that prevented you from being wrinkled and losing your teeth. He made a desperate effort to take the Controller's meaning.

"Yes," Mustapha Mond was saying, "that's another item in the cost of stability. It isn't only art that's incompatible with happiness; it's also science. Science is dangerous; we have to keep it most carefully chained and muzzled."

"What?" said Helmholtz, in astonishment. "But we're always saying that science is everything. It's a hypnopædic platitude."

"Three times a week between thirteen and seventeen," put in Bernard.

"And all the science propaganda we do at the College . . ."

"Yes; but what sort of science?" asked Mustapha Mond sarcastically. "You've had no scientific training, so you can't judge. I was a pretty good physicist in my time. Too good—good enough to realize that all our science is just a cookery book, with an orthodox theory of cooking that nobody's allowed to question, and a list of recipes that mustn't be added to except by special permission from the head cook. I'm the head cook now. But I was an inquisitive young scullion once. I started doing a bit of cooking on my own. Unorthodox cooking, illicit cooking. A bit of real science, in fact." He was silent.

"What happened?" asked Helmholtz Watson.

The Controller sighed. "Very nearly what's going to happen to you young men. I was on the point of being sent to an island."

Another kind of totalitarian society was created by George Orwell in his novel *1984*, published after World War II and no doubt influenced by it. This society was the opposite of the world of perfect contentment depicted in Huxley's book. In Orwell's world, man is controlled so as to heighten his worst characteristics.

71. The All-Powerful State
George Orwell

"How does one man assert his power over another, Winston?"

Winston thought. "By making him suffer," he said.

"Exactly. By making him suffer. Obedience is not enough. Unless he is suffering, how can you be sure that he is obeying your will and not his own? Power is in inflicting pain and humiliation. Power is in tearing human minds to pieces and putting them together again in new shapes of your own choosing. Do you begin to see, then, what kind of world we are creating? It is the exact opposite of the stupid hedonistic Utopias that the old reformers imagined. A world of fear and treachery and torment, a world of trampling and being trampled upon, a world which will grow not less but *more* merciless as it refines itself. Progress in our world will be progress toward more pain. The old civilizations claimed that they were founded on love and justice. Ours is founded upon hatred. In our world there will be no emotions except fear, rage, triumph, and self-abasement. Everything else we shall destroy— everything. Already we are breaking down the habits of thought which have survived from before the Revolution. We have cut the links between child and parent, and between man and man, and between man and woman. No one dares trust a wife or a child or a friend any longer. But in the future there will be no wives and no friends. Children will be taken from their mothers at birth, as one takes eggs from a hen. The sex instinct will be eradicated. Procreation will be an annual formality like the renewal of a ration card. We shall abolish the orgasm. Our neurologists are at work upon it now. There will be no loyalty, except loyalty toward the Party. There will be no love, except the love of Big Brother. There will be no laughter, except the laugh of triumph over a defeated enemy. There will be no art, no literature, no science. When we are omnipotent we shall have no more need of science. There will be no distinction between beauty and ugliness. There will be no curiosity, no employment of the process of life. All competing pleasures will be destroyed. But always—do not forget this, Winston—always there will be the intoxication of power, constantly increasing and constantly growing subtler. Always, at every moment, there will be the thrill of victory, the sensation of trampling on an enemy who is helpless. If you want a picture of the future, imagine a boot stamping on a human face—forever."

He paused as though he expected Winston to speak. Winston had tried to shrink back into the surface of the bed again. He could not say anything. His heart seemed to be frozen. O'Brien went on:

"And remember that it is forever. The face will always be there to be stamped upon. The heretic, the enemy of society, will always be there, so that he can be defeated and humiliated over again. Everything that you have undergone since you have been in our hands —all that will continue, and worse. The espionage, the betrayals, the arrests, the tortures, the executions, the disappearances will never cease. It will be a world of terror as much as a world of triumph. The more the Party is powerful, the less it will be tolerant; the weaker the opposition, the tighter the despotism. Goldstein and his heresies will live forever. Every day, at every moment, they will be defeated, discredited, ridiculed, spat upon—and yet they will always survive. This drama that I have played out with you during seven years will be played out over and over again, generation after generation, always in subtler forms. Always we shall have the heretic here at our mercy, screaming with pain, broken up, contemptible—and in the end utterly penitent, saved from himself, crawling to our feet of his own accord. That is the world that we are preparing, Winston. A world of victory after victory, triumph after triumph after triumph: an endless pressing, pressing, pressing upon the nerve of power. You are beginning, I can see, to realize what that world will be like. But in the end you will do more than understand it. You will accept it, welcome it, become part of it."

As long as people can experience and suffer the pain of others, there may be hope. Yevgeny Yevtushenko, a Russian poet, a non-Jew, wrote this poem as an anguished protest —mourning an episode that took place in the past, and crying out against anti-Semitism.

Babi Yar is the name of a ravine near Kiev, in the U.S.S.R., where many thousands of Jews were massacred by the German army dur-

ing World War II. After years of delay——35, to
be exact——a monument was erected with the
following inscription on it:

> Here in 1941–1943, the German Fascist invaders
> executed over 100,000 citizens of Kiev and prisoners
> of war.

As the Jews of Russia are persecuted in their
lives, so the dead Jews of Kiev are denied their
identity as martyrs. They were massacred not as
"citizens of Kiev," but as Jews.

72. Babi Yar

Yevgeny Yevtushenko

No monument stands over Babi Yar.
A drop sheer as a crude gravestone.
I am afraid.
        Today I am as old in years
as all the Jewish people.
Now I seem to be
        a Jew.
Here I plod through ancient Egypt.
Here I perish crucified, on the cross,
and to this day I bear the scars of nails.
I seem to be
        Dreyfus.
The Philistine
        is both informer and judge.
I am behind bars.
        Beset on every side.
Hounded,
        spat on,
        slandered.
Squealing, dainty ladies in flounced Brussels lace
stick their parasols into my face.
I seem to be then
        a young boy in Byelostok.
Blood runs, spilling over the floors.

The bar-room rabble-rousers
give off a stench of vodka and onion.
A boot kicks me aside, helpless.
In vain I plead with these pogrom bullies.
While they jeer and shout,
                              "Beat the Yids. Save Russia!"
some grain-marketeer beats up my mother.
O my Russian people!
                    I know
                           you
are international to the core.
But those with unclean hands
have often made a jingle of your purest name.
I know the goodness of my land.
How vile these anti-Semites—
                              without a qualm
they pompously called themselves
"The Union of the Russian People"!
I seem to be
            Anne Frank
transparent
           as a branch in April.
And I love.
           And have no need of phrases.
My need
        is that we gaze into each other.
How little we can see
                     or smell!
We are denied the leaves,
                          we are denied the sky.
Yet we can do so much—
                        tenderly
embrace each other in a dark room.
They're coming here?
                    Be not afraid. Those are the booming
sounds of spring:
                  spring is coming here.
Come then to me.
                Quick, give me your lips.
Are they smashing down the door?
                                No, it's the ice breaking . . .

The wild grasses rustle over Babi Yar.
The trees look ominous,
               like judges.
Here all things scream silently,
                  and, baring my head,
slowly I feel myself
              turning gray.
And I myself
           am one massive, soundless scream
above the thousand thousand buried here.
I am
    each old man
             here shot dead.
I am
    every child
           here shot dead.
Nothing in me
        shall ever forget!
The "Internationale," let it
             thunder
when the last anti-Semite on earth
is buried forever.
In my blood there is no Jewish blood.
In their callous rage, all anti-Semites
must hate me now as a Jew.
For that reason
         I am a true Russian!

Claude McKay, one of eleven children of a Jamaican farmer, distinguished himself as a novelist, short story writer, and poet. He became the first Black man awarded the medal of the Institute of Arts and Sciences in Jamaica in 1912. In the 1920s he was a prominent figure in the Harlem Renaissance and in the American radical press. The bulk of his work, of course, was given over to the Black experience. This poem, written out of that background, could speak for the anguish of an inmate in a concentration camp or a Jew in the Warsaw ghetto.

73.   If We Must Die

Claude McKay

If we must die—let it not be like hogs
Hunted and penned in an inglorious spot,
While round us bark the mad and hungry dogs,
Making their mock at our accursed lot.
If we must die—oh, let us nobly die,
So that our precious blood may not be shed
In vain; then even the monsters we defy
Shall be constrained to honor us though dead!
Oh, Kinsmen! We must meet the common foe;
Though far outnumbered, let us show us brave,
And for their thousand blows deal one death-
    blow!
What though before us lies the open grave?
Like men we'll face the murderous, cowardly
    pack,
Pressed to the wall, dying, but fighting back!

The following two selections present views about human behavior that certainly can be applied to Nazi Germany, but that have relevance to our own society as well.

Arthur Koestler, in an excerpt from his book *Darkness at Noon*, argues that a humane society is impossible because political leaders will always sacrifice the individual to the needs and goals of the larger group.

Eric Hoffer, in an excerpt from the book *The True Believer*, describes how easily people become true believers, in any doctrine, and then block out everything that contradicts the truth they have accepted. This view clearly

agrees with what we know about the behavior
of the German people (and others) under Hitler.

74. Why There Has Never Been a Humane Society

Arthur Koestler

"There are only two conceptions of human ethics,
and they are at opposite poles. One of them is Christian
and humane, declares the individual to be sacrosanct,
and asserts that the rules of arithmetic are not to be
applied to human units. The other starts from the basic
principle that a collective aim justifies all means, and
not only allows, but demands, that the individual
should in every way be subordinated and sacrificed to
the community—which may dispose of it as an ex-
perimentation rabbit or a sacrificial lamb. The first
conception could be called anti-vivisection morality,
the second, vivisection morality. Humbugs and dilet-
tantes have always tried to mix the two conceptions;
in practice, it is impossible. Whoever is burdened with
power and responsibility finds out on the first occasion
that he has to choose; and he is fatally driven to the
second alternative. Do you know, since the establishment of Christianity as a state religion, a single example
of a state which really followed a Christian policy?
You can't point out one. In times of need—and politics are chronically in a time of need—the rulers were
always able to evoke 'exceptional circumstances,' which
demanded exceptional measures of defense. Since the
existence of nations and classes, they live in a permanent state of mutual self-defense, which forces them to
defer to another time the putting into practice of hu-
manism. . . ."

75. On Blind Faith

Eric Hoffer

The readiness for self-sacrifice is contingent on an imperviousness to the realities of life. He who is free to draw conclusions from his individual experience and observation is not usually hospitable to the idea of martyrdom. For self-sacrifice is an unreasonable act. It cannot be the end-product of a process of probing and deliberating. All active mass movements strive, therefore, to interpose a fact-proof screen between the faithful and the realities of the world. They do this by claiming that the ultimate and absolute truth is already embodied in their doctrine and that there is no truth nor certitude outside it. The facts on which the true believer bases his conclusions must not be derived from his experience or observation but from holy writ. "So tenaciously should we cling to the world revealed by the Gospel, that were I to see all the Angels of Heaven coming down to me to tell me something different, not only would I not be tempted to doubt a single syllable, but I would shut my eyes and stop my ears, for they would not deserve to be either seen or heard." To rely on the evidence of the senses and of reason is heresy and treason. It is startling to realize how much unbelief is necessary to make belief possible. What we know as blind faith is sustained by innumerable unbeliefs. The fanatical Japanese in Brazil refused to believe for years the evidence of Japan's defeat. The fanatical Communist refuses to believe any unfavorable report or evidence about Russia, nor will he be disillusioned by seeing with his own eyes the cruel misery inside the Soviet promised land.

It is the true believer's ability to "shut his eyes and stop his ears" to facts that do not deserve to be either seen or heard which is the source of his unequaled fortitude and constancy. He cannot be frightened by danger nor disheartened by obstacle nor baffled by contradictions because he denies their existence. Strength of faith, as Bergson pointed out, manifests itself not in moving mountains but in not seeing mountains to move. And it is the certitude of his infallible doctrine that renders the true believer impervious to the uncertainties, surprises and the unpleasant realities of the world around him.

Thus the effectiveness of a doctrine should not be judged by its profundity, sublimity or the validity of the truths it embodies, but by how thoroughly it insulates the individual from his self and the world as it is. What Pascal said of an effective religion is true of any effective doctrine: It must be "contrary to nature, to common sense and to pleasure."

———————————

Jacob Stroyer, once a slave himself, wrote about the experience of slavery in the United States in a series of volumes entitled *Sketches of My Life in the South*. This selection describes in moving terms the departure of a group of slaves who have been sold to new masters in Louisiana. Stroyer's depiction of this scene is a haunting parallel to the accounts of Jews who were rounded up and deported to concentration camps.

76. Sold to Louisiana

Jacob Stroyer

. . . the victims were to take the cars from a station called Clarkson turnout, which was about four miles from master's place. The excitement was so great that the overseer and driver could not control the relatives and friends of those that were going away, as a large crowd of both old and young went down to the depot to see them off. Louisiana was considered by the slaves as a place of slaughter, so those who were going did not expect to see their friends again. While passing along, many of the Negroes left their master's fields and joined us as we marched to the cars; some were yelling and wringing their hands, while others were singing little hymns that they were accustomed to for the consolation of those that were going away, such as,

> *When we all meet in heaven,*
> *There is no parting there;*
> *When we all meet in heaven,*
> *There is parting no more.*

We arrived at the depot and had to wait for the cars to bring the others from the Sumterville Jail, but they soon came in sight, and when the noise of the cars died away we heard wailing and shrieks from those in the cars. While some were weeping, others were fiddling, picking banjo, and dancing as they used to do in their cabins on the plantations. Those who were so merry had very bad masters, and even though they stood a chance of being sold to one as bad or even worse yet they were glad to be rid of the one they knew.

While the cars were at the depot, a large crowd of white people gathered, and were laughing and talking about the prospect of Negro traffic; but when the cars began to start and the conductor cried out, "all who are going on this train must get aboard without delay," the colored people cried out with one voice as though the heavens and earth were coming together, and it was so pitiful, that those hardhearted white men who had been accustomed to driving slaves all their lives, shed tears like children. As the cars moved away we heard the weeping and wailing from the slaves, as far as human voice could be heard; and from that time to the present I have neither seen nor heard from my two sisters, nor any of those who left Clarkson depot, on that memorable day.

From fiction and philosophy to fact. Tragedies, smaller in scope, but similar in other respects to the Holocaust, have taken place in recent history. This article reprinted from *Newsweek* Magazine, July 2, 1973, describes events, chillingly familiar, that happened in the early 1970s.

77. Slaughter of the Innocents
Newsweek

In terms of sheer brutality, few events in post-World War II history can equal the massacre that took place last year in the beautiful central African republic of Burundi. At that time, members of the Bahutu tribe, which makes up 85 percent of the country's population, rose up against the towering Watutsi overlords who have dominated them for centuries. The insurrection failed, and the "Tutsi" government of Col. Michel Micombero exacted a frightful vengeance—slaughtering up to 250,000 "Hutu" men, women and children. Some died from bullets or razor-sharp *panga* knives; others from long nails driven through their heads. Finally, the Tutsis' blood lust was sated and the killings came to an end. But last month, the Tutsis resumed the pogrom against their onetime vassals with a ferocity that smacks of outright genocide.

Once again, the murderous round of fighting was sparked by a Hutu rebellion, this one hatched in the refugee camps at Tabora and Kigoma in neighboring Tanzania. The Hutu strategy called for a three-pronged invasion—from Tanzania, Zaïre and Rwanda—and the seizure of the Burundian capital of Bujumbura. In order to instill the spirit of bravery in their Hutu followers, the organizers of the venture—students just back from France and Belgium—asked Zaïrois witch doctors to administer potions that were supposed to render the recipients immune to harm from bullets. The signal for the attack was given and on May 12 some 4,000 ill-equipped Hutus marched across the border. But the magic potions apparently failed, and soon the outgunned Hutus were fleeing for their lives. It was then that the latest slaughter of innocent Hutus began.

Entrusted to carry out the blood bath this time was the *"Jeunesse Révolutionnaire,"* an ill-disciplined paramilitary group of young men attached to Micombero's ruling party. Armed with machetes, spears and guns, they have been roaming the countryside, burning Hutu villages and murdering Hutus whenever they are found. Witnesses coming from Burundi report seeing open mass graves in Bujumbura and truckloads of bodies in the town of Gitega. Best estimates are that some 10,000 Hutus have been killed so far in the current outbreak—and the massacre is not yet over.

Not all of the Hutus have gone meekly to their death. Many thousands of them have fled to U.N.-administered refugee camps in neighboring countries, chiefly Tanzania. And in those squalid camps, the scenes of human misery are appalling. At the camp in Tabora last week, one 80-year-old Hutu woman stared blankly as doctors cleaned off the stump that once was her hand; before letting her cross the border, the Tutsis had hacked it off. And at Kigoma, 225 miles to the west, another exhausted Hutu woman arrived with two babies strapped to her back. When they were untied by the Portuguese nurse, it was discovered that one of the babies was dead, its spine crushed by a Tutsi spear. "The refugees tell me," says the Rev. Ramón Vicens, a Catholic priest who heads a mission in Tanzania, "that women and girls had their bellies opened and breasts cut off. Pregnant women had their children cut out and left for dead by their sides."

The savage repression of the Hutus is in one way even worse than last year's. Then, the Tutsi government appeared to be selective in its campaign of murder, killing only the educated or influential Hutus. This year, the killing is indiscriminate, and officials in Rwanda—where the Hutus are in control—charge that Burundi has embarked on a program of calculated genocide. They insist that a secret Burundian document known as the "Simbananiye White Paper" specifically calls for the elimination of the "surplus" Hutu population in order to achieve numerical parity between the Tutsis (600,000) and the Hutus (3.6 million)—a parity that would require nothing short of an African holocaust. "Micombero," says one Hutu exile, "is a madman."

Madman or not, Micombero is once again shedding the blood of thousands of innocent people. And once again, the international community—including the major powers, the United Nations and the Organization of African States—appears to be helpless or even indifferent to the tragedy of the Hutus.

The Armenians were the victims of genocide in 1915—almost thirty years before the term was coined. The Armenians, who have lived around Mount Ararat since before recorded history, share a common language, culture, and church—they were the first nation to adapt Christianity. Although they had been conquered by many empires, they were especially oppressed—and many times massacred—under the Ottoman Empire (now Turkey) in the nineteenth century.

The motives of the leaders who ordered their death may be compared to those of the Nazi leaders who authorized the extermination of the Jews. Following the 1908 victory of the Young Turks, a faction among them, who seized power in 1913, espoused the doctrine of Pan-Turanianism, a formula for justifying the domination of the Turks over the non-Turkic peoples (who were also non-Muslim and had been only tolerated by tradition). The Turkish government, soon after it entered World War I as Germany's ally, ordered the extermination of the Armenian minority. The government used the opportunity the war presented them with—lack of observation by and immunity of sanctions from the Allies—to conceal their crime, just as Hitler used World War II to conceal the "Final Solution." Like Hitler, the men who ordered the Armenians slain labeled their victims as enemies who were planning to attack them. After World War I, the ruling junta authorizing the genocide fled, but their successors were responsible for the massacre of Greek Christians in Smyrna in 1922.

The following passages are taken from *Accounting for Genocide: National Responses and Jewish Victimization During the Holocaust* by Helen Fein (New York: The Free Press, 1978).

78. The Armenians: An Example of Genocide

Helen Fein

There was never any doubt as to who the victims were; no need to require their registration as Jews were registered in Germany in 1935. Their identity was known to tax collectors, public officials, and neighbors. The campaign began with measures to strip them of the means to resist and to segregate them sexually. Armenians were ordered to hand in their weapons, and they usually hastened to find weapons to hand in even if they had to buy them, for fear that charges of noncooperation would be brought, used as evidence of disloyalty, and then employed to provoke violence against them. Armenian men in the army were segregated into special units ("labor battalions"), disarmed, and later slain. On the night of 24 April, some 1,000 prominent Armenians were arrested in the capital and secretly murdered, leaving the others numbed by terror. The remaining males in each village were summoned by the town crier to report immediately, 'led out of town, and slain. Women, children, and a few infirm males previously exempted were then bidden by the crier to prepare themselves for deportation. They were driven into the desert by soldiers, staggering along until they dropped from drought, starvation, the lash, or their festering wounds. Women might elect or be selected to become wives of Muslims, thus gaining exemption but also requiring them to part with their children. The military was aided by surrounding Kurdish and Circassian tribesmen who looted and raped the women, kidnapping a few favorites and murdering many. For months, packs of bedraggled survivors wound through the deserts of western Asia until they fell or were slain. Toynbee, assessing all the evidence, estimated that two thirds of the 1,800,000 Armenians in the Ottoman Empire in 1914 were annihilated or deported to the desert.

———

The internment of civilian west coast Japanese and Japanese Americans in World War II was not one of America's proudest moments. In the spring of 1942, through an Act of Congress, a series of evacuation orders were issued designating the western half of the states of Washington and Oregon, the entire state of California, and a portion of Arizona a military defense zone from which anybody of Japanese descent, even "one-sixteenth of Japanese blood," had to remove himself. Many Japanese were sent to barbed wire enclosed internment centers. One Japanese-American, Gordon Kiyoshi Hirabayashi, convicted of violating the restrictions, appealed the conviction to the U.S. Supreme Court, where he lost. In his comment on the case, Justice Frank Murphy noted: "In this sense it bears a melancholy resemblance to the treatment accorded to members of the Jewish race in Germany and in other parts of Europe."

79. Instructions To All Persons of Japanese Ancestry

**WESTERN DEFENSE COMMAND AND FOURTH ARMY
WARTIME CIVIL CONTROL ADMINISTRATION**
Presidio of San Francisco, California
May 3, 1942
INSTRUCTIONS
TO ALL PERSONS OF
JAPANESE
ANCESTRY
Living in the Following Area:

All of that portion of the City of Los Angeles, State of California, within that boundary beginning at the point at which North Figueroa Street meets a line following the middle of the Los Angeles River; thence southerly and following the said line to East First Street; thence westerly on East First Street to Alameda Street; thence southerly on Alameda Street to East Third Street; thence northwesterly on East Third Street to Main Street; thence northerly on Main Street to First Street; thence northwesterly on First Street to Figueroa Street; thence northeasterly on Figueroa Street to the point of beginning.

Pursuant to the provisions of Civilian Exclusion Order No. 33, this Headquarters, dated May 3, 1942, all persons of Japanese ancestry, both alien and non-alien, will be evacuated from the above area by 12 o'clock noon, P. W. T., Saturday, May 9, 1942.

No Japanese person living in the above area will be permitted to change residence after 12 o'clock noon, P. W. T., Sunday, May 3, 1942, without obtaining special permission from the representative of the Commanding General, Southern California Sector, at the Civil Control Station located at:

Japanese Union Church,
120 North San Pedro Street,
Los Angeles, California.

Such permits will only be granted for the purpose of uniting members of a family, or in cases of grave emergency.

The Civil Control Station is equipped to assist the Japanese population affected by this evacuation in the following ways:

1. Give advice and instructions on the evacuation.

2. Provide services with respect to the management, leasing, sale, storage or other disposition of most kinds of property, such as real estate, business and professional equipment, household goods, boats, automobiles and livestock.

3. Provide temporary residence elsewhere for all Japanese in family groups.

4. Transport persons and a limited amount of clothing and equipment to their new residence.

The Following Instructions Must Be Observed:

1. A responsible member of each family, preferably the head of the family, or the person in whose name most of the property is held, and each individual living alone, will report to the Civil Control Station to receive further instructions. This must be done between 8.00 A.M. and 5:00 P.M. on Monday, May 4, 1942, or between 8:00 A.M. and 5:00 P.M. on Tuesday, May 5, 1942.

2. Evacuees must carry with them on departure for the Assembly Center, the following property:
    (a) Bedding and linens (no mattress) for each member of the family;
    (b) Toilet articles for each member of the family;
    (c) Extra clothing for each member of the family;
    (d) Sufficient knives, forks, spoons, plates, bowls and cups for each member of the family;
    (e) Essential personal effects for each member of the family.

All items carried will be securely packaged, tied and plainly marked with the name of the owner and numbered in accordance with instructions obtained at the Civil Control Station. The size and number of packages is limited to that which can be carried by the individual or family group.

3. No pets of any kind will be permitted.

4. No personal items and no household goods will be shipped to the Assembly Center.

5. The United States Government through its agencies will provide for the storage, at the sole risk of the owner, of the more substantial household items, such as iceboxes, washing machines, pianos and other heavy furniture. Cooking utensils and other small items will be accepted for storage if crated, packed and plainly marked with the name and address of the owner. Only one name and address will be used by a given family.

6. Each family, and individual living alone, will be furnished transportation to the Assembly Center or will be authorized to travel by private automobile in a supervised group. All instructions pertaining to the movement will be obtained at the Civil Control Station.

Go to the Civil Control Station between the hours of 8:00 A.M. and 5:00 P.M., Monday, May 4, 1942, or between the hours of 8:00 A.M. and 5:00 P.M., Tuesday, May 5, 1942, to receive further instructions.

> J. L. DeWITT
> Lieutenant General, U. S. Army
> Commanding

SEE CIVILIAN EXCLUSION ORDER NO. 33.

---

80. Kiyoshi Hirabayashi v. United States

Supreme Court Decision

An Executive Order has given a military commander the right to designate a military area and make restrictions to govern this area. The Act of Congress of March 21, 1942, makes it a misdemeanor to knowingly disregard these restrictions. Gordon Kiyoshi Hirabayashi was convicted in the District Court (California) of violating the Act of Congress. The decision was appealed and the judgment of conviction affirmed.

The particular restriction presently being discussed states that all persons of Japanese ancestry residing in the military area must be within their place of residence daily between the hours of 8:00 P.M. and 6:00 A.M. It has been contended that the curfew order and other orders on which it rested were beyond the war powers of the Congress, the military authorities and of the President (as Commander in Chief of the Army). It is also being questioned whether the restriction violated the Fifth Amendment by unconstitutionally discriminating between citizens of Japanese ancestry and those of other ancestries.

Gordon Kiyoshi Hirabayashi (appellant) asserted that the indictment should be dismissed because he was an American citizen who had never been a subject of and had never pledged allegiance to the Empire of Japan. In addition, the Act of March 21, 1942, was thought to be an unconstitutional delegation of Congressional power.

The appellant was born in Seattle in 1918 of Japanese parents who had come from Japan to the United States, and who had never afterward returned to Japan. He was educated in the Washington public schools and at the time of his arrest was a senior in the University of Washington. It was also maintained that Mr. Hirabayashi had never been in Japan or had any association with Japanese residing there.

Gordon Kiyoshi Hirabayashi felt that he would be giving up his rights as an American citizen in obeying the curfew imposed by the military commander. For this reason he was away from his place of residence after 8:00 P.M. on May 9, 1942. The jury returned a verdict of guilty on both counts: 1) failure to report to the Civil Control Station on May 11 or May 12, 1942, to register for evacuation from the military area, and 2) failure to remain in his place of residence from 8:00 P.M. to 6:00 A.M. Hirabayashi was sentenced to imprisonment for a term of three months on each, the sentences to run at the same time.

Certain social, economic and political conditions existed when the Japanese came to the United States. These conditions are believed to have caused the Japanese to stick together and prevented their assimilation as a part of the white population. In addition, large numbers of children of Japanese parentage are sent to Japanese language schools after public school is over.

Some of these schools are thought to be sources of Japanese nationalistic propaganda, encouraging the children to pledge allegiance to Japan. Considerable numbers, estimated to be approximately 10,000, of American-born children of Japanese parentage have been sent to Japan for all or part of their education.

As a result of all these conditions affecting the life of the Japanese in the Pacific Coast Area, there has been little social intercourse between them and the white population. Because persons of Japanese ancestry have been faced with many restrictions while residing in the United States, they may have become more isolated from the rest of the population and more attached to Japan and Japanese institutions.

The Executive Order permitted establishment of military areas for the purpose of protecting national defense resources from sabotage and espionage. The Act of Congress ratified this Executive Order. Both were an exercise of constitutional power to wage war. Once the Executive and Congress have this power, they also have the freedom to use their own judgment in determining what the threat is and how it can be resisted. A court should not decide whether the Executive and/or Congress did the right thing nor should a court substitute its own judgment for that of the Executive or Congress.

Measures adopted by the Government may point out that a group of one nationality is more dangerous to the country's safety than any other group. This is not entirely beyond the limits of the Constitution and should not be condemned just because racial differences are usually irrelevant.

Appellant, however, insists that the exercise of the power is inappropriate and unconstitutional because it discriminates against citizens of Japanese ancestry, in violation of the Fifth Amendment.

Distinctions between citizens solely because of their ancestry are hateful to a free people whose institutions are founded upon equality. For that reason, discrimination based on race alone has often been considered a denial of equal protection. These considerations would be in effect here were it not for the fact that the danger of espionage and sabotage makes it necessary for the military authorities to look into every fact having to do with the loyalty of populations in the danger areas.

Mr. Justice Frank Murphy concurring statement

Distinctions based on color and ancestry are utterly inconsistent with our traditions and ideals. They are at variance with the principles for which we are now waging war. We cannot close our eyes to the fact that for centuries the Old World has been torn by racial and religious conflicts and has suffered the worst kind of anguish because of inequality of treatment for different groups. There was one law for one and a different law for another. Nothing is written more firmly into our law than the compact of the Plymouth voyagers to have just and equal laws. To say that any group cannot be assimilated is to admit that the great American experience has failed, that our way of life has failed when confronted with the normal attachment of certain groups to the lands of their forefathers. As a nation we embrace many groups, some of them among the oldest settlements in our midst, which have isolated themselves for religious and cultural reasons.

Today is the first time, so far as I am aware, that we have sustained a substantial restriction of the personal liberty of citizens of the United States based upon the accident of race or ancestry. Under the curfew order here challenged no less than 70,000 American citizens have been placed under a special ban and deprived of their liberty because of their particular racial inheritance. In this sense it bears a melancholy resemblance to the treatment accorded to members of the Jewish race in Germany and in other parts of Europe. The result is the creation in this country of two classes of citizens for purposes of a critical and perilous hour—to sanction discrimination between groups of United States citizens on the basis of ancestry. In my opinion this goes to the very brink of constitutional power.

Except under condition of great emergency a regulation of this kind appplicable solely to citizens of a particular racial extraction would not be regarded as in accord with the requirement of due process of law contained in the Fifth Amendment.

. . . a denial of due process of law as that term is used in the Fifth Amendment. I think that point is dangerously approached when we have one law for the majority of our citizens and another for those of a particular racial heritage.

Nor do I mean to intimate that citizens of a particular racial group whose freedom may be curtailed within an area threatened with attack should be generally prevented from leaving the area and going at large in other areas that are not in danger of attack and where special precautions are not needed. Their status as citizens, though subject to requirements of national security and military necessity, should at all times be accorded the fullest consideration and respect. When the danger is past, the restrictions imposed on them should be promptly removed and their freedom of action fully restored.

In his excellent book, *Crisis in Black and White*, Charles E. Silberman, the distinguished journalist and teacher, draws an unsparing and cogent analogy between the traumas suffered by Africans at the hands of the slave traders and the appalling experiences of prisoners in concentration camps. This selection speaks for itself.

81. The Greatest Trauma of All
Charles Silberman

What happened to transform the heroic African into the submissive slave?

For one thing, the process of enslavement subjected the African to a series of traumas that tended to sever him from his culture and institutions and destroy his sense of identity. First, there was the physical torment of the long march to the sea from the point of capture: tied together by their necks, the slaves walked barefoot for weeks through the steaming jungles; those who wearied were abandoned to die a slow death by starvation. (The British abolitionist Thomas Fowell Buxton wrote of having seen hundreds of skeletons lining one of the caravan routes.) Arriving at a coastal trading port, the slaves were subject to the further shock of being exhibited naked to the European slave traders. The slaves who were bought were branded like cattle and, like cattle, herded on shipboard; those considered unfit or undesirable were abandoned to starve to death.

Then began the greatest trauma of all: the dread Middle Passage, a trip so brutal that only an age which has been debased by the existence of the Nazi crematoria could believe it really happened. Here is one description:

> . . . The height, sometimes, between decks, was only eighteen inches; so that the unfortunate human beings could not turn around, or even on their sides, the elevation being less than the breadth of their shoulders; and here they are usually chained to the decks by the neck and legs. In such a place the sense of misery and suffocation is so great that the Negroes . . . are driven to frenzy. They [the slave traders] had on one occasion taken a slave vessel in the river Bonny: the slaves were stowed in the narrow space between decks, and chained together. They heard a horrid din and tumult among them, and could not imagine from what cause it proceeded. They opened the hatches and turned them up on deck. [The Negroes] were manacled together, in twos and threes. Their horror may be well conceived, when they found a number of [Negroes] in different stages of suffocation; many of them were foaming at the mouth, and in the last agonies— many were dead. The tumult they had heard was

the frenzy of those suffocating wretches in the last stage of fury and desperation, struggling to extricate themselves. When they were all dragged up, 19 were irrecoverably dead. Many destroyed one another, in the hopes of procuring room to breathe; men strangled those next to them, and women drove nails into each other's brains. Many unfortunate creatures, on other occasions, took the first opportunity of leaping overboard, and getting rid, in this way, of an intolerable life.

It is estimated that approximately one-third of the Africans taken prisoner died en route to the coast and at the embarkation station, and that another third died during the Middle Passage and the "seasoning" that followed. Most slaves were landed first in the West Indies, where they were "seasoned" or broken in to their new roles as slaves; only afterward were they transshipped to the United States.

Concentration camp prisoners went through an analogous series of shocks. The first was the shock of "procurement": Gestapo policy was to make arrests at night, to heighten the element of shock, terror, and unreality. A day or two later came the second shock, transportation to the camp, which "involved a planned series of brutalities inflicted by guards making repeated rounds through the train"; prisoners transported in cattle cars were sealed in, under conditions much like those of the Middle Passage. When they arrived at the camp, there were sham ceremonies designed to reassure the prisoners—so that the next round of terrors would have even greater impact. Those not marked for early extermination would go through "registration," filled with indignities, including inspection while naked. (Descriptions of this process in the concentration camps is remarkably similar to descriptions of the inspection of slaves in the 18th century.) In the concentration camp, registration ended with perhaps the most devastating weapon of all: being marked with a number—which symbolized the prisoners' loss of his name, hence of his identity. "Because he . . . had become a number," the psychologist Elie Cohen has written, "the prisoner belonged to the huge army of the nameless who peopled the concentration camp." Without question, the African slave's loss of his own name—slaves were given new names by the traders or by their new masters—was even more devastating, for in preliterate society, a man's name is considered an essential part of his personality. Surely it is significant that the Black Muslims insist on discarding their "slave names" and taking new names instead.

————————

OMINOUS SIGNS

Does history repeat itself? This selection, reprinted from *The New York Times* of September 17, 1976, describes the desperate plight of Indochinese (Vietnamese, Cambodians and Laotians) seeking an escape from communist rule. To people who know the history of the 1930s, these pathetic incidents call to mind vividly the situation of Jews who managed to leave Germany or other countries on board ships or even small boats, only to discover that no government would permit them to land. The best known of these episodes was the voyage of the *St. Louis,* which left Hamburg, Germany, in May 1939 bound for Havana, Cuba. Aboard were 937 Jewish passengers, all with American quota permits and special permits to wait in Cuba while their American visas were being processed. But the Cubans changed their minds, and the ship was forced to cruise aimlessly in the Atlantic while urgent pleas were sent to one government after another. Finally, after 35 days at sea, England, France, Holland, and Belgium agreed to share the refugees between them. Other ships, however, were not so fortunate; some had to return to their ports of origin; others, unseaworthy to begin with, went down at sea.

82. Voyages of the Damned
The Associated Press

Fleeing Indochinese Often Rebuffed by Passing Ships

Bangkok, Thailand, Sept. 16—Ships on the high seas are tending to pass up boatloads of refugees fleeing Indochina as nations in the area become more reluctant to grant them a haven.

Over the last few months, ship captains have discovered that taking on refugees may well mean a great deal of time and money lost in trying to discharge them at one in hospitable port after another.

A Panamanian-registry freighter picked up 31 Vietnamese refugees in the South China Sea more than two months ago. The refugees, refused entry into Singapore and Yemen, are reported still aboard the freighter on their way to Japan after a journey of 16,000 miles.

A group of 33 Cambodians, after having fled to Vietnam in 1975, escaped recently aboard a fishing smack only to find Thai and Malaysian officials pushing them out to sea. The boat is now in Thai waters for the second time, its voyagers hoping for a change of heart on the part of the authorities.

Giving help to foundering vessels is required by international law, and refugee sources said some cases of ignoring refugee appeals on the high seas had led to violations of seafaring traditions and laws.

Twenty-two Vietnamese, cramped aboard a 20-footer, said they had been passed up by five vessels while limping toward Thailand in August. The refugees said that one of the ships stopped and towered over them, its crew staring down but ignoring their pleas.

Another refugee boat from Vietnam, later rescued, was waved away from an oil rig in the South China Sea. The rig's rope ladder was reportedly pulled up as the boat approached.

Explaining some seemingly callous acts, Western refugee officials said captains—under pressure from their companies to speed along the sea lanes and not delay in ports of call—must sometimes make a difficult assessment of just how badly off a refugee boat is. There are indications that some escapees may try to exaggerate their distress to get a safe trip to a distant port.

Sea escapes are increasing after a year and a half of Communist government in Indochina. Almost 2,000 refugees have been reported in various corners of Asia this year, with a sharp increase noted after the United States announced last May that it would accept 11,000 more Indochinese.

Singapore has taken the toughest stand and refuses entry to refugees unless a foreign government guarantees it will take them.

Except for refugees with relatives, Hong Kong does not allow Indochinese to come in and settle. The Government says the colony is already overpopulated.

Malaysia, the Philippines and Indonesia take a more flexible attitude, although all three generally will not give permanent exile to refugees. Malaysia, which refugee sources said had pushed some boats out of its waters, makes exceptions for Moslems from Indochina.

Japan does not allow refugees permanent asylum but permits them to stay temporarily and has taken in about 170. Thailand has adopted the most liberal policy and, despite some attempts to discourage refugees, has taken in more than 70,000 fugitives. Almost 600 of them came by boat.

The United Nations High Commissioner for Refugees appealed in July to all "first port-of-call" countries to grant refugees temporary entry on the understanding that the United Nations agency would do its best to resettle them. The agency also appealed to potential countries of resettlement, and some, notably the United States, France, Norway, Australia and Canada, have responded.

Excerpts From a Refugee Log

Following are excerpts from a letter logging the sea escape aboard a 20-foot fishing boat of 26 refugees from Vietnam to Thailand. The letter was written in English and made available by the group's leader, who did not wish to be identified.

Aug. 22: About 1700 I saw a merchant ship 20 kilometers away heading northeasterly. We tried to reach this ship with white flag and great hope to be saved. The ship changed course and increased speed. We were left behind in desperation.

Aug. 23: After a few cups of strong coffee into my empty stomach I regained alertness and kept the wheel till the afternoon so Bich could rest. The sea worsened and reached condition 6, which gave little mercy to our small boat.

At the worst time, the water pump broke down and water kept coming in the boat.

In such a situation we saw a weak light starboard side. Just as seeing heaven, we headed to the light hoping to find a rescue ship. It seemed like we never reached the light. Mostly all of us were on the verge of fainting.

Aug. 24: At daybreak, we found out it was an oil-drilling station. We again approached her with white flag and SOS light signal. Nothing could have been more discouraging when some people signaled for us to go away and when we neared, the rope ladder was pulled up. We were not let on the ship [near the rig] and nobody came down to offer any help.

Later, some arrangements were made and we were allowed to go alongside an oil ship. Food and drinks and other supplies were given generously. Not that receiving food did not make us happy, but the warm way in which the people on the ship had shown toward us made us believe there was still meaning to the word "humanity."

A daring and controversial experiment carried out by psychologist Stanley Milgram in the early 1960s revealed some startling facts about the behavior of "ordinary" Americans under stress, and perhaps helped explain why so many Germans blindly followed orders to commit immoral and inhuman acts. Milgram's work suggests that even in our free society, we are highly conditioned to do as we are told by authority figures, even to do things we know are wrong. This article is from *TV Guide*, August 21, 1976.

83. Obedience to Authority
Stanley Milgram

Sometimes an event occurs during our lifetime that leaves an impression that is both indelible and puzzling. For me that event was the widespread participation of the German people in a system of death camps that destroyed millions of innocent men, women and children. The hapless victims were shot, gassed and burned in ovens.

These deeds were carried out by a people who were as civilized as any people in the world. How was it possible for them to act so cruelly? Did their behavior reveal a potential that is present in all of us? As a social psychologist whose job is to look into the why and how of human behavior, I decided to explore the response of ordinary people to immoral orders.

In order to explore behavior, social psychologists often rely on an important tool, the experiment. Although experiments in chemistry and physics often involve shiny equipment, flasks and electronic gear, an experiment in social psychology smacks much more of dramaturgy or theater. The experimenter carefully constructs a scenario to focus on certain aspects of behavior, a scenario in which the end is unknown and is completed by the experimental subject. The psychologist tries to create circumstances that will allow him to look at the behavior very carefully, note what he observed, and study its causes.

The experiment I set up was relatively simple: a person comes to the laboratory and, in the context of a learning experiment, he is told to give increasingly severe electric shocks to another person (who, unknown to the subject, is a confederate and does not actually receive the shocks). This arrangement gave me a chance to see how far people would go before they refused to follow the experimenter's orders. But a fuller scenario is needed to grasp the flavor of the experiment.

Imagine you had answered an advertisement to take part in a study of learning, and are arriving at the university at a time agreed upon. First, you are greeted by a man in a gray technician's coat; he introduces you to a second volunteer and says you are both about to take part in a scientific experiment. He says it is to test whether the use of punishment improves the ability to learn.

You draw lots to see who is to be the teacher and who the learner. You turn out to be the teacher, and the other fellow, the learner. Then you see the learner strapped into a chair and electrodes placed on his wrist. You are told that, when the learner makes a mistake in the lesson, his punishment will be an electric shock.

As teacher, you are seated in front of an impressive-looking instrument, a shock generator. Its essential feature is a line of switches that range from 15 volts to 450 volts, and a set of written labels that goes from slight shock to moderate shock, strong shock, very strong shock, and so on through XXX—danger, severe shock.

Your job, the experimenter explains to you, is to teach the learner a simple word-pair test. You read a list of words to him, such as blue day, nice girl, fat neck, etc., and he has to indicate by means of an answer box which words were originally paired together. If he gets a correct answer, you move on to the next pair. But if he makes a mistake, you are instructed to give him an electric shock, starting with 15 volts. And you are told to increase the shock one step each time he makes an error. In the course of the experiment the "victim" emits cries of pain and demands to be set free, but the experimenter orders you to continue. The question is: how far will you proceed on the shock generator before you turn to the experimenter and refuse to go on?

Before carrying out the experiment, I wanted to know how people thought they would behave in this situation, and so I asked them to predict their own performance. I posed the question to several groups: psychiatrists, psychologists and ordinary workers. They all said virtually the same thing: almost no one would go to the end.

But in reality the results were very different. Despite the fact that many subjects experience stress, and protest to the experimenter, a substantial proportion continue to the last shock on the generator. Many subjects obeyed the experimenter no matter how vehement the pleading of the person being shocked, no matter how painful the shocks seemed to be, and no matter how much the victim pleaded to be let out. This was seen time and again in our studies and has been observed in several universities where the experiment has been repeated.

But there is more to the experiment than this simple demonstration of obedience. Most of our energy went into systematically changing the factors in this situation to see which ones increased obedience and which led to greater defiance. We studied the effects of the closeness of the victim, the importance of the sponsoring institution and how the sight of other people obeying or defying an authority affected obedience. All of these factors have a powerful effect on whether the subjects obeyed or defied the malevolent authority. This shows that how a person behaves depends not only on his "character" but also on the precise situational pressures acting on him.

When the experiments were published, opinion about them was sharply divided. On the one hand, the

American Association for the Advancement of Science awarded the work its annual socio-psychological prize. At the same time, the experiments attracted fierce criticism, centering mainly on the ethical issues of carrying out the research. The experiments that I had hoped would deepen our understanding of how people yield to authority became themselves the focus of controversy.

But the problem of authority remains. We cannot have society without some structure of authority, and every society must inculcate a habit of obedience in its citizens. Yet these experiments show that many people do not have the resources to resist authority, even when they are directed to act inhumanely against an innocent victim. The experiments pose anew the age-old problem: what is the correct balance between individual initiative and social authority? They illuminate in a concrete way what happens when obedience is unrestrained by conscience.

The Soviet Union today is a prison; citizens of that country are not allowed to leave it without permission, which is granted only in special circumstances. For Jews, who are discriminated against in jobs and education and are denied cultural or religious institutions of their own (unlike the U.S.S.R's other ethnic minorities), emigration is their only hope of living a free life. Since 1971, and largely as the result of pressure from the United States, Soviet authorities have permitted limited numbers of Jews to leave the country. (Between 1971 and the end of 1976, the total Jewish emigration was slightly over 100,000.) This selection, by David K. Shipler, reprinted from *The New York Times*, February 6, 1975, is a grim reminder that 30 years after the Holocaust, Jews are still being persecuted—as Jews.

84.   Visa Is Sweet Sorrow to a Soviet Couple

David K. Shipler

Moscow, Feb. 5—Alekssandr and Lyudmila Lunts have packed their books in suitcases. They have begun to say goodbye to friends. They are finally going to Israel.

They are husband and wife, but are making this journey in contrasting moods and for sharply different reasons. He is a Jew; she is an ethnic Russian. The two facts are central to their definitions of themselves, pivotal in determining where they look to find their roots. For each of them, the sudden, surprising news that they would get their long-sought emigration visas set in motion great, contradictory currents of relief and sorrow, ecstasy and pain.

"It's not only a problem of tickets and visas," Mr. Lunts said. "Almost everybody who decides to leave has to cut out something from the soul."

Many Jews—Jews are officially considered one of more than a hundred non-Russian ethnic groups in the Soviet Union—say frankly that they want to leave not simply because they are Jews or because they are burdened by the anti-Semitism or by the lack of religious freedom, but mainly because they find the political and educational system oppressive, stifling and hypocritical. They want to speak openly, read freely. And they are thinking of their children's future.

Mr. Lunts's motives are not so secular. "If I were not a Jew, I don't think I would leave the country," he said. "The bad features of this social system, for me, would not be enough to make me leave.

"Many years ago there were periods when I began to forget that I was a Jew. But pretty soon I had to remember it—I was forced to remember it. The word, 'Jew,' when pronounced in a trolley bus, is pronounced in a low voice. It is important, but not so important, this cursing in shops and in trolley buses and in stores. When simple people were cursing it was not so important, but when I saw that intellectuals were also anti-Semitic, I felt it very strongly."

Mr. Lunts sat in his sparsely furnished apartment in southwest Moscow, the disorder of moving surrounding him. "To be in your own country is very important," he said intensely. "This is why I want to go to Israel. I feel my country is there, not here."

But his wife's country is here, not there. She is not a Jew, and so she shares none of her husband's compulsion to search for a land that she can feel belongs to her. The forces that tug at her pull back, toward Russia.

He understands. "It is very difficult for her," he said. "It is a sacrifice for me."

In the beginning, it was simply because she loved him, Mrs. Lunts explained. He was a mathematician and computer specialist with a good job in a scientific institute. When he decided to apply for a visa more than three years ago, she agreed to apply also. She was his second wife, they had been married eight years and she did not want to be without him.

"When we began I was not so sure that we should leave the country," she said. "I thought that even here we could survive. But as time went on I realized we could not."

Simply put, she saw in those years the dark sides of the Soviet system, sides she said she never knew existed. Shortly after his application, Mr. Lunts was dismissed from his job, a common fate for those who ask to go to Israel.

She then felt she had to resign her post as a geologist to protect her friends and colleagues at the institute where she worked. They said they would welcome her back if she did not emigrate.

During the jobless years, her husband was jailed twice, for a few days each time. He was picked up on the street for questioning by the KGB—the Committee for State Security—perhaps 20 or 30 times. His apartment became a meeting place for other applicants and for those who had been turned down.

She saw what suffering the Government could bring on people, and now as she pads around the apartment in blue jeans, getting things ready, tears are never far below the surface. "I love the country—it is the system," she said. "The longer we are here, the stronger the feeling we should go as fast as possible."

"I was a geologist," she added. "I was on expeditions many times in Siberia, Central Asia. I like my land very much. I do not want to think that I cannot see this place again. I like this place very much.

"My parents remain here, my sisters and many, many friends. I hope that somewhere, somehow I will be able to come back."

Her husband harbors the same hope, but he dares to say what she must know is true, yet is afraid to put into words. He too leaves people behind. His 18-year-old son by his first marriage is going with them, but his older daughter, married and content, is not. Nor is his 84-year-old father.

"I know that I have no chance of meeting them again," Mr. Lunts said.

A sign now hangs in the corridor of his apartment, hand-painted on brown paper by friends during a party marking his 52d birthday, just a day after he learned on January 21 that the visas would be issued.

It reads, "Visa—the best gift."

———————————

For some Germans, postwar revelations of the full extent of the crimes committed by their government produced feelings of remorse and shame. But with the passage of years, and especially as more and more Germans born after Hitler's time have come to maturity, the collective sense of responsibility for past sins has diminished. Little is taught about the Holocaust in German schools. The possible implications of changing attitudes in Germany, for Jews and for the State of Israel, are discussed here re-

printed from *The New York Times,* July 8, 1976,
by correspondent Craig R. Whitney.

85. Germans and Jews Today
Craig R. Whitney

**Young Germans Say Time Has Come
For "More Normal" Ties With Israel**

Bonn, July 8—Premier Yitzhak Rabin's visit to
West Germany is, from the German point of view, a
turning point.

Chancellors of West Germany have visited Israel,
but when Willy Brandt, visiting Jerusalem in 1973,
asked Premier Golda Meir if she would accept an invitation to Bonn, she replied, "I'll have to think about
it."

Now Premier Rabin is returning the visit of the
former Chancellor, who was succeeded by Helmut
Schmidt last year.

Yet it is still not possible—indeed, it may never
be—to speak of a "normal" relationship between Germans and Jews. The number of Jews who live in West
Germany and West Berlin today—28,000—is certainly not "normal" in the light of history.

There were 500,000 to 600,000 German Jews
before the Nazis took over in 1933. Most had been exterminated by 1945. Few of the survivors wanted to
stay in a country that had shown them such terrible
hate.

The largest West German Jewish Community today is that of West Berlin, about 5,000. "There is a
great conflict here," said one, Hans Rosenthal, a television entertainer. "You are constantly asking yourself,
'Am I a Jew who happens to live in Germany or a
German who happens to be Jewish?" The other main
West German Jewish communities today are in Frankfurt and Munich.

The average West German has learned from the
past that many of the great figures of German history—

Albert Einstein, Arnold Zweig, Heinrich Heine—were both German and Jewish. Today there are no prominent figures in German public life who are Jewish, but a German with even distant Jewish relations is apt to cite the fact almost with pride, as Egon Bahr, the negotiator of much of the Brandt policy of accommodation with Eastern Europe, did recently on a television talk show.

The break with what amounted to a taboo against critical examination of contemporary Jewish or Israeli life came here about the time of the 1973 war between Israel and the Arabs. In the months that followed the war, as a German-born Jew, Secretary of State Kissinger, began an active role in mediating in the Middle East, West German television and magazines began looking at Jews in America.

Der Spiegel, the weekly newsmagazine, published a three-part series on the subject, asking, rhetorically, if American Jews constituted a "secret reserve army" for Israel.

The West German author, Jürgen Thorwald, concluded: "In spite of a real or pretended feeling of guilt or responsibility for the murder of more than four million Jews in the Hitler era"—a widely accepted figure is six million—"the effects of the National Socialist propaganda invention of a Jewish-Bolshevist-capitalist world conspiracy are still felt unconsciously here—the clichés of a Jewish superpower dictating Washington's decisions still live on."

That article could not have been published here 10 years ago. The tone would have been considered too shocking. But the 1973 war, and the Arab oil embargo that accompanied it, forcing the average West German to turn down his thermostat and to do without his traditional Sunday drive for four successive weekends that fall, lifted old inhibitions.

As the historical events of World War II and the German "final solution" to the "Jewish problem" recede farther into the past, the average person here is less and less inclined to feel a sense of individual guilt about that time.

West Germans no longer hang their heads in shame when they are asked about their relationship to the Jewish people. "Why should I feel guilty?" a 26-year-old student from Kiel, Frank Ollmann, asked a questioner a while ago. "I was not born then. I had nothing to do with it."

Mr. Ollmann stands on the political left, which for ideological reasons supports the cause of Palestinian liberation against what it calls the "Zionist imperialism" of Israel.

But there are 26 million men and women like him who were born after 1945, nearly half of the West German population alive today. In what will probably constitute a historic turning point, most of them feel that the awkward, cramped "special relationship" their parents' generation built up with Israel should be replaced by a more normal one, balanced between Israel and the Arab states.

Since World War II West Germany paid billions of dollars to Israel, to Jewish organizations and to victims of Nazism in other countries, and no voices are raised here today to say that that was a mistake. But when the leaders of Israel, or of Poland, come to Bonn asking for new programs of compensation, "no" is the common answer of public opinion.

"We think we have paid enough for the past," a construction worker said in a small pub in Plittersdorf, near here. Asked if he would oppose any new large reparations payments by Bonn to Israel, he and his four companions, three men and a woman, agreed "absolutely."

A doctor in the northern part of the country said recently: "There was a time when I just couldn't hold up my head and have a normal conversation with someone who was Jewish. But I feel the problem has been quite overcome now."

Others worry about this. Just last week a court in Hamburg convicted Ludwig Hahn, a 66-year-old former SS man and chief of the Gestapo in Warsaw, and sentenced him to life imprisonment for murdering at least 230,000 people in the Polish capital during the

Nazi occupation. That conviction received only brief notice in the weekend German papers.

"I know there are more and more people who would prefer not to hear about our dark past," said the West German President, Walter Scheel, on the anniversary of the end of the war in May. "They have had enough, they say, of going around in sackcloth and ashes because crimes were committed in which they had no part.

"But that is not the issue. It is nonsense, of course, to require a young German man or woman to pay for something that was done before they were born. But only if we do not forget may we call ourselves Germans with pride once again."

The situation in India has been changing but this piece shows how easily a nation can abrogate its democratic processes and open the doors to dictatorships. As you read this account of events that took place in India in 1975, try to relate them to the history of the Third Reich. The article, by William Borders, is from *The New York Times* of November 21, 1976.

86. India Limits Civil Rights
William Borders

The lower house of Parliament today passed a sweeping set of constitutional amendments that will significantly shift the balance of power in the Government.

The vote of 366 to 4, with most members of the opposition boycotting and some still in jail, was one of the most significant milestones so far along the authoritarian course that Prime Minister Indira Gandhi's Government set upon 16 months ago, when it suspended civil liberties.

Together with the Government's decision, announced Saturday, to postpone national elections for a second time, the alterations in the Constitution gave a new aspect of permanence to a state of affairs that had originally been presented as temporary.

"They're codifying the state of emergency, giving force of law to the concentration of power in Mrs. Gandhi's hands," said Asoka Mehta, a leader of the dispirited opposition. "After this, there's nothing much for us."

By adjusting dozens of passages in India's 26-year-old Constitution, the bill that was passed today substantially enhances the power of Parliament and the Prime Minister, and diminishes the power of the courts, which have often been a bastion of resistance to the central Government's stern new position.

The following are some of the principal changes:

Judicial review of constitutional amendments is ended, and "there shall be no limitation whatever on the constituent power of Parliament to amend" the Constitution.

Judicial review of ordinary laws is taken away from the lower courts, and the Supreme Court will henceforth be able to declare a law unconstitutional only by a two-thirds majority.

The fundamental-rights section of the Constitution —roughly the equivalent of the American Bill of Rights—is made specifically subordinate to a section outlining "directive principles" of state action, a program of general economic and social goals.

Parliament is empowered to enact legislation banning "antinational" activities and associations.

India's largely ceremonial President is deprived of all political power in a section directing that he "shall act in accordance" with the advice given to him by the Prime Minister and the Cabinet.

The President, acting at the Prime Minister's direction, is given the power for two years to amend the Constitution by executive order in any way that will help give effect to the omnibus legislation.

"In this bill, we have taken many steps which history will show are vital and necessary for the progress of our country and the prosperity of our people," said Law Minister H.R. Gokhale in the ornate, high-ceilinged chamber this afternoon, just before the vote. "The most important thing we are doing is putting beyond doubt the supremacy of Parliament, in unequivocal terms."

Prime Minister Gandhi, who gains the most from the legislation, sat impassive in her front-row seat through the closing moments of the debate, then smiled when the rows of Congress Party members behind her greeted the final vote with vigorous desk-thumping, the traditional form of applause.

The bill must still be passed by the more ceremonial upper house and by a majority of the state legislatures, and signed by President Fakhruddin Ali Ahmed, but no obstacle is expected anywhere along the line. Its passage in the lower house, the chamber with political significance, was never in doubt either, since the Congress Party controls more than two-thirds of the seats, even when everyone is present.

Most of the opposition members have been boycotting ever since the bill was introduced early in September, protesting censorship of news accounts of the proceedings, and the continued imprisonment of more than two dozen members of Parliament.

The set of constitutional amendments is regarded by both the Government and its opponents as momentous, among the most important legislative actions since June of last year, when Mrs. Gandhi declared a state of emergency, in the face of what she said was a grave threat of subversion. The Government contends that the constitutional changes are necessary to achieve "socio-economic revolution," aiding in the war against poverty, ignorance and disease.

Taking part in the debate last week, Prime Minister Gandhi declared: "This bill is a vital step in curing our political system of some of its ills. Those who want to fix the Constitution in a rigid and unalterable frame are entirely out of tune with the spirit of new India."

On the opposition side of the house, most of the seats remained empty. But the general opinion of that side was expressed by P.G. Mavalankar, an independent member from the state of Gujarat, who rose a couple of hours before the vote today to tell his colleagues across the floor that they were "opening the floodgate to regimentation and dictatorship."

"Although you are in a strong majority, you are not sustained by morality," he declared. "God will not forgive the sin you are about to commit."

As we have seen in our readings up to now, the defeat of Hitler did not spell the end of his particular form of madness. The world is still in danger. Other leaders have used, and are using, similar methods in order to achieve unlimited power, and to destroy groups and individuals they regard as undesirable, for whatever reason.

The final selections carry important messages about the future. In the first, taken from the book *The Destruction of European Jews,* Raul Hilberg warns us to beware of administrative measures directed against any one group; if not stopped in time, they can lead to measures of physical extermination. He points out, too, that destructive minds today have access to technological tools for killing large numbers of people such as Hitler never even dreamed of.

In the final selection, Elie Wiesel, the writer who has done more than any other to transmit the message of the Holocaust, asks, "Could it happen again?" He is referring specifically to Jews. The events he refers to were current at the time the article was written, in 1974, and undoubtedly influenced the writer's mood. Nevertheless, his basic feeling is one of uncertainty and fear.

87. The Occurrence Is Past; The Phenomenon Remains

Raul Hilberg

Let us point out at once that the Germans have not been the only ones in history who have had a reason to embark upon a destructive course of action. When we examine the world historical scene, we may note that many times, in many countries, bureaucracies have launched the opening phases of a destruction process. Even now, in the Union of South Africa and elsewhere, specialists are selecting, exploiting, and concentrating new victims. Very often, seemingly harmless bureaucratic activities—such as the definition of a particular group and the exclusion of its members from office—contain the seeds of administrative continuity. Potentially, these measures are steppingstones to a killing operation, but as a rule insurmountable barriers from without and within arrest and disrupt the destructive development. Externally, the opposition of the victims may bring the process to a halt; internally, administrative and psychological obstacles may bar the way. The discriminatory systems of many countries are the leftovers of such disrupted destruction processes.

The German destruction of the Jews was not interrupted. That is its crucial, decisive characteristic. At the threshold of the killing phase the flow of administrative measures continued unchecked. Technocratic and moral obstacles were overcome. An unprecedented killing operation was inaugurated, and with the beginning of this operation the Germans demonstrated once and for all how quickly even large groups, numbering in the millions, could be annihilated. . . .

As time passes on, the destruction of the European Jews will recede into the background. Its most immediate consequences are almost over, and whatever developments may henceforth be traced to the catastrophe will be consequences of consequences, more and more remote. Already the Nazi outburst has become historical. But this is a strange page in history. Few events of modern times were so filled with unpredicted action and unsuspected death. A primordial impulse had suddenly surfaced among the Western nations; it had been unfettered through their machines. From this moment, fundamental assumptions about our civilization have no longer stood unchallenged, for while the occurrence is past, the phenomenon remains.

Before the emergence of the 20th century and its technology, a destructive mind could not play in fantasy with the thoughts that the Nazis were to translate into action. The administrator of earlier centuries did not have the tools. He did not possess the network of communications; he did not dispose over rapid small arms fire and quick-working poison gases. The bureaucrat of tomorrow would not have these problems; already, he is better equipped than the German Nazis were. Killing is not as difficult as it used to be. The modern administrative apparatus has facilities for rapid, concerted movements and for efficient massive killings. These devices not only trap a larger number of victims; they also require a greater degree of specialization, and with that division of labor the moral burden too is fragmented among the participants. The perpetrator can now kill his victims without touching them, without hearing them, without seeing them. He may feel sure of his success and safe from its repercussions. This ever-growing capacity for destruction cannot be arrested anywhere.

Since the end of the Jewish catastrophe, basic decisions have been made about the future. In the Christian world the remaining alternatives are gradually moving toward polar ends. After 2,000 years there is no defensible middle ground. The ancient compromise, with all its contradictions, is weakening day by day. To the Jewish community that growing dichotomy conveys unique opportunities and unprecedented vulnerabilities. Jewry is faced with ultimate weapons. It has no deterrent. The Jews can live more freely now. They can also die more quickly. The summit is within sight. An abyss has opened below.

88. Ominous Signs and Unspeakable Thoughts

Elie Wiesel

I admit it sadly: I feel threatened. For the first time in many years I feel that I am in danger. For the first time in my adult life I am afraid that the nightmare may start all over again, or that it has never ended, that since 1945 we have lived in parentheses. Now they are closed.

Could the Holocaust happen again? Over the years I have often put the question to my young students. And they, consistently, have answered yes, while I said no. I saw it as a unique event that would remain unique. I believed that if mankind had learned anything from it, it was that hate and murder reach beyond the direct participants; he who begins by killing others, in the end will kill his own. Without Auschwitz, Hiroshima would not have been possible. The murder of one people inevitably leads to that of mankind.

In my naïveté I thought, especially in the immediate postwar period, Jews would never again be singled out, handed over to the executioner. That anti-Semitism had received its death-blow long ago, under the fiery skies of Poland. I was somehow convinced that—paradoxically—man would be shielded, protected by the awesome mystery of the Event.

I was wrong. What happened once, could happen again. Perhaps I am exaggerating. Perhaps I am oversensitive. But then I belong to a traumatized generation. We have learned to take threats more seriously than promises.

There are signs and they are unmistakable. The sickening spectacle of a diplomatic gathering wildly applauding a spokesman for killers. The scandalous exclusion of Israel from UNESCO. The arrogant self-righteousness of certain leaders, the cynicism of others. The dramatic solitude of Israel. The anti-Semitic statements made by America's top general. Anti-Semitism has became fashionable once more both in the East and in the West.

No wonder then that suddenly one hears discussions on a subject that many of us had thought buried long ago: Jewish survival. Can Israel—the country, the people—survive another onslaught? How many times must it sacrifice the best of its children? How long can one go on living in a hostile world? Is it conceivable that Hitler could be victorious posthumously?

For those of us who have lived and endured the human and Jewish condition in its ultimate depth know: at this turning point in history, the Jewish people and the Jewish State are irrevocably linked; one cannot survive without the other. As a community, we have rarely been so united. And never so alone.

And so, the idea of another catastrophe is no longer unthinkable. I say it reluctantly. In fact, it is the first time I say it I have chosen until now to place the Holocaust on a mystical or ontological level, one that defies language and transcends imagination. I have quarreled with friends who built entire theories and doctrines on an event which, in my view, is not to be used or approached casually. If I speak of it now, it is only because of my realization that Jewish survival is being recalled into question.

Hence the fear in me. All of a sudden, I am too much reminded of past experiences. The enemy growing more and more powerful, more and more popular. The aggressiveness of the blackmailers, the permissiveness of some leaders and the total submissiveness of others. The overt threats. The complacency and diffidence of the bystanders. I feel as my father must have felt when he was my age.

Not that I foresee the possibility of Jews being massacred in the cities of America or in the forests of Europe. Death-factories will not be built again. But there is a certain climate, a certain mood in the making. As far as the Jewish people are concerned, the world has remained unchanged: as indifferent to our fate as to its own.

And so I look at my young students and tremble for their future; I see myself at their age surrounded by ruins. What am I to tell them?

I would like to be able to tell them that in spite of endless disillusionments one must maintain faith in man and in mankind; that one must never lose heart. I would like to tell them that, notwithstanding the official discourses and policies, our people does have friends and allies and reasons to advocate hope. But I have never lied to them, I am not going to begin now. And yet . . .

Despair is no solution, I know that. What *is* the solution? Hitler had one. And he tried it while a civilized world kept silent.

I remember. And I am afraid.

Glossary of Terms

Anti-Semitism—prejudice against Jews; dislike or fear of Jews; discrimination against or persecution of Jews.

Aryan—has no validity as a racial term. It has been used by the Nazis to mean a superior, Nordic-type Caucasian Gentile.

Auschwitz—a city in southwestern Poland where there was one of over 100 Nazi extermination camps.

Bismarck, Otto von—Prussian prince and chancellor (1815–1898) who unified Germany; later called the "Iron Chancellor."

Demagogue—a person who obtains power by means of appeals to emotions and prejudices.

"Final Solution"—the term used by Nazis to mean the mass physical extermination of the Jews.

Genocide—the systematic killing and annihilation of a whole people or nation.

Gestapo—the German internal security police organized in 1933 under the Nazi regime to operate against political opposition.

Holocaust—complete destruction of people or animals by fire; the destruction of European Jews 1933–45. From the Greek "burnt whole."

Juden—"Jews" in the German language.

Nationalism—devotion to one's nation; excessive patriotism; doctrine that national interests are more important than international considerations.

Nihilism—the general rejection of customary beliefs in morality, religion, or, loosely, any violently revolutionary movement involving some use of terrorism.

Nuremberg—city in Germany where the Nazis held large rallies, and later where an International Military Tribunal held trials of Nazis accused of War Crimes (1945–46).

Pogrom—an organized massacre of, or attack on, the Jews or other minority groups. Term used in Eastern Europe. From the Russian "like thunder; devastation."

Prejudice—a judgment or opinion formed before the facts are known (pre-judge); a preconceived idea, usually unfavorable, of intolerance or hatred of other races, creeds, religions, etc.

Prussia—a former state of Germany regarded as militaristic.

Racism—program or practice of discrimination, segregation, persecution, and domination on the basis of race. Scientists claim that there is no such thing as "race." "Race" has generally been used to recognize three major groups of mankind as Caucasian, Negroid, and Mongoloid. The Nazis considered non-Aryans (Jews, Gypsies, Poles, and Blacks) as "racially" inferior and undesirable.

Scapegoat—a person, group, or thing that bears the blame for the mistakes or crimes of others.

Stereotype—a fixed image or notion of a person or group; having no individuality; to assign the characteristics observed in a few members of that group to the whole group.

Third Reich—the Third Republic, referring to Hitler's administration in Germany (1933–45).

Totalitarianism—a government or doctrine in which one political party or group maintains complete control and makes all others illegal.

Treaty of Versailles—the Treaty which was signed at the end of World War I that stripped Germany of her lands, treasury, and pride.

Treblinka—a Nazi concentration camp. Extermination center northeast of Warsaw, Poland.

Weimar Republic—the German Republic from 1919 to 1933. Its constitutional assembly met in the city of Weimar in 1919.

Index

ABOUT THE EDITORS

ROSELLE CHARTOCK, 34, is a teacher at Monument Mountain Regional High School in Great Barrington, Massachusetts. She is doing doctorate work on the teaching of the Holocaust at the University of Massachusetts. Her husband, Alan, is a political science professor. They have two children, Jones, 3, and Sarah, 1.

JACK SPENCER was born in Adams, Massachusetts. A product of the 1950s, he earned a B.A. from Amherst; a M.A. from Purdue and a M. Ed. from North Adams. He taught social studies for fifteen years at Williams High School and Monument Mountain Regional in the Southern Berkshires. At present, he is assistant superintendent of schools for the Berkshire Hills Regional School District in Massachusetts. He lives in Stockbridge, Massachusetts.

Here are the Books that Explore the Jewish Heritage-Past and Present.

Fiction

☐	20816	**My Michael** Amos Oz	$2.95
☐	20570	**Preparing for the Sabbath-** Nessa Rapoport	$2.95
☐	20105	**Brothers Ashkenazi** Singer	$4.50
☐	22967	**Mila 18** Leon Uris	$3.95
☐	20807	**Night** Elie Wiesel	$1.95
☐	13564	**Holocaust** Gerald Green	$2.50

Non-Fiction

☐	20818	**Where The Jackals Howl & Other Stories** Amos Oz	$2.95
☐	01339	**Jewish Family Book** Strassfeld & Green	$9.95
☐	01369	**Season's of Our Joy** Arthur Waskow	$8.95
☐	01265	**The Jewish Almanac** Siegel & Rheins, eds.	$9.95
☐	22500	**Children of the Holocaust** Helen Epstein	$3.95
☐	13810	**World of Our Fathers** Irving Howe	$3.95
☐	13807	**A Treasury of Jewish Folklore** Nathan Ausubel, Ed.	$3.95
☐	14420	**The New Bantam-Megiddo Hebrew & English Dictionary** Levenston & Sivan	$2.95
☐	20212	**Chaia Sonia** Don Gussow	$2.50
☐	20530	**The War Against the Jews** Lucy S. Dawidowicz	$3.95